ORDER OF THE HOLY CROSS
WEST PARK, NEW YORK

The Age of Illusion

901.933
Lav

The Age of Illusion

Manners and Morals 1750-1848

James Laver

Monastic Library
Holy Cross Monastery
West Park, NY 12493

David McKay Company, Inc.
New York

ORDER OF THE HOLY CROSS
WEST PARK, NEW YORK

909.75
L

THE AGE OF ILLUSION

Manners and Morals 1750-1848

Copyright © 1972 by

James Laver

All rights reserved, including the right to reproduce
this book, or parts thereof, in any form, except for
the inclusion of brief quotations in a review.

Library of Congress Catalog Card Number: 70-173893

Printed in England

Bliss was it in that dawn to be alive,
But to be young was very heaven.

WORDSWORTH

The Sensual and the Dark rebel in vain,
Slaves by their own compulsion! In mad game
They burst their manacles and wear the name
Of Freedom, graven on a heavier chain!

COLERIDGE

Contents

Illustrations

Picture research by Rowena Ross

1 Society and Religion in the Mid-Eighteenth Century

Louis XIV had died in 1715, and the defeats suffered by France in the closing years of his reign had reduced her political domination; but her prestige, especially in the social and cultural fields, was still prodigious. French furniture and French porcelain were to be seen in the houses of the rich all over Europe; and even in the matter of dress, French modes were accepted as the appropriate garb of the upper classes, both men and women. If one reads the memoirs of Saint-Simon or of Lord Hervey, or the letters of Lady Wortley Montagu, one gets the impression of a common European civilization, aristocratic and French.

In fact, by the deliberate policy of Richelieu, Mazarin and Louis XIV himself, the French nobility had been shorn of much of its power. The nobles for the most part had ceased to be local magnates and had become courtiers whose first duty was to contribute to the glory of the Court at Versailles.

It is true that they retained many of their feudal privileges, although less completely than the nobility of other European countries, where the condition of the peasants (i.e. of the bulk of the population) varied widely. In Austria, Poland, Prussia, Russia and Spain they were still serfs, but in France the peasant was no longer bound to the soil; he could sell his land if he wished, could marry without his lord's consent and could come and go as he pleased. But he was still compelled to grind his corn in his lord's mill, bake his bread in his lord's oven and press his grapes in his lord's wine press. The *corvée*, the work he had to do in his lord's fields, was probably less arduous than in some other countries, for we hear of a Hungarian peasant complaining that 'he owed four days of his labour to his lord, spent the fifth and sixth hunting and fishing for him, while the seventh belonged to God'. James Harvey Robinson writes:

In central, southern and eastern Europe, the medieval system still prevailed; the peasant lived upon the same manor and worked for his lord in the same way that his ancestors had worked a thousand years before. Everywhere the same crude agricultural instruments were still used, and most of the implements and tools were roughly made in the village itself. The wooden ploughs commonly found even on English farms were constructed on the model of the old Roman plough; wheat was cut with a sickle, grass with an unwieldy scythe, and the rickety cartwheels were supplied only with wooden rims.[1]

But even if those who laboured on the land in England were still using primitive instruments, the services due to the local lord had long since been commuted into money payments. Also the vast increase in commercial activity and the rise of a prosperous middle class had begun to modify the whole social picture. Moreover the line between the rich merchant and the aristocracy was less sharply drawn than in other European countries.

In France the nobility was a privileged class, exempted from most of the taxes levied on townsmen and peasants, on the ground that they were supposed to serve their King with the sword. They were forbidden to take part in industry or commerce (except maritime trade). The Church, the Army and the Law were, however, open to them. In England the ban on trade was less harshly imposed, and the nobility enjoyed no special exemption from taxation, nor from the normal operation of the law. The French were astonished that Lord Ferrers should be condemned to death and actually executed for killing his coachman; the English peerage enjoyed certain immunities but these did not extend to murder.

But the chief difference, perhaps, between England and the rest of Europe was that a title was inherited only by the eldest son. It is true that if a very exalted person, a duke for example, was also in possession of a marquisate or an earldom, his eldest son was allowed to use the second honour as a courtesy title during his father's lifetime, but this did not entitle him to a seat in the House of Lords. The sons of dukes and marquises were allowed to call themselves Lord John Grosvenor or whatever it might be, but *their* sons were merely Mr So-and-so, the peer's family name. In this way the continental proliferation of counts, viscounts, barons and the rest was avoided, and the distinctions between the younger sons of the nobility and those of the non-titled upper classes were happily blurred. Also the English aristocracy seldom showed any reluctance to marry the daughters of commoners and this has certainly been a major cause of its survival and continuing importance in the life of the country.

Horace Walpole himself was extremely annoyed when his young nephew Lord Orford refused to marry the heiress who had been chosen for him, a certain Miss Nicoll with 'an immense fortune of a hundred and fifty thousand pounds'. The other side of the picture is seen when Lady Elizabeth Seymour, who was considered the best catch in the country, being the heiress of both the Seymours of Somerset and the Percys of Northumberland, was captured by the London banker Sir Hugh Smithson. He duly changed his name to Percy. It is recorded that he asked the King for the Garter and when it was refused said: 'I am the first Percy to be refused the Garter.' To which George III, not usually considered a witty man, replied: 'You are the first Smithson to ask for it.' Yet Smithson-Percy soon found himself accepted into the ranks of the aristocracy.

The opposite extreme was to be seen in Germany where the horror of a misalliance was pushed to fantastic lengths. In England the landowner without a title – the squire – thought himself just as good as his neighbour the earl; but in Germany the hereditary nobility was itself sharply divided into an upper and a lower stratum. The former possessed a seat and a vote in the Reichstag, the latter were originally the household officials of the electoral princes or other magnates and had been granted land and aristocratic privileges, both of which became hereditary.

It is a complication almost incomprehensible to the English reader that the lower nobility was further divided into two groups: the imperial knights and the territorial nobility.

The imperial knights, who were to be found chiefly in Swabia and south-west Germany, were, until the disappearance of the Holy Roman Empire in 1806, immediately subject to the Emperor . . . whilst the territorial knights were subject to the prince of the territory within which their estates lay. According to centuries-old tradition, intermarriage between upper and lower nobility was interdicted; it was regarded as a misalliance.[2]

The matter was further complicated by the fact that the Emperor Joseph II at the end of the eighteenth century had ennobled large numbers of bankers and merchants; but this had not dispelled the prejudice against 'degrading occupations', and at the end of the nineteenth century it was still impossible for the son of a shopkeeper to become a lieutenant in the reserve. That he should even aspire to become a lieutenant in the regular army was, of course, unthinkable.

The aristocracy remained fixed in its feudal prejudices. Germany was still full of small princely courts with all the rigid etiquette which they involved. Not only the prince but members of his court were regarded with immense reverence, and the ordinary bourgeois took off his hat when they passed in the street. There was much use of titles, and even when these titles were not of nobility but of office or profession, their omission would have caused great offence. Wives shared in these honours. Not only was the wife of a Baron a Baronin (this was usual throughout Europe) but the wife of a judge was Frau Justizrath, the wife of an army captain Frau Hauptmann, the wife of a court preacher Frau Hoffrediger; even the wife of the head forester expected to be addressed as Frau Oberforstmeister.

Except in the great commercial cities the rigid demarcation of rank or caste was carried into every department of life. In the court theatres, for example, the stage boxes were reserved for the court, the front row of the

3

stalls for army officers, the front row of boxes for the nobility. Then came tradespeople and the rest. It would have been out of the question for any of these categories to stray from their appointed place.

The ranks were the more easily distinguished because of the German passion for uniforms. Everybody wore them, from the Emperor to the village postmaster. And nearly everyone managed to acquire a cross or a medal of one sort or another.

Between the aristocracy and army officers and the commercial middle classes of the big cities, there was undoubtedly in Germany an antagonism unparalleled in the other countries of Europe. Certainly there was nothing like it in England or France. The German aristocracy despised all careers except those in diplomacy, administration and the army, and did its best to exclude all other classes from these fields. They left commerce to the bourgeoisie and banking and finance to the Jews.

Snobbery was not, of course, entirely absent from the English scene. Horace Walpole professed a great contempt for manufacturers and, later in the century, for those 'nabobs' who had made huge fortunes in India. He was equally scornful of those who solicited posts in government from powerful ministers. He boasted that he himself was independent, oblivious of the fact that the King had rewarded Sir Robert Walpole for his long services by giving his three sons offices under the Crown. The eldest was Auditor of the Exchequer, the second Clerk of the Pells. Horace Walpole himself was Usher of the Exchequer and shared with his brother Edward a Collectorship of the Customs granted to Sir Robert for three lives. All that the Usher of the Exchequer had to do was 'to shut the gates of the Exchequer and furnish paper, pens, ink, wax, sand, tape, penknives, scissors, parchment etc.' to the officials, and to pay tradesmen's bills. He did not even perform this onerous task himself; the work was done by his deputy, a certain Mr Bedford.

This was indeed a common practice and sometimes the deputy himself had a deputy who obtained, as may be imagined, a very small reward for his services. We learn that the duties of Lord George Sackville's post in the Irish government were carried out by a man who, himself growing too old and feeble, passed the job on to a nephew who received fifty pounds a year.

Meanwhile, on the other side of the Atlantic a form of society was coming into being which had no parallel in the Old World, and this society took shape almost entirely in what was later to be the United States of America. In South America the conquistadors had imposed on the native population a servitude resembling that of feudal Europe. The land was divided into large estates, the owners of which continued the aristocratic tradition, living in large houses with many servants. There was little difference between the manner of life of a Spanish grandee at home and his counterpart in the New World.

4

But most of the early immigrants to North America were of the English middle classes either rural or urban, yeoman farmers, or shopkeepers and craftsmen. One of their main reasons for coming to America was their dislike of the European class system and they had no intention of setting it up again in their new home. Also, in England they had had little chance of bettering their condition, whereas America seemed to offer unlimited opportunities to the sturdy and industrious. They could acquire and work a farm without paying any rent to a landowner and they rejoiced in their independence. They had already undergone a sifting process, for it was naturally the most enterprising who had taken the chance of coming to America. 'In a sense,' says Henry Bamford Parkes in his excellent survey of *The American People*, 'America was from the beginning a state of mind and not merely a place.'[3]

Even in the English colonies, however, there were considerable differences in social conditions and social attitudes. The earliest English colonists were mostly men of the upper classes who were granted ownership of land in the new territories by the King of England. The founders of the new colonies did not find them very profitable and most of them eventually passed into the direct control of the Crown. Some colonies (such as Virginia) were founded by companies of merchants who hoped to reap a profit from their investment.

In New England, however, the motive was different. What the Pilgrim Fathers desired, far more than money, was freedom to worship in their own way. They were nearly all Calvinists and they sought to set up a Puritan theocracy which could impose its own Presbyterianism instead of having Episcopalianism forced upon it. The New Englanders had none of the religious toleration of William Penn, the Quaker founder of Pennsylvania. Yet the Puritan spirit encouraged a high degree of independence and sturdy self reliance and contributed in no small measure to the gradual emergence of what can only be described as a new kind of man.

The situation was somewhat different in the southern part of the country. To a lesser, but still considerable, extent the conditions resembled those of South America. Some of the early settlers acquired large plantations worked first by indentured servants shipped out from England, and later by Negro slaves. Yet among themselves the landowners had the same spirit of self reliance as the colonists in the north and they too, by the middle of the eighteenth century, had begun to feel themselves to be Americans, and showed themselves to be so when the time came to fight the War of Independence.

The English at home were completely unaware of this. The year 1750 was a time of tranquillity. The War of the Austrian Succession had ended with the Peace of Aix-la-Chapelle and there was no other major conflict in sight. War at this period was very different from the great national struggles

5

of the nineteenth century. Wars were fought for dynastic reasons by small professional armies who marched and countermarched, besieged and relieved cities, and who cheerfully went into 'winter quarters' when weather conditions made mobility difficult. And even the dynastic wars were hardly felt in England. Battles were essentially something to be fought out on foreign fields. And nothing is more extraordinary to the modern mind than the freedom with which the French and English were able to visit one another's country even in time of war. One should perhaps add: if they belonged to the upper classes.

Indeed the eighteenth century, up to the French Revolution, was a halcyon time for aristocracy all over Europe. French was universally spoken. The court of Frederick the Great conversed in French and so, more surprisingly, did the court of George II. This is shown by the well-known story of the last conversation the King had with his dying Queen. She urged him to marry again and he replied: '*Non, non. J'aurai des maîtresses.*' '*Ça n'empêche pas,*'[4] riposted the Queen, drawing on the depth of her experience of married life.

There was indeed a unity of culture at this period which had not existed since Roman times and was never to exist again. This is curiously exemplified in the extraordinary career of Elizabeth Chudleigh, Countess of Bristol and Duchess of Kingston. Married (perhaps) in early life to the future Earl of Bristol, she was the mistress of the Duke of Kingston until he married her shortly before his death. She was a striking figure at the court of Frederick, Prince of Wales, and it seems to have made little difference to her position in society that she was not yet married to the Duke. He took a house for her in Knightsbridge and gave a grand ball attended by royalty. She led off the minuets partnered by the Margrave of Anspach. Her life with the good-natured Duke of Kingston was generally harmonious, but after one of their occasional quarrels she decided to travel abroad by herself. She could not however have quarrelled with her lover very seriously for the Duke lent her nearly two thousand pounds for the expedition and provided her with a spacious travelling coach. She certainly travelled *en princesse* with two maids, an apothecary, her own jeweller, a manservant, and even a hussar who was detached from his regiment to ride beside the coach and serve as an escort. Their first port of call was Dresden and there she gave a demonstration of the extraordinary fascination she could exercise over anybody when she chose. The Duke of Saxony had just died but his widow the Dowager Electress was delighted with Elizabeth, no doubt because she was a cheering influence on a rather gloomy court.

She was received with equal graciousness by Frederick the Great, who, after giving several fêtes in her honour, passed her on to his brother-in-law, the Duke of Brunswick. On this visit we have an unexpected glimpse of her from the pen of no less a person than Casanova. He claims in his memoirs

6

that he had met her before when, having been thrown from his horse immediately outside her house in Knightsbridge, she had rushed out and helped him to his feet. This may be fantasy; at all events he gives a very vivid picture of her at a review of troops at Brunswick.

In 1769 she managed to secure a divorce from her first husband and the Duke of Kingston, after some hesitation, married her. When he died shortly afterwards it was found that he had left everything to her, cutting off his eldest son, Evelyn Meadows, with a miserable five hundred pounds. Naturally Evelyn Meadows decided to contest the will and the method he chose was to involve the Duchess in the most spectacular *cause célèbre* of the century.

She was now a woman of immense wealth and in the meantime decided to go abroad once more. Her first port of call was Rome. An English duchess was indeed almost a queen and the reception which the Pope gave her did not surprise anyone in the eighteenth century, however astonishing it may seem to us. She arrived in the Tiber and anchored by special permission near the Castel Sant'Angelo. She did not have to pay toll fees or submit to a customs inspection. Clement xiv received her in the Vatican and had long conversations with her. She responded by giving some enormous parties and even on one occasion having the whole Colosseum illuminated for a fête. But at home the clouds were gathering and on her return from Rome she was faced with the charge of having committed bigamy. This was a very dangerous situation for her: as a peeress she could not, even if convicted, be branded on the hand and sent to prison; but was she a peeress? Her first husband had not yet succeeded to the Earldom of Bristol. He was still Mr Augustus Hervey, and if she had really been married to him then she had never been legally married to the Duke of Kingston. The danger of branding and imprisonment was still present.

Her trial was one of the most extraordinary spectacles ever offered to the British public, or rather to those who could afford to pay ten to twenty guineas for a seat. Special stands were erected in Westminster Hall for the four thousand people who actually witnessed the trial. The ladies were decked out in their finest clothes and richest jewels, the Royal Family themselves attended and all the nobility of the land; and outside in the street there was a large crowd of less exalted persons who were all, or nearly all, on Elizabeth's side. It is impossible to follow all the ups and downs of the trial which dragged on and on and exhausted everybody's patience. In the end she was found guilty of bigamy. She successfully pleaded the privilege of the peerage, so although humiliated and in many minds disgraced she was given no further punishment.

She decided to travel abroad once more and her plans included visits to Rome, Munich, Vienna and St Petersburg. Vienna was a great disappointment for the rigidly puritan Maria Theresa did not approve of Elizabeth at all. She refused to receive her unless she was presented by the British ambassador. He declined to present her as Duchess of Kingston but offered to do so if she were Countess of Bristol. This for obvious reasons she could not admit and so she was never received at court at all. She thought that perhaps the other great Empress, Catherine II, would be more welcoming and decided to go to St Petersburg. She travelled in splendid style, in her own yacht which had been fitted up at Calais. It is astonishing that this could take place while France and Great Britain were at war. The French had gone to the aid of the American rebels in 1778, and although, of course, the fighting was not taking place in Europe, it still seems extraordinary to the modern mind that in these circumstances an Englishwoman, however exalted, should have been free to come and go as she pleased.

Elizabeth was not disappointed by her reception at St Petersburg. Catherine the Great saw her at once in private audience, installed her in a handsome house in the Russian capital, gave her a country estate and showered her with gifts. On her way back she was entertained by the Polish Prince Radziwill. He met her on his estate at Berg with a procession of forty carriages, followed by six hundred Polish knights on splendid horses, followed in their turn by grooms, huntsmen and keepers with a thousand hounds on the leash. A troop of hussars and cossacks formed the escort. It was even rumoured that she was about to marry the Prince, but nothing came of this, and she established herself early in 1788 in a magnificent palace near Fontainebleau which had previously belonged to the French King's brother. She died in the very year that Louis XVI was compelled to summon the States General. The French Revolution had begun but the Duchess of Kingston did not live to witness it. She remains one of the most astonishing characters of the eighteenth century and her life is an example of the privileges enjoyed by the upper classes all over Europe during the *ancien régime*.

If the English went abroad, considerable numbers of foreigners came to England, and many of the French adopted English fashions in dress. They took back with them English horses, English dogs and English post-chaises, all these being generally acknowledged to be the best in the world. William Knox, visiting France in the 1760s, records his astonishment that: '*la mode Anglaise* is the *haut ton* [high fashion] throughout . . . The clothes were cut in English fashion and roast beef is brought to the politest tables at supper.' So completely anglicized were some French circles that Horace Walpole complained that he found nothing but dullness, which he could have had 'in such perfection at home'.

He was also rather shocked to find that many French people would talk of nothing but the writings of David Hume, the sceptical Scottish philosopher. Indeed they were all determined to be philosophers; and Walpole remarks in his sensible way: 'Free-thinking is for oneself; surely not for

8

Society.' What particularly shocked him was that atheistic remarks were made *in front of the servants*: 'The conversation was much more unrestrained, even on the Old Testament, than I would suffer at my own table in England, if a single footman were present.'

Walpole had the foresight to realize how dangerous the doctrines of the philosopher might be. 'They have no time to laugh; there is God and the King to be pulled down first; and many women . . . are devoutly employed in the demolition. They think me quite profane for having any belief left.' But he adds, concerning some of his aristocratic friends: 'They are ashamed to defend the Roman Catholic religion because it is quite exploded; but I am convinced that they believe it in their hearts.'

In England the situation was somewhat different. Professed atheists and even professed deists were rare. In fact it was not considered good manners to discuss religion at all. The Bench of Bishops was almost entirely composed of men who owed their preferment to the soundness of their Whig principles: Erastians to a man, believing that the Church should be under the control of the State. To appoint them was the deliberate policy of the Government which thought, probably correctly, that the bulk of the English people had had enough of religious interference and fanaticism in the preceding century. Every manifestation of 'enthusiasm'[5] was looked on askance. The services in the Anglican churches were of an extreme dullness: the scene is vividly portrayed for us in Hogarth's engraving *The Sleeping Congregation*. Only two persons present seem to be awake: the preacher droning on, and the clerk in the box below the pulpit leering at the sleeping servant-girl who sits nearby. Such truly pious men as there were must often have asked themselves the Old Testament question: 'Can these dry bones live?'

However, the movement which was to be known as Methodism was, by the middle of the century, already under way. Its founders, Wesley and Whitefield, had realized that if they were to reach the people they must go outside the churches and preach in the open. They did this with some hesitation and the move provoked great resentment, especially among the country clergy.

John Wesley's own ancestry was a kind of epitome of the religious conflicts of the seventeenth century. His father, Samuel Wesley, was brought up as a Dissenter and was the son and grandson of ministers who had been deprived of their livings by the Act of Uniformity, which prescribed the use of the Anglican Prayer Book. However, both Samuel Wesley and his wife Susanna accepted in early life the teaching of the Church of England. Both were 'high church' in the days when the term had a political rather than a religious meaning. Both regarded Charles I as a martyr and professed the doctrine of non-resistance to established authority. But with Samuel Wesley, as with many high churchmen, passive obedience came to an end when James II showed signs of wishing to bring back Catholicism, and he welcomed William of Orange with sufficient ardour to be made one of the King's chaplains.

Susanna did not agree with him about this. 'Sukey,' said Samuel Wesley, after concluding family prayers in his rectory at Epworth some time in the summer of 1701, 'why did you not say *amen* this morning to the prayer for the King?'

'Because,' answered his wife, 'I do not believe the Prince of Orange to be King.'

'If that be the case,' said he, 'you and I must part; for if we have two kings, we must have two beds.'

Part they did, and it is a solemn thought that if King William had not died the following year and been succeeded by Queen Anne who satisfied the loyalties of both, they would never have met again and John Wesley would never have been born.

In his early days, John Wesley was a striking example of the different currents which swayed religious life at the time. The influences to which he reacted were extremely complex. There was the Catholic strain which came from reading the ascetic Thomas à Kempis. Wesley fasted on Wednesdays and Fridays and considered obligatory the devotions of the third, sixth and ninth hours. In 1732 we find him discussing with his mother the doctrine of the 'Real Presence'. He believed in the oblation of the elements and even, it would seem, in prayers for the dead. His view of the 'intermediate state' between Heaven and Hell was hardly distinguishable from the Catholic doctrine of Purgatory. It is almost as if he was destined to anticipate Newman by a hundred years.

Wesley's notions of the ecclesiastical function were of the most exalted order. Also he detested the predestinarian doctrines of the Calvinists, and so it was natural that, when he decided to go to America as a missionary, he should avoid the New England colonies and go to Georgia where the Church of England was 'by law established'. His brother Charles decided to go with him as secretary to General Oglethorpe, the founder of the colony, and on 10 December 1735 the Atlantic crossing was begun. On 2 February the land was sighted and the following day the *Simmonds*, the tiny vessel in which they had travelled, dropped anchor in the Savannah River.

John Wesley's original intention had been to evangelize the Indians but he soon found that there was enough for him to do in Savannah itself. The settlers, who began by liking him, found his opposition to 'Sabbath-breaking' and his insistence on fasting and long and frequent church services not at all to their taste. His brother Charles became equally unpopular for, hearing shots from a fowling-piece on a Sunday, he thought it his duty to obtain from General Oglethorpe an order forbidding all shooting on the Sabbath.

John's position was further undermined by the complications of his private life. He fell in love with a girl of eighteen, niece of one Causton, storekeeper and chief magistrate of Savannah. She had two other suitors, named Williamson and Millichamp, but she was taking French lessons from Wesley, and he by his earnest discourse turned her thoughts to religion. It was perhaps natural that the impressionable girl should fall in love with a man who was both her tutor and her spiritual director. Wesley earnestly desired to marry her if he could do so without hindering his work.

He was in great perplexity, but the girl herself, between the importunities of her other suitors, Wesley's vacillation and her own desires, was almost distracted, and her relations, to give her a breathing space, sent her to stay with some friends in another town in Georgia. Wesley visited her there and on the first occasion found her full of piety, good works, and serious conversation. But he still hesitated to propose marriage and on his second visit found her sadly changed. She had become careless and worldly – a very natural reaction – and was so unhappy that she talked of leaving America by the next boat for England.

In the end she married Williamson. He objected to religious asceticism and very strongly to her private conversations with Wesley. She began to neglect such religious duties as fasting and early morning prayer. Wesley admonished her on several occasions, but she paid no heed, and one Sunday he took the outrageous step of repelling her from the Communion Table.

A priest may, for good and sufficient reason, repel any of his flock from the ceremonies he dispenses, but if that priest be also an unsuccessful suitor, even if unsuccessful by his own will and deed, he does so at the cost of obloquy as universal as it is deserved. Causton had a warrant issued for Wesley's arrest on a charge of defamation, and Wesley decided that any chance he had ever had of doing good in Georgia had now vanished. He escaped to Charleston and thence to England.

His mission to Georgia had ended in disaster, but it had a profound influence on Wesley himself. In fact, because of what had happened on the voyage out, it might be regarded as the turning point in his life. Travelling in the same ship were the Moravians, Protestant Dissenters fleeing from their homes to escape the persecution of the Archbishop of Salzburg. Wesley was much impressed by their piety and by their behaviour during a storm. Alone among the passengers they remained completely unmoved.

Their patron was Count Zinzendorf, who had allowed them to settle on his estate in Saxony. He represented the new pietistic wave of German Lutheranism. Wesley, having returned to London, was once more in touch with the Moravians and met Zinzendorf himself. He read Luther's *Commentary on the Epistle to the Galatians* and through it found the central thread which runs from Saint Paul through Saint Augustine to Luther. Clinging to this, he parted company – although he did not know it – from the Catholic Church, of which the Church of England has always considered itself a part.

It is not impossible to accept both Justifications by Faith (in the Lutheran sense) and the Apostolic Succession, but although the doctrines are not incompatible, it is very difficult for them to remain together in stable equilibrium. Newman came down on one side and went to Rome; Wesley came down on the other and (even against his will) became founder of a new Dissent.

It would be difficult to over-estimate the importance of this in the religious life of England, at least so far as the lower stratum of English society was concerned. In a long life of evangelical endeavour, Wesley and his conversions transformed other lives to an incalculable extent. His influence even reached down to the brutalized workers in the coal-fields. It has been claimed that by bringing religion to the working classes, he saved England from its own French Revolution and if this is an exaggeration there is at least a grain of truth in it. No English mobs in the late eighteenth century pulled down churches or chapels (except, of course, Catholic chapels, as in the Gordon Riots of 1780, for the prejudice against the Church of Rome was still intense).

Wesley even influenced the Church of England itself. It began to stir from its torpor and produced from its own ranks an evangelical movement which had a profound influence on English life. Its influence was, perhaps, not entirely to the good, for if it promoted many humanitarian projects, especially the abolition of slavery, it was fanatically puritanical, sabbatarian and intolerant of ordinary people's pleasures. All the same it is impossible to see the period clearly if we think of such figures as Sandwich and John Wilkes, or even of Horace Walpole and Dr Johnson, and forget to include men like John Wesley.

I

FOOTNOTES

1 J.H.Robinson, *Medieval and Modern Times*, Boston 1919.
2 Ernst Kohn-Bramstedt, *Aristocracy and the Middle Classes in Germany*, London 1937.
3 Henry Bamford Parkes, *The American People*, London 1949.
4 'No, no. I will have mistresses.' 'That will be no obstacle.'
5 We should remember that in the eighteenth century 'enthusiasm' (='filled with the god') was a term of abuse, equated with religious fanaticism. Even John Wesley said: 'I can be accused of many things but not of enthusiasm if I can help it.'

2 Crime and Punishment

The typical criminal of the eighteenth century was the highwayman or the footpad; the former, armed with pistols, frequented the high roads; the latter, armed with cutlasses and knives, waited at places where foot travellers might be expected to pass. The favourite locations for both were the commons which then surrounded London, such as Hampstead Heath, Bagshot, Finchley Common, Epping Forest, Hounslow Hill and Blackheath. The highwaymen were as a rule excellently mounted and could easily overtake the lumbering coaches on which they preyed. The names of Jack Shepherd, Tom King, Dick Turpin, Sixteen String Jack and Paul Clifford have passed into legend, some of them because of the chivalry they allegedly displayed, being especially polite to ladies and even (like Tom King) restoring to them any article of jewellery for which they had a sentimental attachment. Their audacity knew no bounds. In the previous generation there was actually a scheme to stop the coach of Queen Caroline, the wife of George II, on her way to St James's Palace and rob her of her jewels; and later in the century the Prince of Wales (afterwards George IV) and the Duke of York were stopped one night in a hackney coach in Berkeley Square and robbed.

In 1744 the Lord Mayor and the Aldermen of London made a petition to the King which said that 'diverse confederacies of a great number of evilly disposed persons, armed with bludgeons, pistols, cutlasses and other dangerous weapons, infest not only the private lanes and passages but likewise the public streets and places of usual concourse, and commit the most daring outrages upon the persons of His Majesty's good subjects'; and they called for a more rigorous application of the law. It is true that the law was not very effective and the novelist Tobias Smollett comments:

This defect, in a great measure, arose from an absurd notion that laws necessary to prevent these acts of cruelty, violence and rapine would be incompatible with the liberty of British subjects; a notion that confounds all distinction between liberty and brutal licentiousness, as if that freedom was desirable in the enjoyment of which people find no security for their lives or effects.

13

Smollett's contemporary, the novelist Henry Fielding, who was also a magistrate, brought out 'An Enquiry into the causes of the Increase of Robbers' in which he stated that some of the best known highwaymen have:

... committed robberies in open daylight, in the sight of many people and have afterwards rode silently and triumphantly through the neighbouring towns without any danger of molestation. This happens to every rogue who has become eminent or whose audaciousness is thought to be desperate ... Officers of justice have owned to me that they have passed by such with warrants in their pockets against them without daring to apprehend them.

A similar story is told by Horace Walpole (in a letter to Sir Horace Mann, 30 September 1750): 'I was sitting in my own dining room on Sunday night – the clock had not struck eleven – when I heard a loud cry of "Stop thief". A highwayman had attacked a post-chaise in Piccadilly, within fifty yards of the house. The fellow was pursued, rode over the watchman, almost killed him and escaped.' In a later letter to Sir Horace Mann, in 1752, he remarks: 'One is forced to travel, even at noon, as if one were going to battle.'[1]

The pedestrian in the streets of London and other cities was given very little protection by the authorities; the watchmen, or 'charlies' as they were called, were frequently recruited from elderly men who had applied to the parish for relief. They were provided with a rattle, a cudgel and a greatcoat and housed in a little wooden box. They were also provided with a lantern and were expected to walk round their beat once an hour calling out the time of night and a comment on the weather. Thieves and footpads paid little attention to them and the watchmen knew only too well what treatment was likely to be accorded to them if they interfered; they were also much harassed by the young 'bloods' who frequently after a drunken orgy sallied forth to 'tease the charlies'. The box would be overturned or more often placed with its door against the wall so that the occupant could not get out.

There was no day watch and of course no detective police, but a beginning was made with what afterwards became known as the Bow Street Runners (they were first called after the name of the magistrate to whose office they were attached, as Justice Wright's people or Sir John Fielding's people). These primitive police were quite efficient in a limited way and were certainly more respectable than their predecessors, the thief takers, the most notorious of whom was Jonathan Wilde, who were often the accomplices of the men they afterwards turned in.

The *Annual Register* for 21 October 1763 notes that 'a horse patrol, under the direction of Sir John Fielding, is fixed upon the several roads near the metropolis, for the protection of His Majesty's subjects. The patrol consists of eight persons well mounted and armed.' Twenty years later we read that 'patrols on horse and foot were stationed from Sadler's Wells Lane, around the new road to Tottenham Court Road Turnpike; likewise from the City

Road to Moorfield; it was found necessary to do the same at other places.'

Evidence was hard to get. A man called Burnworth was the leader of a gang of robbers and the Government offered a reward of three hundred pounds (which was a very large sum in those days) if any of his accomplices would help to arrest him. Out of fear or loyalty none came forward, and Burnworth became so bold that, according to the *Newgate Calendar*, on one occasion he sat down at the bar of a public house in Holborn, called for a pint of beer and drank it holding a pistol in his other hand by way of protection. He then went out with the greatest apparent unconcern.

To be a tollgate keeper was a hazardous occupation. The *Annual Register* for 23 July 1762 notes that 'one Richard Watson, Tollman of Marylebone Turnpike, was found barbarously murdered in his tollhouse; upon which, and some attempts made on other Tollhouses, the trustees of Turnpikes have come to a resolution to increase the number of toll-gatherers and to furnish them with arms, strictly enjoining them, at the same time, not to keep any money at the toll bars after eight o'clock at night.'

Gentlemen of this period usually carried swords, and simple citizens found it prudent to arm themselves with cudgels when going home at night or coming away from some place of entertainment. They also tried to form companies of vigilantes; the *British Spy* for 21 September 1782 recorded that 'the inhabitants about Moorfield have come to a resolution of going armed in a body about their neighbourhood, every night until eleven o'clock, to clear it of thieves.'

Dick Turpin and Tom King were among the most noted highwaymen of their day. They worked together for some years but an unfortunate (for them) accident brought their partnership to an end. A horse which had been stolen one Saturday night was discovered the following Monday by a certain Mr Boyes (presumably an officer of the Watch) at the Red Lion Inn at Whitechapel. King's brother went to collect it and was seized; after being promised his liberty he disclosed that there was 'a lusty man in a white duffle coat waiting for the horse in Red Lion Street'. Boyes went there, recognized King and attempted to take him into custody. King drew a pistol and pointed it at Boyes but it did not go off; when Turpin, who had been waiting nearby, rode up, King called out to him: 'Dick, shoot, or we are taken, by God!' Turpin fired at Boyes but missed him and shot King instead. King died a week afterwards of the wound but Turpin got away.

The most famous Englishman of the century was Dick Turpin who long eluded pursuit and whose most spectacular feat was to 'ride to York' jumping over all the turnpike gates on the way. This was the subject of innumerable broadsheets. The sympathies of the public were not always on the side of law and order. A few years later MacLean was the admired highwayman. His gentlemanly deportment was extolled and a sort of admiration kindled for him in the public mind; his crimes were gaily recounted by those who did not suffer from them; and the excited tales told produced no doubt a crop of young aspirants to succeed him on the road and to end like him on the gallows. The ladies took great notice of him while he was in Newgate prison and kept him well supplied with money. But they could not save him from being hanged on the gallows at Tyburn. MacLean is immortalized in *The Beggars' Opera*, the moral effect of which was so much deplored by Dr Johnson. At most public executions, in fact, the sympathies of the mob seem to have been on the side of the criminals. One such, the *Annual Register* for 1764 tells us, 'addressed himself to the populace of Tyburn, and told them he could wish they would carry his body and lay it at the door of Mr Parker, a butcher in the Minories, who, it seems, was the principal evidence against him; which being accordingly done the mob behaved so riotously before the man's house that it was no easy matter to disperse them.' The astonishing thing about this story is that the authorities allowed or were unable to prevent the body being carried from the place of execution through the heart of the city, a distance of seven miles. Respect for authority was indeed at a low ebb, for many of the London magistrates at that time were notoriously corrupt. One of the exceptions was Henry Fielding, who declared that in his career as a Middlesex magistrate he reduced the profits of his office from five hundred to three hundred pounds a year by refusing to accept bribes. In his comedy *Rape Upon Rape* he shows a picture of one of his venal colleagues in the person of Justice Squeezum.

The gallows was a familiar sight in the City outskirts. To quote Alexander Andrews:

Enter it at every point, and you have to pass a line of gibbets. Pass up the Thames, there would be gibbets along its bank, with the rotting remains of mutineers or persons who had committed murders on the high seas, hanging from them in chains. Land at Execution Dock, and the gallows were being erected for the punishment of some fellow of the same club. Enter from the west by Oxford Street, and there were the gallows at Tyburn . . . cross any of the heaths, commons or forests near London, and you would be startled by the creaking of the chains from which some gibbetted highwayman was dropping piecemeal.[2]

Nor was the gallows an unfamiliar sight in the town itself. We hear of them being erected in Fleet Street, in the Strand, in Covent Garden and opposite the end of Panton Street.

One of the causes of the law's ineffectiveness was its failure to distinguish between serious crimes and minor offences. Murder, highway robbery, burglary, forgery were classified as capital crimes, but the term also included returning to England after being transported, arson, incendiarism, horse and sheep stealing, falsifying certificates of marriage and even, under a law of George I, the illegal destruction of ornamental trees. The *Annual Register* for 24 October 1763 tells us that 'since the middle of July, more than one hundred and fifty persons have been committed to the new prison at Clerkenwell, for robberies and other capital offences'. Twenty years later, in 1786, there were forty-four public executions in London and in the following year a hundred and one; 'it was the custom to execute them in batches'.

Persons convicted of high treason were still subject to the old barbaric sentence of being hanged, drawn and quartered; after they had been hanged their genitals were cut off, their bodies ripped up and the intestines torn out and burnt; they were then beheaded, the head being exposed until it rotted on a spike; the bodies were then cut in four pieces and despatched to the four corners of the kingdom to be exposed as a warning to others. The courts sometimes decreed that this barbaric procedure should take place before the victim finally expired. It was expressly laid down in the case of de la Motte, who was convicted of high treason in carrying on a secret correspondence with the enemy, 'that he should be drawn to the place of execution on a hurdle and there be hanged by the neck but not until he was dead, and that his bowels should be taken out and burnt before his face.' In executions where quartering was not practised, i.e. for crimes considered less heinous than high treason, the body was given to the surgeons for dissection. In the final piece of Hogarth's *The Four Stages of Cruelty*, we can watch this being done.

In *The Countryman's Magazine* for March 1754, we read that twelve malefactors were executed at Tyburn: 'Dennis Neale, John Mason, John Walsh, Robert Keys, Grace Grammitt and Joshua Kim for diverse highway robbery; John Smith and William Ford, for horse stealing; Richard Hutton, for returning from transportation; Daniel Wood for sheep stealing; Thomas Barnard and William Jiggs for burglaries.' It will be noted that one of these was a woman; a more horrible fate awaited those women who were convicted of what was called 'petit treason' or murdering their husbands – they were sentenced to be burnt alive. They could also be burnt alive for coining. It is curious that coining cases often included a woman either as principal or as accomplice. A writer of the period explains that 'as the decency due to their sex forbids the exposing and publicly mangling of their bodies their sentence is to be drawn to the gallows, and there to be burnt alive'; but, he goes on, 'the humanity of the English nation has authorized by a tacit consent, the almost general mitigation of such part of these punishments as savours of torture and cruelty; a sledge or hurdle being usually allowed such traitors as are condemned to be drawn and there being few instances, but those accidental or by negligence, of any persons being embowelled or burnt, not to be previously deprived of sensation by strangling.' But this 'human' proviso was not altogether effective, for when Katherine Hayes was burnt at Tyburn for the murder of her husband the hangman slackened the rope before she was dead and it was some time before she died.

Accused persons who refused to plead were still subject to the *peine forte et dure*, or pressing to death. John Chamberlayne in his *Present State of Great Britain* tells us what this implied:

The criminal to be sent back to prison from whence he came, and there laid in some dark room on the bare ground on his back, all naked, his arms and legs drawn with cords fastened to the several corners of the room; and then should be laid upon his body irons and stones, so much as he can bear, or more; the next day he shall have three morsels of barley bread without drink, and the third day he shall have drink of the water next to the prison door, except it be running water, without bread, and this shall be his diet till he dies. Which grievous type of death some stout fellows have chosen, and so, not being tried and convicted of their crimes, their estates may not be forfeited to the King but descend to their children, nor their blood stained.[3]

However, in a later edition of his book (1755) he adds: 'But yet we so abhor cruelty that of late they are suffered to be over-charged with the weights laid upon them, that they expired presently.' Pressing to death was not abolished until 1771.

Less horrible but still extremely unpleasant was exposure in the pillory. Such pillories were set up at Charing Cross, Cheapside, St Paul's church-yard, Cornhill and Aldgate. The victim's head was inserted in the hole between two planks and his ears nailed to the wood. Sometimes he was also stripped to the waist, tied to the back of a cart and whipped through the streets. He could also have his tongue bored by a red-hot iron or his nose slit, or be branded with capital letters indicating his offences, as 'SO' for seditious libeller, on either cheek; 'M' for manslaughter; 'T' for thief on the left hand; 'R' for rogue and vagabond on the shoulder; and 'P' for perjury on the forehead. The *Westminster Journal* of 29 October 1774 records that 'Ann Leaver, convicted of grand larceny, was sentenced to be branded in the hand'; and on 25 October, Catherine Clark 'for petit larceny to be privately whipped'. Whipping of women either in public or in private was not abolished in England until 1820. It is curious to note that the fee for whipping a woman was threepence at the beginning of the century, but by 1759 had risen to two shillings and sixpence – it is suggested that one-and-six of this was for hiring the cart. Nor was one whipping always enough, for the *Public Ledger* for 1764 records: 'On Wednesday the 14th a woman, an old offender, was conveyed in a cart from Clerkenwell Bridewell to Enfield, and publicly whipped at the cart's tail by the common hangman, for cutting down and destroying wood in Enfield Chase. She was to undergo the same discipline twice more.' Even unconvicted prisoners were sometimes whipped in prison, as is related in Smollett's *Roderick Random* (1748), in which one of the characters who had been arrested on suspicion of a felony was, she relates, 'often whipped into a swoon, and lashed out of it'. Her attempt to commit suicide 'was punished with thirty stripes, the pain of which bereft her of her senses'.

Although most of the English penal code had been taken to America by the first colonists, it would seem that on the whole it was not so drastically enforced. Malefactors were whipped, placed in the pillory and the stocks and hanged just as they were in England, but the arm of the law was even less effective and in an underdeveloped country did not reach so far. In New England the 'ecclesiastical' discipline of the Puritans was drastic enough. The adulteress was compelled to wear the 'scarlet letter' 'H' on the bodice of her dress. In the late seventeenth century there was the episode of the 'witches of Salem', but even they were hanged and not burned alive. And by the time our study commences these excesses had long been over.

It is something of a shock to realize that foreign observers in general regarded the English penal code as more merciful than their own. Judicial torture was practised in France up to the time of the Revolution; the method varied according to the part of France in which it occurred. At Rouen the thumb-screw was in use; in Brittany the bared feet were placed in front of a fire and were gradually pushed nearer to it; at Besançon the prisoner was hung from the ceiling by his hands and increasing weights attached to his feet; in Paris the victim was tortured by being made to swallow enormous quantities of water. There was also the torture known as 'the boot'; Damiens, who had attempted to assassinate Louis XV, was tortured in this manner for several hours before being led off to execution. Prisoners could still be tortured in order to extract an admission of guilt; they could still be sent to the galleys, flogged and branded, have their hands cut off, or their tongue cut out or pierced.

Enlightened minds were beginning to think all judicial torture repugnant. The great Montesquieu protested against it, as did also Voltaire; the Marquis Beccaria published an essay on crime and punishment in which he pleaded for more humane practices. Judicial torture in France was finally abolished in 1788.

In Paris the traditional scene of executions was the Place de la Grève. The process of putting to death was of three kinds: the criminal could be hanged, or burned alive, or broken on the wheel. Damiens was pulled to pieces by having his limbs attached to four horses which were then driven off in opposite directions, but this was the only time this punishment was inflicted in the eighteenth century. We have noted that in England women condemned to death were sometimes burned but were strangled beforehand. In France people were still burned alive; sometimes the victim was clad in a shirt soaked in sulphur, which meant he was truly burned instead of being slowly roasted. Sometimes he was strangled either by decision of the justices or secretly by the executioner himself, presumably in return for bribes. Sometimes, before being attached to the stake, the victim had his right hand cut off at the wrist. Burning at the stake fell out of use some years before the Revolution.

The most horrible of all the punishments inflicted in France under the *ancien régime* was that of being broken on the wheel. This was the usual punishment for murder, highway robbery and arson. It is said to have been imported from Germany by a law of 1534 and lasted in France until 1789. The victim was tied to a wheel, placed horizontally upon a stake, in such a way that his limbs crossed the spokes of the wheel; his bones were then broken with an iron bar. During this torture a priest stood beside the condemned man holding a crucifix and exhorting him to confess his sins. Sometimes the victim was on the wheel for hours before death came to his relief; sometimes he was removed from the wheel while still alive and burned at the stake.

The penalty of being broken on the wheel was imposed in other parts of Europe. Oliver Goldsmith, visiting Lisbon shortly after an attempt on the life of the King of Portugal, reports: '*Our merciful Sovereign* has been for some time past recovered of his fright: though so atrocious attempt deserved to exterminate half the nation, yet he has been graciously pleased to spare the lives of his subjects, and not above five hundred have been broken upon the wheel, or otherwise executed upon this horrid occasion.'

At least one thing had vanished in the eighteenth century from the penal codes of England and France: the death sentence for heresy. This was still in force in Portugal and Spain and, to quote once more from Oliver Goldsmith's account of his visit to Lisbon, 'yesterday we had an *auto da fé*, at which were burnt three young women accused of heresy, one of them of exquisite beauty, two Jews and an old woman, convicted of being a witch. One of the friars, who attended this last, reports that he saw the devil fly out of her at the stake in the shape of a flame of fire. The populace behaved on this occasion with great good humour, joy and sincere devotion.'

The French form of the pillory consisted of a gibbet to which was attached an iron collar into which the neck of the victim could be locked. The device was used to punish nearly all criminals not condemned to death and often for crimes which in modern times would be considered petty, such as picking the coins out of a church alms box by means of a stick with a little glue on the end. Coachmen being found guilty of insolence were similarly punished (a mark of the still aristocratic system in France), domestic servants who were guilty of carrying a stick or cane, usurers and men who lived on the immoral earnings of women. For most of these exposure in the pillory was by no means the end of the matter; they could then be whipped, branded, banished, imprisoned or sent to the galleys.

Whipping at the cart-tail was practised in France as well as in England; branding was performed in public with a red-hot iron in the form of a letter 'V' for *voleur* (thief), a fleur-de-lys, or the letters 'GAL' for those condemned to the galleys. Special care was taken to make the mark indelible. A curious addition to these punishments was known as *la promenade à l'âne*, which consisted of seating a condemned man on the back of an ass with his face towards the tail; the beast was then led through the streets and the rider was subjected to the insults and missiles of the mob. This punishment, which had fallen into disuse in Paris, was revived in 1750; it was abolished in 1791.

Prison conditions were bad in England and France, even worse in Italy, Spain and Portugal. If we count the seignorial dungeons, there were about twenty prisons in Paris at the end of the seventeenth century. In these, prisoners were often detained without trial for many years. A woman prisoner arrested in 1774 spent thirty years in the prison of Saint-Martin and when she finally came up for trial it was found impossible to pass judgement upon her 'in view of the death of all parties concerned in the case'.

The prisoners were divided into three principal categories. There were the *pailleux* (those who were given merely straw to lie on), who slept in a kind of dormitory, and in one of these in Le Châtelet there was at one moment a count of more than a hundred. Those who could afford to pay were a little better off: for five *sous* a day they had a room to themselves and for three *sous* a room for two. Really rich prisoners were allowed a room with a fireplace and a supply of coal.

One advantage the prisoners in the eighteenth century had over those in the nineteenth was that they were released from their cells during the day and were able to walk about the prison as they pleased; the only obligation seems to have been to hear mass at nine o'clock in the morning and prayers in the evening. The wives of those detained were allowed into the prison on condition that they entered no other room than that of their husbands. Rich prisoners could have provisions brought in from outside, but of course the jailers and *concierges* exploited this to their own advantage. The *pailleux* were less fortunate; they were provided with little more than straw, water and bread, and it was bread of very poor quality. This was the cause of frequent riots. Sometimes the prisoners fought among themselves or attacked the jailers; pistols and other weapons were sometimes smuggled in from outside. Escapes were numerous and the remedy found by the authorities was to load some of their prisoners with chains or even to attach them to the wall by means of an iron band passing round their necks. Few survived such treatment as the cells in which they were enclosed were damp and insanitary and sometimes almost entirely without ventilation. The sanitation of the cells was of a most primitive kind and disease was rampant. Even in England the judges were sometimes provided with nose clips against the appalling stench when prisoners were brought before them.

A committee of the House of Commons appointed in 1727 to inquire into the condition of the Fleet Prison and its internal discipline revealed a shocking state of affairs.[4] Prisoners were in chains in waterlogged dungeons and tortured without any process of law. Perhaps the worst aspect was the extortions practised by the jailers; the slightest privileges had to be heavily paid for, and if the prisoner had no help from outside he was likely to starve to death. Prisoners were, however, allowed to call out through a grating to passers-by, 'Pray remember the debtors', for debtors were confined in the same cells as felons. Debtors who had somehow retained some money of their own were charged a heavy rent for separate rooms. The treatment of lunatics in the eighteenth century was particularly shocking. They were half-starved, lodged in filthy cells, chained to the wall and frequently whipped. All this took place in Bedlam and it is a commentary on the insensitivity of the age that Bedlam – the old Bethlehem Hospital – was the scene of an exhibition to which the public flocked. *The World* for 7 June 1753 says: 'to satisfy the curiosity of a country friend I accompanied him a few weeks ago to Bedlam. It was in Easter week, when, to my great surprise, I found a hundred people at least, who having paid their twopence apiece, were suffered, unattended, to run up and down the wards, making sport and diversion of the miserable inhabitants.'

Sensitivity to suffering varies from age to age. It is appalling to think that more people have died by violence, *in our own century* than in the previous three hundred years. The battle fronts in two world wars, Auschwitz, Dachau, Hiroshima – it is a horrifying catalogue. Future ages will probably condemn us for our cruelty as we condemn the eighteenth century. The difference would seem to be that while we are insensitive to human suffering if it is sufficiently remote from our own experience, the eighteenth century positively revelled in it at first hand. Every public execution was a gala, a holiday. There can be no denying that seeing their fellow creatures put to death gave pleasure to people of all classes.

The paradox is exemplified in the life of George Selwyn. He was certainly a highly cultivated man, popular in the numerous clubs to which he belonged. He passed for a wit and had a wide circle of friends, including Horace Walpole who said of him when he died: 'From eight years I have known him intimately without a cloud between us; few knew him so well and consequently few knew so well the goodness of his heart and nature.' Yet he had an obsession with death and never missed an opportunity to see a corpse. This was so well known that Lord Holland, on his death-bed, is alleged to have said to his servant: 'If Mr Selwyn calls, show him up. If I am alive I shall be very pleased to see him; and if I am dead I am sure he will be very pleased to see *me*.'

Selwyn had a passion for attending executions. He saw Lord Lovat's head cut off on Tower Hill, and he made a special journey to Paris in order to see the execution of Damiens. And when he found some difficulty in pushing his way through the crowd, the executioner, recognizing him, called out, *'Faîtes place pour Monsieur; c'est un Anglais et un amateur.'*[5] It was not as if he were collecting evidence for some projected reform; in fact he would probably have resisted this. Perhaps there is more unacknowledged sadism in the human heart in any period than we are willing to admit.

2

FOOTNOTES

1 Horace Walpole, *Letters*, ed. Mrs Paget Toynbee, Oxford 1914.
2 Alexander Andrews, *The Eighteenth Century*, London 1856.
3 John Chamberlayne, *Magnae Britanniae Notitia, or The Present State of Great Britain*, London 1705.
4 There is an appalling account of prison life at this period in the opening chapters of Henry Fielding's *Amelia*, 1752.
5 'Make way for the gentleman; he is an Englishman and an enthusiast.'

3 Sports and Pastimes

It is impossible to deny that many of the so-called sports popular in the eighteenth century were extremely brutal and cruel. Bull-baiting and bear-baiting had been practised in England from the twelfth century at least. In Queen Elizabeth I's time, as every student of Shakespeare knows, the building on Bankside erected for bear-baiting stood side by side with the Globe Theatre, and patrons passed indifferently from one kind of entertainment to the other. After being prohibited under Cromwell – the Puritans deserve credit, at least for *that* – the old sports were revived after the Restoration and carried on for another century.

Few found anything wrong with them, but they convinced some foreign observers of the natural barbarity of the English nation. In the *Tatler* in the early years of the century, Sir Richard Steele, writing of the cock-shy, in which a cock was tied by the leg and sticks were thrown at it until it died, remarked that some:

... French writers have represented this diversion of the common people much to our disadvantage, and imputed it to a natural fierceness and cruelty of temper, as they do some other entertainments peculiar to our nation; I mean those elegant diversions of bull-baiting and prize-fighting, with the like ingenious recreations of the bear-garden. I wish I knew how to answer this reproach which is cast upon us, and excuse the death of so many innocent cocks, bulls, dogs, and bears, as have been set together by the ears, or died an untimely death, only to make us sport.[1]

By this time bull-baiting seems to have been more frequent than bear-baiting, due possibly to the difficulty of obtaining bears. There was no scarcity of bulls in an England still so largely rural, and baiting them took place in some districts almost every Sunday. The bull was tied by a fairly long rope to a stake and the dogs were loosed at him one by one.[2] The horns were sometimes blunted or tipped with metal buttons, so that the dog would be tossed rather than gored. If, however, the dog was tossed high he was quite likely to break his back in the fall.

Many kinds of dogs were used but the favourite was, naturally enough, the bulldog, bred over the centuries for this very purpose; and when a good dog of this breed once fastened his teeth in the nose of the bull nothing could prise him off. Sometimes the bull lived to fight again and sometimes he was slaughtered, the flesh of a baited bull being much esteemed. Occasionally the bull not only killed some of the dogs but broke loose and mauled the spectators. He was then beaten to death with cudgels. It was one of the 'humane' rules introduced in the eighteenth century that such cudgels should not be tipped with iron!

The practice of bull-baiting was long thought to have been particularly prevalent in Warwickshire, in the region round Birmingham.[3] There was a curious connection between bull-baiting and church services, as for example in the 'Chapel Wake' held on Snow Hill, Birmingham, 'in commemoration of the building of St Bartholomew's Chapel'. At this celebration in 1798 the whole of the local militia turned out with drums beating and flags flying. Nearly all local wakes included bull-baiting and as few of them fell on the same date it was possible for a 'good' bull to take part in a whole succession of them. We hear of one baited at Madeley, Broseley and Ironbridge, all small towns in Shropshire.

The cruelty practised was almost unbelievable, for the bull was not only attacked by dogs but roused to fury by being pricked with sharp stones or surrounded with burning straw. It is not surprising that less hardened Englishmen began to protest and some local authorities tried to put a stop to these barbarous practices. Under the Turnpike Act it was made an offence to bait a bull in a street or other public place, but it was not an offence to bait it on private property, a curious example of the roundabout way in which reforms in England were sometimes brought about.

Various attempts had been made to suppress bull-baiting by law, but the attempt to do so by Act of Parliament failed in 1802, and it was not until 1835, two years before the accession of Queen Victoria, that an act was passed forbidding the keeping of any 'house, pit or other place for baiting or fighting any bull, bear, dog or other animal'.

Another cruel sport popular throughout the period was cock-fighting. It had a long tradition behind it for it was known to the Greeks and the Romans. It was practised in England even before the Romans arrived, for, astonishing as it may seem, specimens of the spurs used in cock-fighting have been found among the relics of the prehistoric lake-dwellers at Glastonbury. It is also surprising to learn that in medieval times schoolmasters (some of whom were monks) gained considerable profits from matches organized by their own scholars.

Cock-fighting was very popular in Elizabethan times; prohibited during the Commonwealth, it burst out again under Charles II. It was, indeed, patronized by royalty and there were 'royal' cock-pits at Windsor and

Newmarket and several in London, the most famous being that in Birdcage Walk, much resorted to by Members of Parliament.

We need not concern ourselves with the elaborate rules drawn up for regulating the contests. In most cock-pits the arena was a round table, about a foot lower than an ordinary table, and around this were two rows of the most highly-priced seats. Behind these, and separated from them by a low barrier, were two or three rows of benches and behind these again, standing room.

Hoyle's *Games* of about 1750 includes elaborate instructions for the breeding and rearing of game-cocks. The diet of these birds included wheat-flour, eggs and butter worked into a stiff paste and baked; also hot wine. It is no wonder that the phrase 'fed like a fighting cock' passed into the language. The birds, after being exercised by attacking a mere 'dunghill cock', were carried back to their pens and anointed with a salve of fresh butter mixed with leaves of rue, hyssop and rosemary. The massage was completed by *licking* the head and eyes; some breeders licked the birds all over. Then the comb was cut off, the tail clipped close to the body and head-feathers pulled out, and the spurs cleaned and sharpened. For the actual contest the bird was fitted with steel spurs to make the fight more deadly.

In the cock-pit the birds were held beak to beak and then released. They immediately flew at one another with much flapping but as they grew tired and began to bleed from their wounds they ceased to waste their strength in such displays and began to work in close to one another like boxers in the ring. Sometimes a cock was able to dispatch its opponent with a single stroke. Usually even the victorious bird was severely wounded, and its keeper instructed to 'search and suck your cock's wounds, and wash them well with hot urine. . . . If he be hurt in the eye, chew a little ground ivy and spit the juice in it.' One can only wonder how many human patients at this period were treated with equal care.

One of the most notable patrons of the sport in the eighteenth century was that same Earl of Derby who gave his name to the most famous of horse races. He is said at one time to have had three thousand game-cocks on his estate, and his chief 'feeder', a man called Potter, was famous all over the country. Joseph Gilliver was even more celebrated, enjoying the patronage of both George III and George IV. The profession was carried on by the Gilliver family for generations and there is today a cock-fighting museum at Polesworth near the hamlet where they lived. In *Old English Sports*, Frederick W. Hackwood tells us that the name of this hamlet was changed from Birchmoor to Cockspur and is still listed under that name in the postal directory.

There can be no doubt of the immense popularity of cock-fighting in the eighteenth century. Its patrons ranged from kings to costers. Even fine ladies did not disdain to watch it and to stake large sums on the performance of their birds or those of their friends. Parsons too joined in the sport, even on Sundays, for we hear of clerics like the 'Parson of Willenhall' who had almost to be dragged from the cock-pit when the time came for him to conduct the service in the neighbouring church.

The fights which frequently broke out among the humans at cock-fights, especially if the cock-pit stood near the ale-house, were a cause of grave concern to the parish authorities, and some attempt was made to put them down. At Wednesbury in 1750 publicans were warned that 'all such persons who shall in future aid, encourage, or abet in any way whatever in carrying on cock-fighting, or any such sports, shall have their licences withdrawn, and all cockers who shall be caught stirring up or inciting any assembly to riot shall be whipped at the common whipping-post'.

Gradually, as the century progressed, the voice of humanity began to make itself heard. As early as 1747, the *Gentleman's Magazine* published some verses which show that some people at least were beginning to realize the essential cruelty of cock-fighting:

> Come Hogarth, thou whose art can best declare
> What forms, what features, human passions wear;
> Come, with a painter's philosophic flight,
> Survey the circling judges of the fight.
> Touch'd with the sport of death, while ev'ry heart
> Springs to the changing face, exert thy art;
> Mix with the smiles of cruelty at pain
> Whate'er looks anxious in the lust of gain;
> And say, can aught that's gen'rous, just or kind,
> Beneath this aspect, lurk within the mind?

More than a generation later, the poet Crabbe expressed similar sentiments:

> Here his poor bird th' inhuman cocker brings,
> Arms his hard heels and clips his golden wings;
> With spicy food the impatient spirit feeds,
> And shouts and curses as the battle bleeds.
> Struck through the brain, deprived of both his eyes,
> The vanquished bird must combat till he dies –
> Must faintly peck at his victorious foe,
> And reel and stagger at each feeble blow.
> When fallen, the savage grasps his dappled plumes,
> His bloodstained arms for other deaths assumes,
> And damns the craven fool that lost his stake
> And only bled and perished for his sake.

Cock-fighting survived, however, and was never more popular than in the Regency period. At last, in 1849, it was made illegal by Act of Parliament.

Hunting and hawking at least give the quarry a chance. They all have a long history in England, the learned Strutt devoting almost a whole chapter of his book, *The Sports and Pastimes of the People of England* (London 1801), to their practice among the Saxons, Danes and Normans and in medieval and later periods. Nearly all our kings, at least from Alfred the Great, were passionately devoted to the chase, and in early times there was plenty of scope in the extensive forests which almost covered the land. By the beginning of the eighteenth century these had been considerably diminished and what remained no longer harboured the wolf and the wild boar. Deer remained and so did hares and foxes and birds of many kinds. In early days most of the latter were caught in nets or killed by trained hawks, but as firearms became more efficient so hawking declined. Strutt tells us that it seems to have been at its zenith at the commencement of the seventeenth century; by the close, it was rarely practised, and a few years afterwards hardly known.

We need not here concern ourselves with the medieval distinctions between 'beasts of venery' (the hart, hind, hare, boar and wolf) and 'beasts of the chase' (buck, doe, fox, marten and roe), nor with the extraordinary names given to these creatures at different ages. Nor need we trouble ourselves with all the legal apparatus erected for the punishment of poachers. The organization of royal hunting was extremely elaborate, involving as late as the seventeenth century a whole series of officers: Masters of the Game, Sergeants of the Staghounds, Lumberman of the Buckhounds, Yeoman and Pages of the Leash, with an army of underlings.

The fox at this period was little hunted, being regarded as vermin to be exterminated by trap and snare, but as it became more and more difficult to hunt the stag, the fox gradually came into prominence. The historians of the chase tell us that in the reign of William III several packs of staghounds had recently been changed to packs of foxhounds. One of the first to be so transformed was the Charlton Hunt (now Goodwood) in Sussex. The dates of the establishment of hunts still extant is not without interest: for instance in Leicestershire, the Quorn was established in 1698, the Pytchley in 1750 and the Belvoir in 1740. We may therefore conclude that from the middle of the eighteenth century the principal sport of the English country gentleman was fox-hunting.

It was very different in France. The tradition of the chase in that country started with the early Capets in the tenth century and all French kings from then until the French Revolution hunted almost every day; moreover, they hunted with a degree of lavish splendour attained by no other kings in Europe. It has been estimated that the accommodation at Versailles for the men engaged in venery was a hundred times greater than that occupied by the rooms and offices for state business. When the King hunted it was like an army setting forth. There was first the *grand veneur* and his lieutenant, four more lieutenants, nobles all, and four more who actually did the work, four under-lieutenants and forty-four *gentilshommes de vénerie*, a squire, an under-squire, several pages, a *piqueur* (whipper-in), nearly thirty men to look after the dogs and sixty-six to water the horses. There was a pack of hounds for chasing the deer, another pack which hunted the hare, and more than a hundred other hounds for hunting the wild boar, needing four lieutenants, four under-lieutenants, and a corps of dog handlers and guards. Hunting the wolf required a similar organization.

Hawking was practised up to the French Revolution. The official in charge of falconry followed the King in all his travels, even accompanying him in war. He actually asked for and received passports from the enemy general to allow him to continue his sport unhindered. When Napoleon came to power, although he judged that hunting was necessary for his prestige, he cut down the organization severely and abolished falconry altogether. He even cut down the annual expense of hunting to less than half a million francs; it must have been at least ten times as much during the *ancien régime*. After the Restoration Charles x, who was passionately devoted to hunting, tried to revive the ancient splendour, and it was one of the counts against him at the Revolution of 1830 that he had wasted the public money on a sport which was by then so far out of fashion.

As the eighteenth century progressed many Englishmen began to be more interested in horse-racing than in hunting. Horse-racing can be traced at least to Saxon times, and in the Middle Ages there seem to have been regular meetings, particularly at Chester and Stamford. In the seventeenth century horse-racing took place in Hyde Park and at Newmarket, the latter being specially favoured by Charles II, and we read in the *Spectator*, early in the eighteenth century, of what would now be called a 'selling plate' to be run on Coleshill Heath in Warwickshire. Queen Anne was fond of the sport and kept and raced horses in her own name. In 1713 she gave a cup to be competed for at York. The meetings at Doncaster were started in 1703, although the St Leger (named after Colonel St Leger, a noted Yorkshire sportsman) was not established until 1778.

The other famous race to be named after a patron of the Turf is, of course, the Derby. In 1780 the twelfth Earl sponsored an event which was known as the Derby Stakes. Horse-racing had been going on at Epsom (or Banstead Downs as it was sometimes called) for more than a generation, the annual races being instituted in 1730. It was probably the amount of money involved in prizes and stakes which led to the popularity of the races at Epsom. The course was within driving distance of London and foreign observers even at this early period were immensely impressed by the great crowd of vehicles of all kinds which on Derby Day passed Hyde Park Corner for Epsom: the carriages of the nobility, post-chaises, wagons, donkey-carts; there were even those who went on foot, including the gipsies who from the beginning were a conspicuous feature of the Epsom Downs.

Stands were erected for those who could afford to purchase places but the vast majority of the spectators watched the race from the rails.

Another aspect which surprised and impressed foreign observers was the informality allowed in the heterogeneous crowd. Aristocrats who would never have dreamed at ordinary times of paying the slightest attention to tradesmen and the like greeted them with the greatest geniality on the course and even exchanged bets; the grooms and jockeys were treated with amiable familiarity and a French observer noted with astonishment the sight of a peer of the realm walking arm in arm with his own jockey.

Ascot attracted a more socially acceptable crowd. While Epsom, remarks F.W. Hackwood rather primly, is 'noted for being the saturnalia of a vast crowd', Ascot is 'distinguished for its genteel quietness and aristocratic assemblage'. The earliest recorded meeting there was in 1727. In 1772 the famous race for a Gold Cup was instituted, followed in 1785 by the establishment of a Gold Plate of one hundred guineas in value. The Ascot races, so conveniently near Windsor, were usually attended by royalty, who from an early date drove down the course in an open carriage, a tradition which is still maintained.

At Goodwood in the early eighteenth century the first Duke of Richmond purchased a hunting seat and summer residence; he seems to have been more interested in hunting than in racing. It was the third Duke who in 1801 laid out a race-course in the park, but it was not at first very successful in attracting the public to its meetings. Not until the 1820s did it begin to deserve the name of 'Glorious Goodwood'.

By the second half of the eighteenth century the English thoroughbred had become famous throughout Europe. The breed, slender, highly-strung and very fast, was made possible by crossing the sturdier English horse with an Arab, brought to England in the early eighteenth century by a Yorkshire sporting squire named Darley who had business connections with the Near East. The offspring resulting from the mating was the Duke of Devonshire's Flying Childers, one of the fleetest horses in racing history. The famous horse Eclipse, who was descended from the 'Darley Arab', not only was very successful as a racer but was the sire of 334 winners. He attained the extraordinary age of seventy-five years, dying in 1789, and his skeleton is preserved in the Oxford Museum. A portrait of Eclipse was painted by George Stubbs, and indeed it became the fashion to commission pictures of famous horses. Sartorius, a pupil of Stubbs, painted Diomed, who won the Derby in 1780; Marshall, John Fernley the Elder and many other painters both excellent and indifferent continued the style and the tradition. Their pictures in modern times change hands in sale-rooms for fantastic amounts.

Horses expected to race 'over the sticks' never attained such celebrity. They were for the most part cavalry horses or hunters and of a more sturdy build. It is in some ways surprising that steeplechasing as a public event lagged behind racing 'on the flat' for so long. The famous Grand National run at Aintree, near Liverpool, was not established until 1827 with the encouragement and patronage of William IV. The very term steeplechase only came into use during the Regency. It originated from a group of officers, probably intoxicated, who decided in the middle of the night to get on their horses and ride in a straight line towards a church steeple on the distant horizon, jumping over every obstacle in their path.

Other rural sports popular in England were coursing, angling and shooting. As we have noted, the gun had already in the seventeenth century replaced the hawk as a means of killing game-birds, but the weapons were still far from perfect and it was more usual to 'net' the birds. However, before the end of the eighteenth century a serviceable shot-gun had been evolved and we begin to find a number of sporting prints representing shooting.

Fishing has been practised from the very earliest times, not at first as a sport but out of sheer necessity; and it is interesting to note the antiquity of some of the devices used by primitive man. The Palaeolithic chipper of flints could hardly shape an effective hook but he had already invented the 'gorge', a narrow strip of flint with a groove in the middle round which the line could be fastened. This was buried in the bait and the fish swallowed it end first. The tightening of the line fixed it crosswise in the gullet. A similar device is still used in 'sniggling' eels. The first line was probably a trailing tendril and the first rod a pliant sapling. In the third century AD, a Greek writer described a line composed of coloured wool and feathers: the first known mention of a 'fly'.

In the eighteenth century the rod consisted of seasoned twigs spliced together. The line was of horsehair until this was replaced by gut. Baits of all kinds were used including, oddly enough, cows' brains. Freshwater fish might be taken at any time, except on private property; there was a close season for salmon and sea trout. The fly-fishing season lasted from April or May until September or October.

Another favourite amusement was prize-fighting. This, as a sport or as a spectacle, did not really establish itself until the eighteenth century. It is true that in 1681 we hear that 'a match of boxing was performed before his Grace the Duke of Albemarle between the Duke's footman and a butcher. The latter won the prize, as he hath done many times before, being accounted, though but a little man, the best of that exercise in England.'[4]

A generation later the famous 'Mr Figg, Master of the Noble Science of self-defence', had a booth at Southwark Fair, as well as a permanent establishment in the Oxford Road. He can be seen in Hogarth's engraving of the Fair, and Hogarth also designed his business card on which he offers to teach gentlemen 'the use of the small sword, backsword and quarterstaff'. There is no mention of pugilism. However, in one of his handbills he

31

promises to exhibit his knowledge in various combats with foil, backsword, cudgel and *fist*. It is plain that boxing was at this time beginning to take the place of the old martial exercises.

There were several other boxing schools, but Figg's 'on the right hand in Oxford Road, near Adam and Eve Court', was the most successful, and many famous fighters of the next generation were trained there. Their names have been piously preserved by one Captain Godfrey, an eye-witness of many of the combats. The aristocracy began to take an interest in the game, and we hear that 'a gentleman of advanced station' asked Figg to find an opponent for a gigantic Venetian gondolier who had been brought to England in the retinue of a nobleman returning from the Grand Tour. Figg produced a man named Whittaker who, having been knocked out of the ring by his opponent, recovered himself and 'with a little stoop, ran boldly in beyond the heavy mallet, and with one English peg in the stomach, quite a new thing to the foreigners, brought him on his breech'. The gondolier regarded this as unsporting and refused to continue the fight. We should perhaps remind ourselves that the 'Queensberry Rules' were in the future and even 'Broughton's Rules' were as yet unheard of. A certain amount of wrestling was still allowed, as in what was known as the 'buttock throw'.

Sometimes boxing matches were arranged between women. As they were thought to be more likely to scratch with their nails than to strike with their fists, they were required to grasp half-a-crown in each hand, the first woman to drop a coin being accounted the loser.

The woman who was willing to take part in such contests must have been a real virago. We find in the newspapers advertisements informing the people that, for example, 'Mrs Stokes, the City championess, is ready to meet the Hibernian Heroine at Figg's.' The results were duly reported in the press, a newspaper of 1768 informing the world that: 'Two women fought for a new shift valued at half-a-crown, in Spaw Fields, near Islington. The battle was won by a woman called Bruising Peg, who beat her antagonist in a terrible manner.'

Sometimes the women fought for a prize (as in this case), sometimes to settle a quarrel, formal challenges being given and answered, as in an announcement of 1772:

'Challenge. – I, Elizabeth Wilkinson, of Clerkenwell, having had some words with Hannah Hyfield, and require satisfaction, do invite her to meet me upon the stage, and box me for three guineas . . .'

The challenged woman replied, again in the daily press:

'I, Hannah Hyfield, of Newgate Market, hearing the resoluteness of Elizabeth Wilkinson, will not fail, God willing, to give her more blows than words, desiring home blows from her and no favour. She may expect a good thumping.'

The value of the prize leads one to suspect that the pretended quarrel between the two women was just a bit of clever publicity on the part of the promoters of the contest. It is difficult to conceive of two market women, who were probably unable to read or write, paying for advertisements in the newspapers.

Figg himself, as we have noted, was more of a swordsman and cudgel player than a boxer, but his successor, John Broughton, was solely a boxer. He established his fame at George Taylor's, Taylor having taken over Figg's amphitheatre and also opened another one, the Great Booth, in Tottenham Court Road. Broughton was the real founder of the London prize-ring. He seems to have been not only a brave fighter but an admirable character. He was born in 1705 and began life as a waterman's apprentice. As such he learned not only to row but to use his fists to some purpose, watermen being notorious for their rowdy behaviour. During his long career (he died aged eighty-four in 1789) he was only defeated once.

According to another account he was at one time the Duke of Cumberland's coachman; certainly he enjoyed His Royal Highness's patronage, and that of Frederick, Prince of Wales, until the unlucky day, 10 April 1750, when he accepted a challenge from a Norwich butcher named Slack. Broughton's supporters had no doubt of the issue and the betting was ten to one in his favour. The Duke wagered £10,000 and, when Slack temporarily blinded Broughton with a terrific blow between the eyes and won the match, was naturally furious. He patronized Broughton no more and, what was worse, now that the royal protection had been withdrawn, the authorities closed the amphitheatre which had seen so many of Broughton's triumphs.

Still, Broughton is justly remembered for his endeavour to lay down rules for prize-fighting. He established the 'round' or 'set-to' and a time limit between the rounds. He laid it down that 'no person is to butt his adversary when he is down, or seize him by the ham, the breeches, or any part below the waist; a man on his knees to be considered down'. He also insisted on 'rails' (or ropes, as we should say). The earlier prize-fights were simply fought in an open space of bare ground on which had been scratched a square of one yard each way. The fight went on until the seconds of one of the combatants were unable to 'bring him up to scratch' (the origin of that curious phrase), that is, to place one of his feet on the mark in the ground. Broughton also introduced 'mufflers', i.e. boxing-gloves, for practice fights, the real battles being, of course, conducted with bare fists.

After Broughton's disaster, boxing seems to have fallen out of favour with the aristocracy, and for some years there are no accounts of fights in the *Advertiser* or the *Gentleman's Magazine*. They still went on in the provinces and the outskirts of London, but it was not until the 1780s that the young Prince of Wales (the future 'Prinny') and his friends began to take an interest in 'the fancy' and to patronize its exponents once more. The new generation of boxers was an improvement on the old school of bruisers, in both

33

technique and manners. 'Gentleman Jackson' won the esteem of his contemporaries for his conduct in the ring and out of it, and the Jew Mendoza
made up for his lack of weight by his agility and technical skill. It became
the fashion for men like Lord Barrymore and the Duke of Hamilton to take
a chosen prize-fighter into their employment, the fighter not only to win
prize money for his patron but to act as a bodyguard when he walked abroad.
By the 1790s gentlemen had ceased to wear swords, and quarrels in such
places as Vauxhall tended to degenerate into affairs of fisticuffs. The upper
classes began to take lessons in the 'noble art' themselves, and Angelo's
Academy in St James's Street became a favourite haunt of the young bloods
of White's and other clubs in the vicinity. William B. Boulton makes the
interesting point that aristocratic young men were beginning to acquire:

... a mild taste for physical exercise, not athletic by any means as yet, but still a
step forward from the eternal lounging in card-rooms which had held the field as
the main diversion of the young man about town for nearly a century. Mr Charles
Fox and his friends at Brooks's had made a fashion of an affected negligence in
dress and the gradual disappearance of the lace ruffle, powdered wig and embroidered waistcoat ... made the change easier. The sporting young men of the
period began to take an interest in driving and even in hunting, and to dress more
like their stud grooms. Boxing as an exercise came to share in this gratifying movement, and it was reckoned the correct thing to put on the gloves with a professor at
proper intervals.[5]

Angelo was not the only one to benefit by the vogue of amateur boxing.
Another was John Jackson, who had an establishment at No. 13 Bond
Street. Although he was known as the 'emperor of pugilism' he only fought
three battles in his life. Yet he was an excellent instructor and to list his
clients, says a contemporary journalist, 'would be to copy out one-third of
the peerage'. Even Byron, in spite of his lame foot, thought it necessary to
become one of his pupils and seems to have studied also under another
famous pugilist, Thomas Cribb. It is amusing to recall that King George IV
at his coronation was so much afraid of the hostility of the crowd (angry at
the exclusion of Queen Caroline) that he surrounded himself with a bodyguard including Jackson and Cribb, clad for the occasion in the scarlet and
gold livery of the royal pages.

The fashion for amateur boxing did not last very long. The Fives Court
in St Martin's Lane and the Tennis Court in the Haymarket were the chief
places for professional bouts but these also took place in the country, in
the open air. One of the most celebrated was fought in 1808 in Sir John
Sebright's park, in Hertfordshire, between two professionals named Gully
and Gregson. It lasted for twenty-eight rounds and ended in a victory for
Gully. Gully went on to even greater triumphs for:

After a few years passed in the occupation of a tavern-keeper, he was so fortunate
in speculations and so well served by sound judgment in racing matters, that he

retired and became the purchaser of Ware Park, Hertfordshire. Here he associated with the first circles in the 'county'. He went on to purchase collieries in Yorkshire and crowned his career by being elected Member for Pontefract in the first Reformed Parliament [1832].

Boxing is still with us although under attack; so is fox-hunting. Bull-baiting, bear-baiting and cock-fighting are no more. The two sports dominant in England today – soccer and cricket – were in the eighteenth century only just beginning.

The origins of soccer lie in remote antiquity. In the Middle Ages in England it was a recognized part of Shrovetide rituals, and this aspect of the game survived in Derby until 1846; it survives at Ashbourne in Derbyshire to this day. There was little or no kicking of the ball, which was propelled backwards and forwards by the sheer weight of the massed players. The goals were three miles apart, each being the shutter of a mill-wheel, and to score a goal it was necessary for a player to swim the mill-pond through the narrow archway of the sluice and to touch the mill-wheel with the ball.

Gradually the connection of football with Shrovetide was forgotten every-where but in Derbyshire. It still bore no relation to what would be called either Rugby or Association football, or the American variant of the game. A French visitor to England at the end of the seventeenth century describes the 'ball of leather as big as one's head, filled with air; this is kicked about the streets by any who can get at it; there is nothing of science about'.[6] It was usually played in towns by apprentices and other youths. There was no limit on the number of players, and, as far as can be gathered, no rules at all. In London, football was played in the Strand, to the inconvenience and even danger of passers-by, until the authorities were compelled to intervene.

It was not until the middle of the nineteenth century that there began to take shape in England the two principal kinds of football: Rugby (known as rugger) and Association (known as soccer). This process began in the public schools (which, as every Englishman knows, means the private schools!), where at first there were many different varieties. The peculiarity of rugger is, of course, that the ball is handled; and by 1860 it had become the accepted school game, although both Eton College and Winchester College refused to fall into line. Both rugger and soccer spread to the universities, the Football Association came into being, and by the end of the decade soccer was played in towns and villages all over England. At the end of the century it had become a professional game watched by thousands of spectators, which would certainly have astonished those who were kicking a ball about a hundred years before.

In 1457 an Act of Parliament was passed in Scotland forbidding football and golf. It has been conjectured, since football alone is mentioned in a similar Act of 1424, that the rise of golf must have taken place during the intervening period. But for centuries it was a quite unregulated affair. 'The modern history of golf begins with the formation of the first Golf Clubs in the middle of the eighteenth century. Courses in those days were wholly natural; the only green-keepers were the rabbits.'[7]

Clubs were formed at Leith and St Andrews, but many years were to elapse before the game made much progress in England. In Scotland, Leith was increasingly eclipsed by St Andrews and it was at the latter place that eighteen holes first became the recognized round. But the game *was* played in England. A regular club was established at Blackheath. This may have been started by Scots, for golf was certainly regarded as a Scottish game.

The Scottish Presbyterian minister Alexander Carlyle records in his *Autobiography* that David Garrick, having invited some friends to dine with him at Hampton,

... told us to bring golf clubs and balls that we might play at that game on Molesly Marsh. We accordingly set out in good time, six of us in a landau. As we were passing through Kensington, the Coldstream regiment were changing guard, and, on seeing our clubs, they gave us three cheers in honour of a diversion peculiar to Scotland. ... Immediately after we arrived, we crossed the river to the golfing ground, which was very good. None of the company could play but John Home and myself, and Parson Black from Aberdeen.[8]

The reason why Acts of Parliament in the fifteenth century had been concerned with football and golf was because neither sport was of much use as a preparation for war. What the authorities wished to encourage was archery, from which other sports were regarded as dangerous distractions. The gradual improvement of fire-arms made such fears obsolete and archery had fallen almost entirely out of use until it was revived in the late eighteenth century by the Toxophilites, a club founded by Sir Ashton Lever in 1780 with the Duke of Bedford as president. The movement spread rapidly, especially when it was discovered that ladies could take part. By the 1780s archery had become a popular (or perhaps it would be truer to say an aristocratic) craze, to be revived half a century later, in early Victorian times.

Football was not an aristocratic pastime, until the public schools began to play it in the nineteenth century. Cricket, however, was beginning to be so even in the eighteenth century, for we find grumbles about 'noblemen, gentlemen and clergy ... making butchers, cobblers or tinkers their companions'.[9]

A less jaundiced writer might well have rejoiced at the mingling of classes, for until the rise of professional cricketers the distinction between 'Gentlemen and Players' could hardly be said to exist. When Lord John Sackville played on the Artillery Ground, Finsbury, in a match attended by the Prince of Wales and the Duke of Cumberland, the Captain of the Eleven was Rumney, the head gardener at Knowle.

The first recorded cricket match was played between the Gentlemen of

Sevenoaks in Kent and the Gentlemen of London in July 1734. Kent was the prominent cricket county and in 1745 played 'All England', a team drawn from Middlesex, Sussex and Surrey. Cricket was also played at this period in Hampshire. The first code of rules was compiled by the London or Artillery Club. It was revised in 1755, in 1774 and again in 1788. The most radical changes were those of 1774. A third stump was added to the original two and the height, which had been twelve inches, was raised to twenty-two. This necessitated the use of a straight bat instead of the old curved kind. The style of bowling changed from underarm to overarm. In a word, the game had assumed the form we know today. The clothes worn were still just summer clothes with the coat left off. Hats were invariably worn: three-cornered hats until the 1790s and top hats thereafter, until they were abandoned altogether in the middle of the nineteenth century. By this time the game was no longer located in the home counties around London but had spread all over the country and, indeed, wherever British influence was paramount, as in such unlikely places as the West Indies and Corfu. Cricket had become the 'English game'.

Another sporting pastime must be mentioned: driving four-in-hand. This would have been impossible in the eighteenth century; the roads were just not good enough. Even as late as the third quarter of the eighteenth century they were bad enough in summer, and in winter impassible. Coaches were without springs, and bumps and jolts were inevitable; moreover, they were frequently upset because of the deep ruts. The pace was slow. In 1753 a new vehicle, 'The Flying Coach', was advertised in Manchester in the following terms: 'However incredible it may appear, this coach will actually (barring accidents) arrive in London in four days and a half after leaving Manchester', a distance of nearly two hundred miles. In 1760 it still took four days for a coach carrying six inside passengers to reach the metropolis from Exeter (170 miles). A few years later the time had been shortened to two days, but it was not until 1784 that the journey was first accomplished in thirty-two hours. It even took two days to do the fifty miles to Brighton when the Prince of Wales first chose the little fishing village as his 'marine residence'. A generation later the Brighton road had become one of the best, and most frequented, in Europe.

What brought about this transformation was the work of two men: Thomas Telford and John Macadam. Both were remarkable examples of Scottish energy and perseverance. Telford, from being a poor shepherd boy, became the engineer-architect of the finest aqueducts built since Roman times, the creator of canals, the improver of roads. Macadam (or, as he himself spelt it, McAdam), whose system of road construction largely replaced that of Telford, was born into a higher class, and it was as a landed proprietor that he became a road trustee. Disgusted by the state of the roads in Ayrshire, he began a series of experiments in which he sought to harden the road

37

surface by covering it with a series of thin layers of broken stone, as nearly as possible of the same size. His theory, which proved correct, was that far from breaking it up, traffic would increase the hardness of the surface by pressing the angular fragments more closely together. Such a process is known as macadamizing, and when its inventor became in 1815 surveyor-general of the Bristol roads, it soon proved its use. The way was open for the construction of lighter vehicles than those which had hitherto been in use, and in consequence for an enormous increase in the speed of travel.

These new facilities for rapid travel between one town and another had considerable effect on the social life of the period. New coaching inns sprang up, with stabling for an astonishing number of horses. At Hounslow, for example, the first stage out of London for the West, one proprietor alone maintained more than a hundred and fifty.

The stage-coaches brought new life to the English towns and villages through which they passed. Their progress was like a blood infusion in the sluggish veins of the ancient countryside. They brought also a touch of gaiety and adventure. They delighted and astonished by what Thomas de Quincey calls 'the absolute perfection of all the appointments about the carriages and the harness, their strength, their brilliant cleanliness, their beautiful simplicity – but more than all, the royal magnificence of the horses'.

The sound of the approaching horn made all the village maidens' hearts beat faster; the ploughman paused in his furrow, the hedger and ditcher looked up from his labour to see the coach go by. Wherever it passed it evoked smiles, and hands were waved in greeting. It brought the sense of speed, the breath of liberty; above all, it brought news.

In our modern world of newspapers, radio and television it is difficult for us to understand the isolation of remote places before the coming of the coaches. World-shaking events might not be known for months. But now the coaches, 'dressed in laurels and flowers, oak leaves and ribbons' to mark the great occasion, were able, as de Quincey tells us, to 'distribute over the face of the land, like the opening of apocalyptic viols, the heart-shaking news of Trafalgar, of Salamanca, of Vittoria, of Waterloo'.

The monarch of the road was the stage-coachman himself, on whose reliability and skill the speed of the vehicle and safety of the passengers depended. To quote the coaching enthusiast Lord William Pitt Lennox:

He was the elect of the road on which he travelled, the imitated of thousands. Talk of an absolute monarch indeed! To him Jim the ostler rushed in eagerness, to him Boniface showed the utmost deference, for him the landlady ever had a wel-come reception, towards him the barmaid smiled and glanced in perpetual amica-bility, and around him the helpers crowded as to the service of a feudal lord. Survey him as he bowled along the road, fenced in coats in winter, or his button-hole decorated with a rose in summer. Listen to the untutored melody of his voice, as he directed the word of exhortation to his spanking tits [coachman's slang for

The Horrors of Punishment

The new gallows at Tyburn in 1783, where ten people could be hanged at a time

Breaking on the wheel, one of the cruellest of punishments, which lasted in France until 1789

A pillory in France; the pillory was the commonest form of punishment for criminals who were not condemned to death

Top Prison ship in Portsmouth harbour

Above Fleet prison – the debtor's prison in London. Eighteenth-century prisoners were free to pass the day as they pleased within the prison walls

Sports and Pastimes

Top Pit ticket for a cock-fight by Hogarth. Cock fighting was finally made illegal in Britain by Act of Parliament in 1849
Above Boxing match between the American Molineaux and the Englishman Cribb in 1811. Boxing did not establish itself until the eighteenth century, but rapidly grew in popularity

Louis xv's hunt in the forest of Compiègne by J.B. Oudry

Above 'The Smoking Club'; coffee houses and clubs became popular in eighteenth-century London encouraging sociability and the art of conversation

Below A game of whist; cards and gambling were one of the main occupations of people of leisure

Above The pump room at Bath in 1798, from the series the 'Comforts of Bath' by Rowlandson. Bath was reborn in the eighteenth century when taking the waters became a fashionable pursuit

Below Sea-bathing at Scarborough – one of the earliest bathing resorts

Above Rowlandson's famous engraving of the pleasure gardens at Vauxhall

Below A Tea Party at Bagnigge Wells by George Morland. Bagnigge Wells was a fashionable spa within easy reach of London

horses] – three chestnuts and a grey – enforcing his doctrine with a silver-mounted whip, the gift of some aristocratic patron of the road, and he will present a feature of social life in England which no other country possessed.

It is the picture of Sam Weller's father, to the life.

The 'aristocratic patrons of the road', the 'swell dragsmen' as they were called, were a numerous band and included some of the greatest names in England. A wave of enthusiasm for everything connected with the road and driving, especially four-in-hand, swept over the upper classes at this period. The 'Driving Club' was established as early as 1808 and its great rival 'The Whip' soon after. And the noble members aped the professional coachmen in everything; one of them even had his front teeth filed so that he could spit through them in the approved fashion.

Nor did these aristocratic Jehus disdain to drive the public stage-coaches. On one occasion, when the driver of the Chichester coach was prevented from completing the journey by an accident, the Earl of March, later Duke of Richmond, took the reins and landed his passengers safe and sound at the White Horse Cellar in Piccadilly. Some aristocrats drove stage-coaches regularly. The Marquis of Worcester could be seen on the box of the 'Evening's Amusement', the Earl of Harborough on the 'Monarch', Sir St Vincent Cotton, of the Tenth Hussars, on the 'Age'. There were some strange results occasionally, when prim ladies who made a point of 'never speaking to outside passengers' found themselves at an inn sitting at the same table as their coachman, who was treated by mine host with far more deference than they were themselves. It is a striking example of the free-and-easy sporting atmosphere of the early years of the nineteenth century, and a curious reflection on the strange vagaries of snobbery, that the 'swell dragsmen' who took such pride in driving the public stage coaches would, in general, have disdained to ride in them as passengers.

By the end of our period the professionals had been driven off the road by the advent of railways. The Liverpool and Manchester railway was opened in 1830 and by 1848 a network of lines had covered much of the country. Yet the sport of driving coaches for pleasure long continued, and, indeed, continues still.

3
FOOTNOTES

1 The *Tatler*, No. 134, Thursday, 16 February 1709.
2 This was certainly the accepted practice and when contemporary prints show

several dogs attacking the bull at once, this should be dismissed as artists' licence.

3 Frederick W. Hackwood in his *Old English Sports*, London 1907, suggests, however, that this is an error, due merely to the fact that records were better kept in this region than elsewhere.

4 *Protestant Mercury*, 12 January 1681.

5 W.B.Boulton, *The Amusements of Old London*, London 1901.

6 M.Misson, *Mémoires et Observations*, Paris 1689.

7 Robert Browning, *A History of Golf*, London 1955.

8 Alexander Carlyle (1722–1805), *Autobiography*, Edinburgh 1860.

9 The *British Champion*, 8 September 1743.

4 Coffee Houses and Clubs

The eighteenth was essentially a *social* century. Communities in the various strata of society were small enough for everybody to know everybody else. There was even more contact between the classes than there was to be in the nineteenth century. They were perforce more huddled together, when even Belgravia had yet to be built and Kensington and Bayswater were open fields. A mid-eighteenth-century newspaper writer, describing London, speaks of:

... the confused Babel which now appears to us with the Hotch-Potch of half-moon and serpentine narrow streets, close, dismal, long Lanes, stinking Alleys, dark, gloomy Courts and suffocating Yards ... if we look into the streets what a Medley of Neighbourhood do we see? Here lives a Personage of High Distinction; next door probably a Butcher with his stinking shambles! A Tallow-Chandler confronts my Lord's nice *venetian* Window; and two or three brawny naked Curriers or leather dressers in their pits shall face the fine Lady in her back Closet, and disturb her spiritual Thoughts: At one end of the Street shall be a Chandler's Shop to debauch all the neighbouring Maids with Gin and gossiping tales, and at the other end perhaps a Brazier, who shall thump out amazing Disturbance, by a ring of Hammerers, for a quarter of a mile around him. In the Vicinity of some good Bishop some good *Mother*[1] frequently hangs out her flag. The Riotous, from their filthy accommodation of a *Spring Garden Bagnio*, shall echo their Bacchanalian Noise to the diversion of the opposite Chapel, which may *perhaps sue in vain for a Remedy*. Thus we *go on in England*.[2]

Sociability was much stimulated by the coffee houses which, in the early years of the century, were springing up everywhere. It has even been suggested that coffee was itself the cause of the increase in conversation so characteristic of the time, caffeine being a real stimulant while alcohol is ultimately a depressant. The end of wine is sleep; the end of coffee is wakefulness. Perhaps without the new drink even the 'philosophers' might have been unable to prolong their discussions throughout the night. Drinking wine or spirits they would have been either at one another's throats with drawn swords, or snoring under the table.

Be that as it may, the habit of drinking coffee, once introduced, grew rapidly. The first coffee house in England seems to have been in Oxford where, early in the reign of Charles II, a Jew named Jacobs opened one 'at the Angel, in the parish of St Peter in the East'. A few years later a house was established in London for the consumption, as Samuel Pepys tells us, 'of the bitter black drink called coffee'. The premises were situated in St Michael's Alley, Cornhill, at the sign of 'Pasqua Rosee's Head', the name being that of the oriental servant whom a Turkey merchant named Edwards had brought back with him from his travels. By the beginning of the eighteenth century it is reckoned that he had three thousand competitors in London alone.

Soon most of the coffee houses, being frequented by people with the same or similar interests, began to acquire a character of their own. Men interested in shipping and foreign trade met at Lloyd's coffee house near the Royal Exchange; City of London merchants congregated at Garraway's in Change Alley, Cornhill; booksellers at the Chapter in Paternoster Row; physicians and apothecaries at Batson's in Cornhill. The most famous literary coffee house was Wills's at the corner of Bow Street and Russell Street, and it was here that the ageing Dryden held court. Later coffee houses frequented by men of letters were Button's and the Bedford. The latter is described in the *Connoisseur* in 1754 as 'crowded with men of parts, almost every one you meet is a polite scholar and a wit'. Habitués included such men as Oliver Goldsmith, Samuel Foote, Henry Fielding, Charles Churchill and Dr Arne.

The fashionable coffee houses of London were further west. The St James's was Whig in tone, just as the Cocoa Tree was Tory. The most fashionable of all was White's, on the site where Boodle's Club now stands. Theoretically anyone with a few shillings or even less in his pocket could enter any of these establishments, but in practice people of a different class from the regular patrons were soon made to feel that they were not welcome. On the other hand any man with the appearance of a gentleman found little difficulty. Roderick Random in Smollett's novel of that name describes how, on his return from France, he began to frequent a certain coffee house in order 'to introduce myself into a set of good acquaintances', and he records that 'my appearance procured all the civilities and advances I could desire'.

Within the English tavern or coffee-house framework there gradually arose little dining clubs, sometimes limited to no more than half a dozen members. One of the earliest, the Saturday, started by Jonathan Swift, consisted merely of Lord Rivers the Lord Keeper, Lord Bolingbroke and himself. Of his other club, the Brothers, he boasted that 'we take none in but men of wit and men of interest', and when one of the members, the Duke of Beaufort, proposed his brother-in-law, the Earl of Danby, as a member, he 'opposed it so warmly that it was waived. Danby is not yet twenty and we will have no more boys'.

It is amusing to note, however, that in general such dining clubs were very happy to make honorary members of such 'noblemen and gentlemen as sent them venison and game'. The club composed of members of the Royal Society which met at 'a house in Dean's Court, between an ale-house and a tavern' introduced, on 3 May 1750, a rule which stated that 'any nobleman or gentleman complimenting this company with venison, not less than a haunch, shall during the continuance of such annuity be deemed an honorary member, and admitted as often as he comes without paying the fee which those members do who are elected by ballot'.

Other famous dining clubs of the period were the Dilettanti Society and the Sublime Society of Beefsteaks. The former was for connoisseurs of the arts;[3] the latter is said to have originated in a room in Covent Garden Theatre, but it was not confined to the theatrical profession. Certainly the actor David Garrick was a member, but so were Hogarth, Charles Churchill, Lord Sandwich and John Wilkes. In 1785 the Society admitted the Prince of Wales.

The club which was formed round Dr Johnson at the Turk's Head in Gerard Street, Soho, was first called merely 'The Club', but later became 'The Literary Club'. It was extremely exclusive. Garrick having remarked to Sir Joshua Reynolds, 'I think I'll be of you,' provoked Johnson to reply, 'He'll be of us! How does he know we will permit him; the proudest duke in England has no right to hold such language.' And Garrick had to wait for some years before he was admitted.

The notion that a club should have a house of its own probably started with the rich and fashionable who frequented White's chocolate house in St James's Street (chocolate in the eighteenth century rivalled coffee in popularity). They felt that they wanted to exclude characters they regarded as undesirable but who had as much right to enter the premises as they had themselves. White's Club was constituted in 1736. It was essentially a club for wealthy men of leisure, and although it included many serious persons, members of the government and the like, its chief attraction was, undoubtedly, gambling. Play ran high. We hear, for example, of Lord Carlisle losing £10,000 at a cast of hazard. The betting book has survived and contains some curious entries. Horace Walpole records that when a man fell down apparently dead at the door of the club, he was carried inside and the members at once made bets on whether he was dead or not; 'and when they were going to bleed him the wagerers for his death interfered, and said it would affect the fairness of the bet'. There were other bets on death. An entry for 4 November 1754 records that 'Lord Montfort wagers Sir John Bland one hundred guineas that Mr Nash outlives Mr Cibber'. The Nash in question was Beau Nash, founder of the prosperity of Bath, and Cibber was Colley Cibber, the Poet Laureate. Both were extremely old, but they outlived the punters, for as Walpole tells us, 'both Lord Montford and Sir John Bland put an end to their own lives before the bet was decided.' Sir John Bland shot himself on the road from Calais to Paris. He had probably gone to France in order to escape his creditors for he had squandered every penny he possessed playing the game of hazard at White's. He is said to have lost £32,000 at a single sitting.

There can be little doubt that one of the main occupations of people of leisure was gambling. There was much play not only in the clubs but in private houses. The favourite games were piquet, basset, ombre and loo. At the beginning of the century there had been a craze for whist. It had fallen for a while out of favour, Dean Swift calling it a game for clergymen and footmen, but became popular again at the beginning of our period. We find Horace Walpole, 2 December 1742, protesting that 'the town is won-drous dull; operas unfrequented, plays not in fashion, amours as cold as marriages – in short, nothing but whist! I have not yet learned to play, but I find that I wait in vain for it being left off'. The same author noted on 9 December 1742 that 'whist has spread an universal opium over the whole nation; it makes courtiers and patriots sit down to the same pack of cards'. Even the Sabbath was not respected for, as we learn from the *True Briton* of 28 January 1746, 'the whole Sabbath is . . . prostituted to these wicked revellings and card-playing goes on as publicly as on any other day! Nor is this only among the young lads and damsels who might be supposed to know no better but men advanced in years, and grey matrons, are not ashamed at being caught at the same pastime.'

In the memoirs of George Anne Bellamy we learn that gambling went on in the greenrooms of the theatres and that thousands of pounds were fre-quently lost there in a night: rings, brooches, watches, professional ward-robes and even salaries in advance. In private homes the housekeeping money was frequently lost, coteries of ladies young and old, single and married, taking part. Ladies of fashion even employed whist masters and professors of quadrille.

The gambling saloons flourished. The *Daily Journal* of 9 January 1751 lists the number of people employed by a typical club proprietor, and these include a director of the gambling room, the dealer, two croupiers and two 'puffs', who had money given them to decoy others to play, a waiter to serve wines, snuff candles and attend the gaming room, an attorney – and a captain 'who is to fight any gentleman who is peevish at losing his money'. The government State Lotteries were widely patronized, drawing of the lotteries generally taking place at about eight o'clock in the evening, a Bluecoat boy (i.e. a pupil at Christ's Hospital in London) being employed to draw the numbers.

Quarrels at the gaming table frequently led to duels. Duelling was very common in the eighteenth century; every gentleman carried a sword by his side and it was likely to leap out of its scabbard on the least provocation. The general feeling of the time was that duelling should be permitted, and even Dr Johnson said:

He, then, who fights a duel, doesn't fight from passion against his antagonist, but out of self defence, to avoid the stigma of the world, and to prevent himself from being driven out of society. I could wish there were not that superfluity of sentiment, but while such notions prevail, no doubt a man may lawfully fight a duel.

Alexander Andrews remarks:

Did the stranger who sat opposite to you in the coffee-house differ from you in opinion; did the blacklegs, with whom you had just lost a few thousands at faro after cozening you out of your estate, insult you upon venturing no more; did your friend refuse to acknowledge the supremacy of his mistress over yours, there was no other remedy than a duel, and a duel was accordingly got up – and fought – frequently in the room.

The general place for duelling was Hyde Park but Pall Mall was another favourite venue. Some of the most prominent men of the day fought duels, including Sheridan, Fox and the younger Pitt. The father of Horace Walpole fought a duel at the foot of the stairs of the House of Commons.

The gambling tradition at White's was taken on towards the end of the century by Almack's, or Brooks's as it was called after the name of the second proprietor, and a generation later by Crockford's. The high play is indicated by the rule that 'every person playing at the new quinze table do keep fifty guineas before him'; and 'every person playing at the twenty-guinea table do keep twenty guineas before him'.

The rule that 'no gaming be allowed in the eating-room except tossing for reckonings' shows that the gambling spirit could not be entirely suppressed even there. It was at Brooks's that Charles James Fox squandered his fortune, and his friendship with the Prince of Wales induced the latter to join the same club, to the great disgust of his father, George III, who was only too well aware of the reckless extravagance of the heir to the throne.

During the Regency, White's and Brooks's became the favourite resort of the dandies, including the 'King of the Dandies', George Brummell. Brummell was elected to White's in 1798 and between then and 1816, when 'he fled to Calais, leaving half the tradesmen of the West End in lamentation, his life work was accomplished. He had placed himself at the head of the male society of his day.'[4] He and his imitators established a complete tyranny at White's, savagely blackballing every candidate for membership of whom they disapproved, appropriating special seats in all the rooms and especially in the famous bow-window, where they took up their position daily, ridiculing the passers-by in St James's Street. Their behaviour had certainly something to do with the founding of other clubs in London, and the erection of splendid buildings to house them.

The London club, as an institution with a large and elaborate club-house of its own, did not, with the few exceptions we have mentioned, really arrive until round about 1815. The Guards Club and the Royal Naval Club were already in existence but the officers of Wellington's armies, accustomed as they were to eat 'in the mess' on active service, needed another institution, and so founded the United Services Club in 1815. The Travellers' had come into existence in the previous year on the initiative of Lord Castlereagh. Ten years later saw the founding of no less than four new clubs: the Oriental, the Athenaeum, the University Club and a City Club called the Union. The Wyndham came in 1828 and the Garrick in 1831, although its club-house was not erected until the 1860s.

According to W.B.Boulton:

It is from the years immediately preceding the passing of the Reform Bill of 1832 that we date the first of the great political clubs. The Tories who surrounded the Duke of Wellington and Sir Robert Peel in those days of strenuous politics 'found White's too neutral in tone' as we learn from Mr Raikes, and established in 1831, in the Carlton, an institution of the right Tory colour. Brooks's ... never lost the Whig flavour which it acquired in the days of Charles Fox, and the great Reform Bill itself may be said to have been incubated in its rooms. But the Brooks's of 1832 included so many reactionaries in its list that the forward spirits of the Liberals felt the necessity of a meeting place of their own, and so founded the Reform Club as a counterblast to the Tory Carlton.[5]

Charles Ollier, writing in 1842, remarks:

Even in its old condition, thirty or forty years ago, Pall Mall was a stately, aristocratical looking street ... Pall Mall has preserved its gentility longer than any other street in London. It was a fashionable place more than a century and a half ago and continues to be so ... Of late years, however, Pall Mall, though it has lost the famous palace of George, Prince of Wales [Carlton House] has improved wonderfully in appearance ... But great as these improvements are, nothing has contributed more to the architectural beauty of the street than the magnificent club-houses recently erected there ... In many respects a great revolution in private life has been brought about by these institutions. On the payment of an annual sum (small in comparison with the splendid accommodations offered) a gentleman, on being elected by ballot, may have for his daily resort a mansion of princely elegance; be waited on by liveried servants; dine in luxury at the mere cost, without profits, of the viands; meet his friends in sumptuous drawing-rooms, and have at his service a costly and extensive library. In fact, with the exception of a sleeping-room, he may live at his club with a degree of state and profuse luxury which nothing but a princely fortune could otherwise command, not to mention the enjoyment, without the expense, of constant society.[6]

He then goes on to describe the Carlton, the Reform ('built from the designs of Barry, architect of the new Houses of Parliament, now in course of erection'), the Travellers', the Athenaeum, and the United Services Club. They were all indeed splendid buildings, for the Carlton Club in its final form was a copy of the Library of St Mark's in Venice, the Reform was an imitation of the Farnese Palace in Rome, the Travellers' was a copy of the Palazzo Pandolfini in Rome, and the Army and Navy, founded in 1838 but not finished until 1851, was erected on the model of Sansovino's Palazzo Cornaro on the Grand Canal in Venice.

Pall Mall was indeed a street of palaces, and as it stands today is a curious monument of one particular epoch of English life. As an anonymous writer of 1851 remarks:

> As at present constituted, the London clubs and club life have produced a new phase of English society, at least in the metropolis – one which will claim the notice of some future Macaulay, as showing the very form and pressure of the time. Until about thirty years ago a club was seldom more than a mere knot of acquaintances who met together of an evening, at stated times, in a room engaged for that purpose at some tavern, and some of them held their meetings at considerable intervals apart ... Quite a new order of things has come up, the clubs of the present time being upon quite a different footing, and also comparatively gigantic in scale. From small social meetings held periodically, they have become permanent establishments, luxurious in all their apartments, and some of the *locales* are quite palatial.

When Thomas Shotter Boys made his drawings, therefore, the club-as-palazzo had only just established itself. The modern observer on the other hand is driven to the reflection that, today, the club in this sense has almost come to the end of its existence. It is practically certain that no more palatial club-houses will be built. Nearly all the old clubs are in financial difficulties, for the 'man-about-town' who kept them going is nearly extinct. We are witnessing the end of the process of which Boys saw the beginning. The club-as-palazzo lasted just about a hundred years.

4
FOOTNOTES

1 'Mother' in this context means brothel-keeper.
2 *Old England*, 2 July 1748.
3 The Dilettanti Society still meets and has been humorously described as a club for peers who like art and art experts who like peers.
4 William B. Boulton, *The Amusements of Old London*, London 1901.
5 *Ibid.*
6 Text by Charles Ollier, *Original Views of London as it is, by Thomas Shotter Boys*, London 1842.

5 'Taking the Waters' and Other Diversions

'Taking the waters' played a considerable part in the life of the English upper classes in the eighteenth century. Tunbridge Wells in Kent had been of sufficient importance in the 1660s for Charles II to transfer his Court there from time to time; and soon Bath became equally popular. Neither of these 'watering places' was, of course, on the sea. It was not until nearly a century later that people began to discover that sea air was just as healthful and very much more pleasant than a chalybeate spring, tasting of iron.

Bath is the proud possessor of the only natural hot springs in the country. The Romans were well aware of their medicinal properties and, once the land had been subdued, resorted there in large numbers, building houses in the neighbourhood and excavating the large bath which is still to be seen. The Saxon invaders do not seem to have had much relish for either bathing in water or drinking it, but in the Middle Ages the splendid Abbey Church was built and Bath was reborn. It did not, however, really rise again as a fine city until the eighteenth century when 'to take the waters' once more became the fashion, and the 'nobility and gentry' began flooding there to enjoy social life and to recover from their dissipations. By the end of the eighteenth century various elegant buildings had sprung up in Bath, the Assembly Room being at the time the largest building of its kind in England.

Beau Nash, as 'King of Bath', was a great reformer of manners. He would not allow the gentlemen to wear swords or the ladies to wear aprons. Everything had to be done with the utmost propriety and he undoubtedly exercised a most civilizing influence. In the reign of Queen Anne ladies and gentlemen were carried to the bath in sedan chairs and, with the greatest decorum, immersed themselves in the healing waters.

The first 'discovery' of the seaside seems to have been Scarborough which in the middle of the eighteenth century became one of the earliest bathing resorts. It is an interesting half-way house between spas like Bath and seaside resorts like Brighton. Scarborough was a spa and as such was visited by Lord Foppington in Sheridan's *A Trip to Scarborough*, but being, unlike

Bath, on the sea it was able to move with the times and develop into a seaside resort. The upper classes began to arrive in their coaches and to plunge (naked) into the health-giving waves. Margate, developing a little later, was another favourite seaside resort. In the Middle Ages it had been quite an important place, allied to the five towns on the English Channel known as the Cinque Ports, with its sailors fighting the French and the Spaniards whenever occasion offered. But by the early eighteenth century it had dwindled away almost to nothing and had acquired a bad reputation as a haunt of smugglers. It was these same smugglers who hollowed out the caves in the cliffs which, known as the 'Grottoes', are now one of the attractions of the town.

Margate owed its prosperity entirely to the fashion for sea-bathing. By the 1760s there were in operation twenty bathing machines – boxes on wheels drawn into the sea by horses. The men still bathed naked but most of the ladies now wore a garment like a long nightgown and, having descended modestly into the sea by the aid of the umbrella-like contraption at the back of each machine, were firmly 'dipped' by professional bathing women who did their best to make their customers drink a quantity of sea-water in the process.

Soon Margate had a Theatre Royal built 'after the mode of Covent Garden', and the greatest actors of the period played there. However, towards the end of the century both Scarborough and Margate had been eclipsed by Brighton. Dr Richard Russell, one of the pioneers of preventive medicine, was a firm believer in the efficacy of sea-water, for both bathing in and drinking, and in the year 1754 he built himself a house in the little fishing village of Brighthelmstone, on the site of what is now the Albion Hotel. From that everything followed. People in search of health – and dissipation – then began to flock there and, in 1783, there occurred the historic arrival of a particularly grand personage: George, Prince of Wales, aged twenty-one and with an annual income of £65,000. He liked Brighton and in the following year rented a house on the Steyne from his chef Weltje. Then he took a house of his own and for the next thirty years set himself to enlarge and beautify it – at enormous expense. The result is the Brighton Pavilion as we know it, with its Hindu exterior and its pseudo-Chinese interior decorations. It was finished in 1817 by which time 'Prinny' had long been Regent and was soon to become King. The famous Regency junketings took place in a much simpler building hardly different from any country house of the period.

It was easy enough for the upper classes to reach any of the new seaside resorts in their coaches and post-chaises, but difficulty of access did not save them all from an influx of the lower orders. Margate in particular was served by the 'hoys' or corn-boats which travelled from London to the estuary and back again. As early as 1765 five of these, starting from Wool

Quay, near the Custom House, were transporting sixty or seventy passengers, each for a return fare of half-a-crown. They were very well conducted for we hear that 'the masters are decent and careful men and allow no impropriety of behaviour which they can prevent. They transact incredible business.' Most of the passenger trade was done, of course, in the summer months and the voyage, in good weather, took eight or nine hours.

Those who did not wish to travel so far to take the waters had to content themselves with the 'wells' in London itself. One of the favourites was Bagnigge Wells which was situated in Clerkenwell. It was named after Bagnigge House, a summer residence of Nell Gwynne. The discovery of two mineral springs in 1760 made it fashionable as a spa. Within easy reach of the centre of London it was much patronized at weekends in summer, and an advertisement of 1779 claims there was served there 'the best tea, coffee and hot loaves'. George Morland's picture, *A Tea Party at Bagnigge Wells*, painted in the 1780s, shows the elegant clientele which resorted there, and George Colman, the Younger, in his prologue to Garrick's play, *Bon Ton* (1775), says:

> Bon Tone's the space 'twixt Saturday and Monday,
> And riding in a one-horse chair on Sunday.
> 'Tis drinking tea on summer afternoons
> At Bagnigge Wells with china and gilt spoons.

Sadler's Wells was an even more frequented resort; and soon other pleasure gardens began to be laid out, for their own sake and without any pretence of taking the waters. There had been such a garden at Lambeth as early as 1663 when we hear of 'lawns and gravel walks ... with hedges of gooseberry trees under which were planted roses'. Two years earlier Pepys' friend, John Evelyn, in his *Diary* records a visit to 'the new garden at Lambeth, a prettily contrived plantation'.

More famous, and destined to a longer life, were the pleasure gardens of Vauxhall and Ranelagh. The name of the former was derived from that of a man who in the reign of King John had built a house there known as Vauke's Hall. A visit to Vauxhall meant for most Londoners crossing the Thames by boat for, until 1750, there was no bridge over the river between London Bridge and Kingston. The fare for a boat with two men rowing was sixpence. Addison devoted a whole number of the *Spectator* to a description of Sir Roger de Coverley's visit in 1712, probably based on his own experience. Sir Roger (or Addison) consumed a glass of Burton ale and a slice of hung beef. He complained, however, of the scarcity of nightingales and the prevalence of 'wanton baggages'.

We do not hear of Vauxhall again until it is mentioned in the *New Guide to London*, published in 1726; but the real founder of Vauxhall as a fashionable resort was Jonathan Tyers who took over two years later. The place was truly launched in 1730 when he staged a 'Ridotto al Fresco' which was attended by the highest in the land, including Frederick, Prince of Wales, who came down the river in his barge from Kew. It is said that it was Hogarth who suggested the fête; he certainly painted pictures for it and designed the little season tickets in silver and bronze.

It was an attractive place, with rows of trees. The Grand Walk was provided with a stately avenue of elms and, parallel with this, was the South Walk, spanned by three triumphal arches; a third avenue called the Grand Cross Walk ran through the whole garden at right angles to these. There were also paths known as the Dark Walk, the Druid Walk and the Lover's Walk. W.B. Boulton remarks that much of the attraction of Vauxhall:

... was provided by the romantic qualities which generations of young people found in Mr Tyers' dark walks. Frisky maidens from the City delighted in braving the dangers of these solitudes and there was not wanting gallant youths who provided the necessary excitement. It was the destiny of most of the famous heroines of fiction from Amelia to Evelina to meet with adventures in the recesses of Mr Tyers' famous solitudes; readers of Fielding will remember how Amelia fared at the hands of Jane and My Lord before the arrival of Booth and Captain Trench, and the meeting of Evelina and Sir Clement Willoughby and the declaration of love which followed.[1]

The behaviour of young people in the dark walks was not always decorous and the magistrates in 1763 compelled Tyers to fence off the walks.

In the Grove, which was the square enclosed by the principal walks and the western wall of the garden, were built temples and pavilions and a covered colonnade for shelter in wet weather. Under this were the boxes for dining. The Prince of Wales allowed Tyers to dedicate to him a pavilion adorned with the Prince of Wales' Feathers. There was space for an orchestra, and concerts were given in which some of the finest singers of the day, such as Mrs Arne and Mrs Baddeley, performed.

The famous engraving by Rowlandson shows us exactly what the scene was like.[2] Many attempts have been made to identify the characters and perhaps W.B. Boulton's is the most persuasive:

The two beautiful women in the centre of the composition are the Duchess of Devonshire and her sister Lady Duncannon; the upright figure on the left with the eye-glass is Captain Popham, proprietor of *The World*, an early specimen of the now common 'society paper'; Admiral Paisley is ... represented as the veteran with the wooden leg on the Duchess's right, and the parson who looks over Lady Duncannon's shoulder is Sir Harry Dudley, the editor of *The Morning Post*. . . . By his side is Jonas Perry, the editor of *The Morning Chronicle*, a great amateur of the claymore and therefore represented in Highland costume. On the right of the picture are His Royal Highness the Prince of Wales and Perdita Robinson clearly trifling with her locket containing her own picture no doubt. Under the orchestra is Dr Johnson with Boswell on his left and Mrs Thrale on his right. Mrs Wechsell is warbling from the orchestra.[3]

The great rival of Vauxhall was Ranelagh on the other side of the river at Chelsea. Horace Walpole in a letter to Sir Horace Mann dated 26 May 1742 describes the opening:

Two nights ago the gardens opened at Chelsea; the Prince, Princess, the Duke of Cumberland, much nobility, and much mob besides were there. There is a vast amphitheatre, finely gilt, painted and illuminated, into which everybody that loves eating, drinking, staring or crowding, is admitted for twelve pence. The building and disposition of the gardens cost sixteen thousand pounds. Twice a week there are to be Ridottos at guinea tickets, for which you are to have a supper and music. I was there last night, but did not find the joy of it. Vauxhall is a little better; for the garden is pleasanter and one goes by water.[4]

However, he was to revise his opinion, for two years later we find him writing to Henry Seymour Conway:

Every night constantly I go to Ranelagh; which has totally beat Vauxhall. Nobody goes anywhere else, everybody goes there. Lord Chesterfield is so fond of it, that he says he has ordered all his letters to be directed there. If you have never seen it, I shall make you a most pompous description of it, and tell you how the floor is all of beaten princes, that you can't set your foot without treading on a Prince of Wales or Duke of Cumberland. The company is universal ... from His Grace of Grafton down to children out of the Foundling Hospital – from My Lady Townshend to the kitten – from My Lord Sandys to your humble cousin and sincere friend.[5]

In 1748 the Peace of Aix-la-Chapelle, which ended the War of the Austrian Succession, was celebrated by 'a jubilee mascarade in the Venetian manner'. Horace Walpole remarks:

It has nothing Venetian in it, but was by far the best understood and the prettiest spectacle that I ever saw: nothing in a fairy tale ever surpassed it. One of the proprietors, who was a German, and belongs to Court, had got my Lady Yarmouth to persuade the King to order it. It began at three o'clock, and, about five, people of fashion began to go. When you entered you found the whole garden filled with masks and spread with tents ... in one quarter was a maypole dressed with garlands, and people dancing round it to a tabor and pipe and rustic music, all masked, as were all the various bands of music who were disposed in different parts of the garden; some like huntsmen with French horns, some like peasants, and a troop of harlequins and scaramouches in the little open temple on the mountain. On the canal was a sort of gondola, adorned with flags and streamers. ... The amphitheatre was illuminated; and in the middle was a circular bar, composed of all types of trees in tubs, from twenty to thirty feet high; under them orange trees, with small lamps in each orange, and below them ... festoons of natural flowers hanging from tree to tree. ... There were booths for tea and wine, gaming tables and dancing, and about two thousand persons. In short, it pleased me more than anything I ever saw.

On another occasion he records that:

On Monday there was a subscription masquerade much fuller than that of last year, but not so agreeable or so various in dresses. The King was well disguised in an old fashioned English habit, and much pleased with somebody who desired him to hold their cup as they were drinking tea. The Duke had a dress of the same kind, but was so immensely corpulent that he looked like Cacofago, the drunken sot in *Rule a Wife and Have a Wife* [by Beaumont and Fletcher]; the Duchess of Richmond was a Lady Mayoress in the time of James I; and Lord Delawarr Queen Elizabeth's porter from a picture in the Guards room at Kensington. There were admirable masks, Lady Washford, Miss Evelyn, Miss Bishop, Lady Stafford and Mrs Pitt were in vast beauty; particularly the last, who had a red veil which made her look gloriously handsome. I forgot Lady Kildare. Mr Conway was the Duke in Don Quixote, the finest figure I ever saw.[6]

During the summer months Londoners were able to disport themselves at the fairs which still played an important part in English life at the period. The principal ones were those held in Smithfield, Southwark and Westminster. The first of these was established as Bartholomew Fair in the twelfth century during the reign of Henry I. It was presided over by the monks of St Bartholomew's Priory and lasted three days. It was originally a cloth fair but by the time of Queen Elizabeth other goods were also sold and the original three-day fair had expanded into a four-day carnival, of which we catch a glimpse in the play by Ben Jonson. It was later extended to fourteen days. Annually on 22 August, the Lord Mayor of London opened it in state, drinking 'a cool tankard of wine, nutmeg, and sugar' at Newgate on his way. When he arrived at Smithfield he read a proclamation. The seventeenth-century Puritans, in spite of all their efforts, did not succeed in having it abolished. In the first year of the eighteenth century there had been an attempt by the Grand Jury of Middlesex to abolish all shows and booths and to make the fair return to its original character for the sale of merchandise, but the gin stall, the gaming booth and the improvised theatre continued to flourish.

There was at this time a very close connection between Bartholomew Fair and the playhouses, for some of the greatest actors of the period did not disdain to appear upon the trestled boards. Quin, Macklin, Woodward, Shuter and Colley Cibber were among the well-known actors who appeared, and, curiously enough, some of the pieces shown were more like the medieval mystery plays than anything found on the contemporary stage. We find such titles as *Jephthah's Rash Vow*, *The Story of the Chaste Susannah* and *The History of Solomon and the Queen of Sheba*. A contemporary playbill or handbill of the 1740s promised the performance of a little opera called *The Creation of the World*, with the addition of Noah's Flood. Several fountains spouted water, and the last scene represented Noah and his family coming out of the Ark:

... with all the beasts two by two and all the fowls of the air seen in the prospect against trees ... a multitude of angels will be seen in double rank ... likewise machines descending from above, with Dives rising out of Hell and Lazarus seen in Abraham's bosom, besides several figures dancing jigs, sarabands, and Country Dances to the admiration of all spectators, with the merry conceits of Squire Punch and John Spendall, completed by an entertainment of singing and dancing with several naked swords by a child eight years of age.

It is difficult to see how such a spectacle could have been mounted in so confined a space. Perhaps the angels and the animals in the ark were only represented on painted canvas. Sometimes plays were removed from theatres like the Haymarket and given at Bartholomew Fair by the same actors. Henry Fielding produced *The Beggars' Opera* at Smithfield. He occasionally appeared himself and the Prince and Princess of Wales did not disdain to visit his entertainment. That Bartholomew Fair was not a mere proletarian junketing we learn from an advertisement of Fielding's that he had provided for a commodious passage for the 'quality' and their coaches, and 'care will be taken that there shall be lights and people to conduct them to their places'.

In spite of the fact that the Lord Mayor opened the proceedings, the Corporation of London was in general puritanical in spirit and made many attempts to suppress the fair altogether. The mob strongly resented this and a Mr Birch and some of the City Marshalls were actually killed in 1751 in attempting to suppress the booths. However, the attempts to cut short the duration of the fair were in the end successful, the number of days being reduced in 1750 from fourteen to three. This put an end to good acting at the Bartholomew Fair. It was hardly a profitable proposition for an established actor to perform there for three days only, and so the promoters turned to other attractions such as menageries and tight-rope walking, acrobatic performances, conjurers and puppet shows. There was even a ventriloquist (although the word itself does not seem to have yet been invented, for he is described as 'the wonderful man who talks in his belly and can fling his voice into any part of the room'). Horace Walpole escorted a party of ladies to Smithfield, and Frederick, Prince of Wales, once visited the fair accompanied by his Beefeaters and leading the future George III by the hand. The proceedings were not always decorous for many fights took place and sometimes the mob set fire to the booths. The fair gradually dwindled away and in 1825 was banished to Islington. Another famous fair was that of Southwark which dated back to the Charter of Edward VI granted in 1550. This was not on the scale of Bartholomew Fair but the same kind of attractions were offered. There is an excellent engraving of it by Hogarth.

The fair which gave its name to Mayfair went back to medieval times. It opened annually on 25 June but it never had the social cachet of the other two and it seems to have led to much more rioting. An attempt to exclude prostitutes caused a fight in which bailiffs and constables were killed; curiously enough the Guards from St James's were on the side of the prostitutes.

One of the favourite diversions of the eighteenth century was play-going, especially in the second half of the period when the middle classes returned to the theatre after what W.J. Lawrence calls 'a long abstinence'.[7] They had been forcibly prevented from going to plays during the Common-wealth, and they had had little taste for the kind of drama offered to them after the return of Charles II. Congreve, Wycherley and the rest of the Restoration dramatists catered for an aristocratic audience whose libertine cynicism found expression in an equally licentious drama. What the audi-ences of 1750 and onwards preferred was something more decent and more emotional. Wit gave place to sentiment and even to sentimentality. What was called 'Genteel' or 'High Comedy' eschewed both vice and vulgarity; unfortunately it often eschewed humour also. All the characters in such a typical example as Whitehead's *School for Lovers* are such models of purity and high-flown sentiment that the play seems to us now to be unreadable and unactable. Yet it had considerable success at the time.

It is thought that the return of the middle classes was hastened by the device of allowing people to come in at a 'second price' when the first piece in the programme was over. The doors were opened at five o'clock and the curtain rose at six, which was too early for the City merchant and his family. But once lured back by cheap prices for the 'after piece' they continued to support the theatre in ever-increasing numbers.

They did so in considerable discomfort. The seats were mere benches without backs and were not bookable. The rich sent their footmen to occupy places in the boxes, but the rest of the audience formed a crowd at the entrance and fought its way in. Orderly queues were unheard of. Ladies fainted, hats were knocked off, sometimes even arms were broken in the struggle. As may well be imagined, those who had gone through such turmoil outside were in no mood to sit quietly through a play they did not like. At Drury Lane and Covent Garden the stage was separated from the auditorium by a formidable row of sharp spikes. These were very necessary for there were serious riots at Drury Lane in 1744 and again, there and at Covent Garden, in 1763. These O.P. (i.e. Old Price) riots, sparked off by the management's abolition of the privilege of coming in after the first piece for half price, caused serious damage to the inside of the theatre, on one occasion to the tune of £4,000.

Lighting was poor, for it was not until Garrick returned in 1765 from his European Tour that he got rid of the chandeliers which hung both in the auditorium and on the stage (even when the scene was supposed to take place out of doors) and substituted for them a number of unseen

E

lights in the wings. These enabled the lighting to be controlled and made possible the scenic effects introduced by Philippe Jacques de Loutherbourg, whom Garrick brought over from the Continent in 1771. He was a well-known battle painter and his advent marks the beginning of a real revolution in decor.

The costuming of plays in the eighteenth century was a very haphazard affair. As the repertoire was changed so often it was unusual for new costumes to be provided for each production, with the result that the players had to make do as best they could with the contents of the theatre wardrobe. Not that the public minded, for knowledge of correct historical costume was almost non-existent. Garrick played Macbeth in the ordinary fashionable dress of the day and Lear in a contemporary coat trimmed with ermine and with some loose white hair attached to the back of a white-powdered conventional wig.

Macklin is credited with being the first to play Shylock in something other than contemporary costume, by wearing a version of mid-seventeenth-century Dutch costume – a long gown rather like a cassock with falling bands. He also played Macbeth, for the first time in theatre history, in something approximating to the Scottish tartan kilt. But any concerted attempt to present 'period' costume with any degree of accuracy had to wait until almost the end of our period.

If we could go back and attend a performance in the eighteenth century we would certainly find it very strange. But we would probably be impressed by the acting of the principal characters. There was little attempt at ensemble acting; the chief players regarded their lines as solo pieces. Even in the nineteenth century Edmund Kean, visiting Liverpool and asked by the subsidiary players for his instructions, merely said: 'Tell them to stand three yards away from me and do their damnedest.' He never rehearsed with them at all. Still, the result must have been impressive, for few periods in the history of the theatre have produced such a galaxy of talent as David Garrick, Spranger Barry, Harry Woodward, John Henderson, Charles Macklin, John Philip Kemble, Mrs Cibber, Mrs Pritchard, Kitty Clive and Peg Woffington.

Among this galaxy the name of Lewis Hallam does not shine very bright. His importance is that he was the real founder of the professional theatre in the United States. He was playing at Covent Garden from 1734 to 1741 and was later at Drury Lane. In 1752 he took the decisive step of carrying his wife and children and a company of ten actors to America. They opened at Williamsburg, Virginia, in September of the same year with a performance of *The Merchant of Venice*. A year later he was in New York, and built a theatre there, on Nassau Street. Here, in spite of opposition from those who regarded the stage as sinful, he presented a fine repertoire of plays.

In the same street was a theatre managed by Thomas Kean who, in

1749, had presented plays in a converted warehouse in Philadelphia. Hallam took this over and played there frequently. He died in 1756 while on tour in Jamaica and his widow married David Douglass, the manager of a company also touring there. The two troupes combined and returned to New York where they were billed as the 'American Company'. This played an important part in the development of early American drama, being the first professional company to present a play by an American author: *The Prince of Parthia* by Thomas Godfrey.

By the Licensing Act of 1737 playhouses in London were strictly limited in number and could be established only by royal letters patent. Apart from the Italian Opera in the Haymarket there were only Drury Lane, Covent Garden and the Haymarket Theatre. But the regulations did not apply to circuses and the like. One of the most successful of London's entertainers in the last quarter of the eighteenth century and the early years of the nineteenth was Philip Astley. As a sergeant-major of dragoons he had served under General Elliot (afterwards Lord Heathfield) at the siege of Gibraltar. The General gave him a horse, which he named Gibraltar, and with this and one other horse he put on a display of horsemanship in a field at Halfpenny Hatch, the site on which Waterloo Station now stands. At first he seems to have intended his establishment to be a riding school, but he also gave displays of acrobatic riding on two horses at once, charging the audience a shilling for a seat and sixpence for standing room. The entertainment became so popular that the regular theatres, jealous of their privileges, tried to have it closed down, and would probably have succeeded if Astley had not been saved by a veritable *deus ex machina*. This was no less a person than King George III, who, riding one day over Westminster Bridge, had some difficulty in controlling his restive horse. Astley who happened to be passing took the matter in hand and so pleased the King by his skill and coolness that he was rewarded by a royal licence. As if this stroke of luck was not enough, Astley shortly afterwards invested £200 he had managed to save in a mortgage on a piece of waste land at Westminster. The mortgagor went abroad and never returned, leaving Astley in possession of the property. On it he built an arena where a much more ambitious show was mounted. This was burned down in 1794 and the building that replaced it was also burned, eight years later. The final amphitheatre lasted until 1862 by which time Astley had been dead for half a century, and Queen Victoria had been on the throne for twenty-five years.

5
FOOTNOTES

1 W.B. Boulton, *The Amusements of Old London*, London 1901.
2 Rowlandson's original drawing for this is now in the Department of Prints and Drawings at the Victoria and Albert Museum, London.
3 W.B. Boulton, *op. cit.*
4 Horace Walpole, *Letters*, ed. Mrs Paget Toynbee, Oxford 1914.
5 *Ibid.*
6 *Ibid.*
7 W.J.Lawrence, *Johnson's England*, 2 vols, London 1933.

6 Le Roi Bien-Aimé

The French Court in the last few years of the reign of Louis XIV had, under the influence of Madame de Maintenon, become sober, pious and dull. When he died in 1715 he was succeeded by his great-grandson, Louis XV, then a young child. The Regent of France was Philippe d'Orléans, of the younger branch of the Bourbons, and he was not a man austere in his own habits or likely to promote austerity in those about him. Politically he was able enough. He was cultivated and witty, and it was during his rule that French gastronomy, in its modern sense, became one of the arts. But his morals were deplorable. His life was one continual debauch, not even stopping short of rape.

This was known even abroad, according to an entry in the diary of Dudley Ryder:

> Went to John's Coffee-House. There was one Mr Doliff lately come over from France. He says the Regent is extremely hated among the generality of people and spoke ill of. They have all a notion that he has a design upon the life of the young King, whom they are prodigiously fond of. He says the Regent gives himself up very much to debauchery, wine and women. It is confidently reported there that the Regent himself ravished Madame Rochefoucauld, the wife of the captain of the Duchess of Berry's guard and that the Duchess of Berry[1] herself assisted him in it by inviting her to take a game of cards with her and then throwing her upon the bed and holding her for the Regent to lie with her.[2]

The anonymous author of *La Vie privée du Maréchal de Richelieu* gives details which confirm this, although the end of the story is different:

> When the Duc d'Orléans became Regent, controlled no longer, he abandoned himself to his appetites. Mesdames Daverne, de Parabère, de Gesvres, d'Argenson, de Châtillon were those to whom he rendered the most lasting homage. They were succeeded by the Duchesse de Phalaris, dead some years ago[3] at a very advanced age. A swarm of women of every class and kind were associated with these ladies and initiated like them into the voluptuous mysteries celebrated by the Regent. Even his own daughters were not exempt. The Duchesse de Berry before, during,

and after her marriage lent herself to the passions of a father even more debauched than herself, and Mademoiselle de Valois only saved her lover, the Duc de Richelieu, from the horrors of the Bastille, by yielding equally to the Regent's desires. . . .

The Duchesse de Berry gathered together in the Luxembourg Palace, where she lived, all the most beautiful women who did not fear to compromise their reputation; her father often supped with her. . . . One day Madame de la Rochefoucauld engaged his lascivious glances; her husband was Captain of the Guard to the Duchesse de Berry, but she avoided that corrupt court. Her reserved conduct inspired even stronger desires on the part of the Regent and he induced Madame de Berry to procure him a tête-à-tête.

The Princess, who eagerly seconded all her father's caprices, soon found a pretext to make Madame de la Rochefoucauld come to her when the Regent was present. His declaration was short and expressive. The young la Rochefoucauld wished to retire but Madame de Berry . . . took her hand, and drew her down on to a chaise longue, holding her firmly in her arms. But Madame de la Rochefoucauld, either because the presence of a third person displeased her, or out of real virtue, defended herself with so much fury that she succeeded in tearing herself from the arms of the Duchesse de Berry. The Regent made a further attempt and was about to triumph over a woman exhausted by a long resistance, when, in the struggle, she gave him a blow in the eye with her elbow, which made him loose his hold. This blow in an eye which was already inflamed (for the Regent's debauches had put him in danger of losing his sight) caused him terrible pain, and gave Madame de la Rochefoucauld time to escape from the danger which threatened her.[4]

In spite of the reputation which he was afterwards to acquire, the young Louis XV seemed to take no interest in women. The courtiers were in despair. They even collected seven ladies of the Court, chosen for their beauty and known for their lack of prudery, and took them all down to Chantilly, where the young King was staying, in the hope that he would be attracted to one of them. It was all in vain. There is a certain irony in what eventually happened, narrated with some wit by the Duc de Castries:

The affaire was nevertheless arranged, or arranged itself. . . . On December 2nd 1723 the Regent died of apoplexy, in the arms of his mistress, the Duchesse de Faloris [sic]. The latter felt that she had obligations to the Crown and, having closed the uncle's eyes, opened those of the nephew, an initiation which took place, it appears, one fine morning in the month of April, 1724.[5]

Louis XV was launched on his long amorous career.

He had been betrothed for political reasons to a Spanish princess who was already resident in France. But she was only six years old and some years must necessarily elapse before the marriage could be consummated: a dangerous interval in which a maîtresse en titre might become all powerful. The child was sent home and another wife for Louis looked for. A list of (it is said) ninety-nine possible princesses was drawn up, but the choice finally fell on Marie Leczinska, daughter of the exiled King of Poland; and the marriage, by proxy, took place on 15 August 1725 in Strasbourg cathedral.

It was an unfortunate decision. At twenty-three, Marie was seven years older than her husband. It is true that at first the timid boy and his pious spouse got on well together, and the conjugal rites were not lacking for, five years after the marriage, when the King himself was a mere twenty years old, he was already the father of five children. In July 1738 the Queen was pregnant for the tenth time. She had a miscarriage and resolved not to have any more offspring, which at that time meant refusing the King's embraces. The author of *La Vie privée du Maréchal de Richelieu* gives a slightly different version, but the result was the same:

The Queen, ruled by a confessor who understood little of his penitent's interests, herself hastened the moment when she was to lose her husband's love. She decreed days of abstinence and when, on one of these mysterious days, the King made his way to her lodgings, some pretext obliged him to return to his own. . . .

One evening the King, who had already decided to return no more to the Queen's apartment, forgot his vows, and flew to her. The day was once again badly chosen and he was refused admission on the pretext that she had just taken medicine. The King insisted and the pious princess persevered in her refusal. Extremely annoyed he swore to try no more and told Le Bel, his principal *valet de chambre*, to go and find him a woman. Not knowing what to do he went to Cardinal Fleury who was already in bed, and asked his advice. The Cardinal, as embarrassed as the *valet de chambre* himself, told him to do whatever his prudence suggested. Le Bel returned to the King and told him that he hadn't been able to find a woman.

This reply did not satisfy the young monarch. . . . 'Go into the galleries,' he said; 'knock wherever you see a light and if you find a woman tell her I want to talk to her.' Le Bel . . . explored the gallery leading to the chapel and meeting there a *femme de chambre* of the Princesse de Rohan, whom he knew and knew to be virtuous, he thought he had found what he was seeking. She was an extremely pretty blonde; he took her to his room under the pretext of speaking to her, and then to the apartment of the King to whom he vouched for the young person's honesty. A sum of money which enabled her to make a good marriage was the price of her sacrifice.

This anecdote, related by Le Bel himself, gives the lie to everything that has been written on this subject. Next day he gave an account of his conduct to the Cardinal who, seeing that providence had abandoned the King to his inclinations, was the first to submit himself to its decrees. He asked Le Bel if His Majesty had shown attention to any particular woman, and on his report that his eye had lighted several times on Madame de Mailly, she was decided upon. She suited the Cardinal who distrusted the ascendancy of a pretty woman; she was neither very young nor very beautiful; she was known to have little taste for intrigue, and the Cardinal instructed him to try to substitute the Countess for the *femme de chambre*.

The occasion was not long in coming. After a further demand for a woman on the part of the King, who had been made to understand that the *femme de chambre* was not suitable for him, Le Bel informed Madame de Mailly that His Majesty had something important to say to her. The Countess was in the middle of an elaborate toilette; Le Bel calculated his master's impatience, and the certainty that a negligée was the attire which was suited to the circumstances, and assured her that the King had ordered him to bring her to him just as she was. Madame de Mailly, not being able to imagine the reason for so extraordinary a message, followed Le Bel who introduced her secretly into the monarch's apartment. She excused herself for her toilette, alleging His Majesty's orders, and her haste to obey them. The King, without listening to her, declared his passion, and without awaiting her response proceeded to prove it. Madame de Mailly surprised, and already loving the King, made a feeble defence and became his conquest, without having had time to think what she was doing . . .

It is known that her sister, Madame de Vintimille, succeeded her, and died in child-bed. Madame de Mailly . . . had also the chagrin of seeing another of her sisters, the Marquise de la Tournelle, later Duchesse de Châteauroux, inherit the right of pleasing her lover.[6]

If Madame de Mailly was the most disinterested of the King's mistresses – she is alleged to have left the Court as poor as when she entered it – the Marquise de la Tournelle was the most exigent. She demanded, in exchange for her favours, to be accorded a handsome apartment in which the King was to visit her without any of the secrecy he had used with regard to her sister, that she should sup with him in full view of the Court, that she should be allowed to draw money, on her mere note of hand, from the royal treasury, that her children if she had any should be legitimized, and that she should be created Duchesse de Châteauroux. To all this Louis xv agreed.

Avid for his glory, she then persuaded her royal lover to join his armies, then engaged in the War of the Austrian Succession. This nearly proved her undoing, for, at Metz, he fell so seriously ill that his life was despaired of. He sent for his neglected Queen, and there was a reconciliation in which she implored him not to ask pardon of her but of God. In plain terms this meant abandoning his mistress and the King agreed. Suddenly he recovered, and the old rhyme was once more played out:

> The Devil was sick
> The Devil a monk would be
> The Devil was well
> The Devil a monk was he.

On the very night of his return to Paris, where he had been received with acclamation, he secretly rejoined Madame de Châteauroux in a house in the Rue du Bac. She demanded an open return to her position at Court and the King yielded. And then, suddenly, she was taken ill with a 'fever' (in the eighteenth century this might mean anything) and died. Louis was overcome with grief and turned to the chase as a means of distraction.

And it was while he was hunting in the Sénart forest that he first set eyes on the woman who was to play the most important part in his life for the next twenty years.

Jeanne-Antoinette Poisson was the daughter of an army contractor of dubious probity, who had been convicted of corruption. Her mother, described as *une femme légère*, nonetheless had a cool head and far-reaching plans. A fortune teller had prophesied that her daughter would, one day, be (almost) Queen of France and, although this must have seemed extremely unlikely at the time, the girl was given an excellent education and prepared in every way for the great destiny it was hoped would be hers. She was introduced to the famous salon of Madame de Tencin and met there men of the calibre of Fontenelle, Montesquieu and Marivaux.

She was married at an early age to a man named Normand d'Etioles and it was under his name that she first appeared in society. Little is known about him, except that he appears to have been as complaisant as most husbands of the period. Madame d'Etioles did everything in her power to attract the attention of the King. She was young and beautiful and had a sense of style which never left her. She appeared at the royal hunt dressed with great elegance in the height of the fashion; one day (according to the Goncourts) dressed in light blue in a phaeton *couleur de rose*, another day in a rose-coloured costume in a phaeton of azure. The King's interest was aroused.

It so happened that her cousin, Monsieur Binet, was *valet de chambre* to Louis XV and it was he who introduced Madame d'Etioles to Versailles, on the occasion of a grand ball on 27 February 1745. Everybody was masked. The King was much taken with one lady (it was all part of the plan) who seemed to him particularly attractive. She was persuaded to remove her mask, and revealed the woman who had so attracted his attention in the Sénart forest. Deliberately, she dropped her handkerchief and the King stooped to recover it. 'The handkerchief was thrown,' said the sharp-eyed courtiers.

Normand d'Etioles put up a certain resistance but was finally placated by being given a lucrative post in far-away Provence. There was a *séparation de biens* (separation of property) and Madame d'Etioles, created Marquise de Pompadour, was installed at Versailles in the apartments which had formerly been occupied by Madame de Châteauroux. In spite of the hostility of the nobility who detested the elevation of '*cette bourgeoise*', she succeeded in maintaining her position for longer than anyone would have thought possible. She became, in fact, the most powerful person in France.

She had some frights from time to time. In 1747 the King cast his eyes on Madame de Périgord who, alarmed, retired to her country estates. In the following year Louis took a fancy to the Princesse de Robecqu, the daughter of the Maréchal de Luxembourg. Then in 1749 the King became the lover of Madame de Forcalquier. There were other alarms but Madame de Pompadour survived them all.

Perhaps her greatest danger was when there was an attempt on the King's life. This, like the previous occasion when he fell ill at Metz, gave Louis one of his rare twinges of conscience concerning his irregular life. Horace Walpole tells us that:

When the King was stabbed, and heartily frightened, the mistress took a panic too, and consulted D'Argenson, whether she had not best make off in time. He hated her, and said, By all means. Madame de Mirepoix advised her to stay. The King recovered his spirits, D'Argenson was banished, and la Maréchale [de Mirepoix] inherited part of the mistress's credit.

Horace Walpole retails another bit of gossip:

that the Chevalier d'Eon 'told people in the Park the other day, that Madame de Guerchy (who is remarkably plain) was going to Paris, to take Madame de Pompadour's place. We do not hear that it is seriously filled up; I mean in the cabinet, for in the Bedchamber it has long been executed by deputies.

Madame de Pompadour took care that it should be so and even established for the King's amusement a kind of harem: the celebrated Parc aux Cerfs. She had hoped (and this is a startling commentary on the *mœurs* of the time) that her daughter would succeed her as royal favourite. She knew Louis xv sufficiently well to realize that incest, far from frightening him, would add a certain piquancy to such a relationship. But the daughter destined for so glorious a career died at the age of ten. Madame de Pompadour then cast around for a means of supplying the King's appetites while still retaining her hold over him in the political field. She appointed herself *Surintendant des plaisirs du Roi.*

In a part of Versailles rather far from the palace stood a small house *entre cour et jardin* which the King's agents selected as suitable. It was purchased in 1755, and did not long lack inhabitants supplied by a considerable number of go-betweens, male and female. The girls were well looked after and care was taken of their education – some of them were no older than twelve. They were handsomely rewarded, even those who failed to please the King being dismissed with a pension.

It is not perhaps astonishing, in view of the moral climate of the time, that even respectable fathers of families tried to get their daughters accepted. A letter is still in existence addressed to the King's agent by an ex-officer of noble birth:

Monseigneur,
Would it be too much to ask of your kindness to try to obtain for my third daughter, aged fifteen, admittance to the happy little house where are trained those of their sex who are reserved for the ardent love of our good King? She is of baptismal innocence, not knowing the difference between the sexes. She has been

brought up by her mother, my worthy spouse, a model of virtue and chaste, who has always laboured to make her daughter fit to please our beloved King.... I await, Monseigneur, your reply with impatience. If it is favourable it will shower the blessings of God on a family which will always be blindly and passionately devoted to you. I have the honour to be, etc.[7]

There was no lack of others (most of them, perhaps, of somewhat lower social standing than the worthy ex-captain whose letter we have just quoted) who were willing to traffic in their own flesh and blood. One of the innumerable stalls, or little shops, in the Palais Royal was kept by a certain Madame Morfi (or Morphi, or Murphy) who had four daughters, whom she sold one after the other. The youngest worked for a dressmaker, Madame Fleuret, who ran a regular business in finding rich lovers for the girls in her establishment. She gave them a certain education and was careful to see that they took their first communion in a convent chapel. That sent up their price.

Louis xv was profoundly afraid of contracting syphilis, and thought this was somewhat less likely if his sexual partners were very young. He sent his *premier valet de chambre*, Le Bel, who acted as his principal procurer, to Paris on a recruiting expedition. The Marquis d'Argenson tells us what happened. Le Bel approached Madame Fleuret who passed him on to Madame Morfi.

He saw *la petite Morfi*, aged fourteen and a half, and thought well of her. He said he was acting for a nobleman at Versailles and despatched her there. He gave a thousand crowns to the mother and a hundred *louis* to Madame Fleuret. The child had wit and pleased the King very much; she has at the moment a pretty little house in the *Parc aux Cerfs*, a housekeeper, a *femme de chambre* and two lackeys.[8]

This was *La Petite Morphil* whose portrait (or back view, rather) has been preserved for us in Boucher's enchanting picture (now in the Wallraf-Richartz Museum Cologne) showing the young woman, naked and lying on her stomach on a sofa.

It is impossible to determine the number of girls and young women who passed through the Parc aux Cerfs, but Raoul Vèze gives a list of some of them which ranges from milliners and servant girls to aristocratic ladies.[9] And aristocratic patrons did not disdain to 'present' candidates themselves. We learn that 'Madame de Sainte-Hélène was presented to the King by the Maréchale de Mirepoix'; and it is even more astonishing to hear of a certain 'Miss Witist, *une Anglaise*' brought to Paris by the Duchess of Devonshire.

Louis xv was insatiable and, as he grew older, increasingly perverse. It is related that one day, visiting the convent of Bonsecours, he found four of the nuns very much to his liking. Next day they were all installed in the Parc aux Cerfs. He found a special exaltation in a sinister mixture of religion and lubricity. He is alleged to have made his mistresses kneel with him in prayer before getting into bed, 'all the while talking of God, the Virgin Mary and the Saints'.[10]

After Madame de Pompadour, Louis' most famous mistress was the future Madame du Barry. Her parentage and ancestry have been laboriously disentangled by historians of the period.[11] There was a certain aristocratic strain entering in the seventeenth century but her immediate forbears were, for the most part, lackeys and *femmes de chambre* (chambermaids) in the service of the nobility. There is a certain irony in the fact that one of her uncles was in the service of Madame de Pompadour.

Jeanne, for such was her baptismal name, was born at Vaucouleurs in Lorraine on 19 August 1743. She was the illegitimate daughter of Anne Bécu and (it is thought) of a monk in the local monastery named Jean-Baptiste Gommard de Vaubernier who had entered the religious life under the name of Frère Ange. Coming to Paris, Anne married in 1749 a lackey named Nicolas Rançon. The family was 'protected' by a financier called Billard-Dumouceaux, who interested himself not only in Anne, who was probably one of his mistresses, but also in her daughter Jeanne, and used his influence to have her admitted by the *Adoratrices du Sacré-Cœur* at the convent of Sainte-Aure. The nine years she spent there gave her some degree of education and a rudimentary taste for letters. She was also sincerely pious and remained so all her life.

Jeanne left the convent in 1758. She was then fifteen years old. She was placed first with a hairdresser and then became *femme de chambre* to the widow of a *fermier-général*, named Madame Delay de la Garde. This was her first introduction to the fashionable world. She was dazzlingly beautiful, as all testimonies agree, and it is probable that her adventures began with one or more of the men in Madame Delay de la Garde's circle. Dismissed by this lady, Jeanne obtained a post with a *marchand de modes* (dress-maker), at the sign of *A la Toilette* in the Rue Neuve-des-Petits-Champs. To accept such an occupation was almost inevitably to embark on a career of *galanterie*, in spite of the severe regime which the *marchand de modes* tried to impose on his employees.

What happened next is a matter of controversy. Her enemies (and she had many after she became the acknowledged mistress of Louis xv) maintained that she had spent some time in the famous brothel kept by Madame Gourdan, but it is at least possible that this notorious woman was bribed to say so. All we know for certain is that she was listed in the police registers for 1761, not as a prostitute but as a *fille galante* (i.e. a kept woman), under the name of Mademoiselle Beauvernier or Vaubernier. A police report describes her as 'a pretty roguish *grisette* [woman of easy virtue], knowing what she was doing and quite content with her lot'.[12]

Between 1760 and 1763 Jeanne acquired a lengthy list of protectors, and among these was Jean du Barry. His aristocratic lineage is undoubted but the fact that he was universally known as *le Roué* (the Rake) is a sufficient commentary on his reputation. Gambler and go-between, he managed to maintain somehow a place in 'good' society. He established a kind of *maison de passe* where wealthy or aristocratic young men could meet beautiful women and when such women were set up *'dans ses meubles'* (that is, provided with a house, servants and a carriage) he collected a commission (or even a regular rent) from their protectors. He also managed, by the favour of men he had 'obliged', to obtain a post as *'fournisseur des armées'* (purveyor to the army). Exactly how he came in touch with Jeanne Vaubernier (as she was now usually called) is not known for certain, but by 1763 he had made her his mistress, not only for her attractions as a bedfellow but with a view to future profit. He did everything possible to attract attention to her, taking her to balls and masquerades and introducing her to as many clients as possible. And, from 1766, people no more spoke of Mademoiselle Vaubernier but of Comtesse du Barry. The pair lived luxuriously and the fact that it was a *faux ménage* (illicit relationship) did not prevent men of distinction from visiting their salon. Among these were famous writers like Marmontel and Crébillon *fils* and it was from people like these that Madame du Barry acquired a certain culture and the ability to take part in an intelligent conversation.

Jeanne had a succession of lovers, some of them, including the Duc de Richelieu, of the highest nobility. The Duc de Lauzun gives a glimpse of the kind of circle she moved in:

I made the acquaintance, at a ball at the Opéra, of a very beautiful girl; she has made too much stir in the world not to speak of her. She was called Mademoiselle Vaubernier: she was nicknamed the Angel on account of her heavenly figure. She was living with Monsieur le Comte du Barry who lived by his wits, practising all kinds of trades. I was asked to supper at the house, which was very well kept and where there were some very pretty women. But it was impossible to see a more amusing spectacle than that of the master of the house. Monsieur du Barry was in a splendid dressing gown, his hat on his head, holding two cooked apples that he had been ordered to put on his eyes. I saw there a Madame de Fontanelle arrived from Lyons with the intention of becoming the King's mistress, and contenting herself, while waiting, with the first-comer. I wanted her, and Monsieur le Comte du Barry, always obliging, managed it for me the following day. I don't think I ever saw Madame de Fontanelle again. Then, the Angel inspired desires in me and did not refuse to satisfy them, but I was restrained by Monsieur du Barry's red eyes and the state of his health. Monsieur de Fitz-James[13] was bolder than I, succeeded and kept her; which did not prevent her from having for me all the small complaisances which might be without danger for either of us.

A few days before my departure for Corsica, I was told that the King had seen the Angel, that he intended to pursue the matter. I went to bid her good-bye and to compliment her on such a brilliant success.

'If you become the King's mistress, beautiful Angel,' I said to her, 'remember that I want the command of an army.'

'That's not enough,' she replied. 'You will be at least Prime Minister.'

The Angel had had some business with Monsieur de Choiseul and to make everything go smoothly had offered to go to bed with him. Monsieur le Duc de Choiseul, who, for just reasons, was incensed with Monsieur du Barry, wouldn't hear of it. It was perhaps the only time he had ever declined a woman's favour, and all Europe knows the consequences of his refusal.[14]

There are many conflicting accounts of the first meeting of Madame du Barry and the King. Du Barry maintained that the King noticed her, *by chance*, as she was walking in the Galerie des Glaces at Versailles, but given du Barry's character this seems somewhat unlikely. The Duc de Castries suggests that there was a plot, concocted by du Barry, Le Bel the King's valet, and the Duc de Richelieu, to throw the beautiful young woman in the King's way. Richelieu's part seems to have been to assure the King that Madame du Barry was a lady of quality married to the Comte du Barry, and that she was only known to have had one liaison, that with the rich financier Sainte-Foy, who had indeed been her principal lover from 1766 to 1768. The King seems to have swallowed this story for, after Madame du Barry had become his mistress, he said to his confidant the Duc d'Ayen: 'They say that I succeed Sainte-Foy.' To which the Duke, with astonishing impertinence, replied: 'Yes, Sire, just as Your Majesty succeeds Pharamond.'[15]

The King, however, was already ensnared, for his new mistress had been able to re-awaken those fires which he was beginning to fear were dying down. For forty years he had exercised his sexual powers to excess, and had recently had one or two failures. Madame du Barry, skilled as she must have been in the arts of love, had been able to restore his confidence. 'I am enchanted with your Madame du Barry,' he confessed to Richelieu. 'She is the only woman in France who can make me forget that I am in my sixties.'

Madame de Pompadour had recently died, aged forty-two, and the King, it seems, had decided that Madame du Barry should take her place as *maîtresse en titre*. But on 24 June 1768 the much-neglected Queen died also and even to Louis xv it appeared improper to proceed too rapidly with the process of elevating his new favourite.

Moreover he had begun to realize that Madame du Barry was not the wife but merely the mistress of the Comte du Barry and that Sainte-Foy had not been the only other man in her life. Also that she could not regularize her position by marrying du Barry because he was married already; and bigamy in France in the eighteenth century was a crime punishable by death.

Du Barry, after consulting Richelieu, produced the most ingenious scheme that even he had ever thought of. He remembered that he had a younger brother, a retired army captain who lived on his estates at a place called Lévignac. He also, in accordance with French usage, was entitled to call himself Comte du Barry; and if he married his brother's mistress, she would become Madame du Barry with an authentic and indisputable title.

The younger brother was therefore persuaded, in exchange for a handsome bribe and the promise of advancement for his family, to agree to this arrangement. The marriage duly took place, although it was necessary to forge quite a number of documents, such as birth certificates, in order to gloss over the irregularities involved. It must have needed some powerful undisclosed influence (that of Richelieu and the possible connivance of the King himself) to push the matter through.

The meeting for the signing of the marriage contract must have provided a scene worthy of the pencil of a Hogarth or the pen of a Marivaux. The future husband and wife were seeing one another for the first time. On the one hand a short, fat, uncouth creature whom contemporaries describe as *une espèce d'imbécile*, on the other one of the most beautiful women in Europe. The actual marriage took place on 1 September 1768, after which the bridegroom, consoled with a pension of five thousand livres a year, took the road to Toulouse, near which his estates lay, and the bride was installed in an apartment in the Château of Versailles. Meanwhile her new brother-in-law and ex-lover busied himself devising a suitable coat-of-arms.

The battle, however, was not yet over. It was one thing to be lodged under the royal roof; quite another to be recognized as *maîtresse en titre* and have the *entrée* to the Court. And the presentation of Madame du Barry at Court presented certain difficulties. A cabal against her had already formed itself led by the Duc de Choiseul, the most powerful man in France, who had himself owed his elevation to the influence of Madame de Pompadour. He saw himself threatened by this new arrival and took every means at his disposal to discredit her. He encouraged, and probably financed, broadsheets and popular songs against her, as well as a whole series of comedies making allusion (and very transparent allusion) to her past life. He even tried to throw in the King's way other possible contestants for the royal favour. The last included his own sister; but it was all in vain. Madame du Barry was already beginning to form a 'clan' of her own, among those courtiers who saw in her triumph a chance to further their own interests.

In order to be presented at Court it was necessary to have a chaperon. Several *grandes dames* were approached but declined the office. Finally Louis found a certain Comtesse de Béarn, up to her eyes in debts, who, in return for a sum sufficient to discharge them and for advancement for her two sons, one in the cavalry and one in the navy, consented to perform the task. Even she lost courage at the last moment and the presentation had to be postponed. And then the King was hurt while hunting in the forest of Saint-Germain. If he should die then all the dreams of Madame du Barry would have been in vain.

However, he recovered and on 22 April 1769 she was duly presented by the Comtesse de Béarn. She made the three curtsies required by custom and went through the ceremony with calm and grace (said her friends) – or with effrontery, as her enemies would have it. Next day she was present at mass in the chapel of the Palace of Versailles in the seat which had formerly been occupied by Madame de Pompadour. Madame du Barry had arrived!

The reign of Madame de Pompadour had lasted nearly twenty years, from 1745 to 1764; that of Madame du Barry lasted a mere five years, from 1769 to the death of the King. She could not compare with the Pompadour in political ability, and it was her misfortune to arrive at a moment when the scandals of the *ancien régime* were becoming intolerable. Madame du Barry became, as it were, the symbol of the complete corruption of the Court of France.

The *Chronique secrète de Paris*, written by the Abbé Baudeau, throws a curious light on the death of Louis xv. The King had taken a fancy to a milkmaid on the Trianon estate and Madame du Barry, for his amusement, had dressed her in one of her own robes and asked her to supper. Everybody drank a great deal and the young woman found herself – inevitably – in the King's arms. The following day the girl's brother died of smallpox. The Goncourts, and other authorities, reject this story, which may or may not be true.

In any case, the King very soon showed the first symptoms of the malady. He was transported to Versailles, his first physician having pronounced the memorable words: '*Sire, c'est à Versailles qu'il faut être malade.*'[16] His doctors treated him as best they could (bleeding was the universal treatment) but it soon became obvious that he was dying. After being visited by several high ecclesiastics he sent for Madame du Barry and told her that, as he was about to receive the sacraments, it would be better if she departed. He told her that he had given instructions that she would want for nothing. He died, horribly disfigured, on 10 May 1774.

6

FOOTNOTES

1 The Regent's eldest daughter.

2 Dudley Ryder, *Diary* (1715–16). Translated from shorthand and edited by William Matthews, London 1939.

3 i.e. some years before 1791 when the book was published.

4 Anon., *La Vie privée du Maréchal de Richelieu*, Paris 1791.

5 Duc de Castries, *Madame du Barry*, Paris 1967.

6 Anon., *La Vie privée du Maréchal de Richelieu*, Paris 1791.

7 Peuchel, *Mémoires tirés des Archives de la Police de Paris*, Paris 1838.

8 Marquis d'Argenson, *Journal et Mémoires*, London 1909.

9 Raoul Vèze, *La Galanterie Parisienne au XVIIIᵉ Siècle*, Paris 1905.

10 Anon., *Anecdotes de la Cour de France pendant la Faveur de Madame de Pompadour*, Paris 1802.

11 Notably by the Duc de Castries.

12 The actual French phrase used in the report – '*une grisette jolie, friponne, éveillé et demandant pas mieux*' – is really untranslatable.

13 Jean-Charles, Comte de Fitz-James, born 1743.

14 Duc de Lauzun, *Mémoires* (1747–83), Paris 1858.

15 That is, the succession is lengthy indeed. Pharamond was one of the earliest of the Frankish kings.

16 'Sire, one ought to be ill at Versailles.'

7 The Pursuit of Love

The student of eighteenth-century mores is compelled to admit that their most striking characteristic is unabashed eroticism. Literature is largely concerned with love-making, and art itself seems to shrink to the decoration of a boudoir. Even more striking is the insouciance and contempt for public opinion evinced by the upper classes in every country of Europe. It is true that several Societies for the Reformation of Manners had been in existence since the end of the seventeenth century, and one of them, started by a group of Anglican ministers, had even, we are told, been joined by 'several Persons of considerable Rank and Fortunes'. By the middle of the eighteenth century such societies were able to claim that they had prosecuted more than one hundred persons for sabbath-breaking, swearing, drunkenness, lewdness, brothel-keeping and sodomy. But it is a fair conclusion that an overwhelming proportion of that number belonged to the lower classes. What more than a century later was to be called the Nonconformist Conscience was already stirring, but not amongst the aristocracy, which was almost untouched by it. In the late nineteenth century, the *Methodist Times* of October 1896 was able to boast that 'Sir Charles Dilke defied the Nonconformist Conscience and is a political outcast today. Parnell despised the Nonconformist Conscience and he destroyed himself and his party. Lord Rosebery ignored the Nonconformist Conscience for a racehorse and the world sees the result.' How men like Lord Sandwich and Sir Francis Dashwood would have laughed at such ideas, that adultery could ruin one's political career, and a mere passion for racing lose one public esteem!

One cannot help feeling that it was political hostility rather than moral fervour that led Junius[1] to denounce the Duke of Grafton for openly flaunting his liaison with the notorious Nancy Parsons: 'It is not the private indulgence, but the public insult of which I complain. The name of Miss Parsons would hardly have been known if the First Lord of the Treasury had not led her in triumph through the Opera House, even in the presence of the Queen.'[2]

Certainly Nancy Parsons did nothing to reinforce the moral lesson set forth in Hogarth's *Harlot's Progress*. Lord Glenbervie, writing at the end of the eighteenth century, tells us of her glittering career:

Our company here consisted of Lord Maynard, a strange character, nephew to Lady Liverpool and the husband of the late Nancy Parsons, or Mrs Haughton, who after being the common spouse of all the town was first the mistress of the Duke of Grafton, when First Lord of the Treasury, afterwards travelled over Europe with the Duke of Dorset, then married Lord Maynard, and again travelled and resided for a year or two, I believe, with the Duke of Bedford at an age to be his mother at least. She had taken the name of Haughton from a West Indian who had found her in a brothel and carried her to Jamaica, and was said to have married [her]. She preceded Lady Hamilton in the favour of the Queen of Naples. I have heard that she would tell some of her intimate friends that in the early part of her life she had once earned, in single guineas, one hundred in one day. Whether she left off lassata or satiata I know not.[3]

Perhaps the most notorious rake of the period was Lord Sandwich. He was by no means unintelligent and had held high office under the Crown. We must also make some allowance, when considering his private reputation, for the hatred loosed against him for his prosecution of John Wilkes. This was the more resented for the fact that both Sandwich and Wilkes had been boon companions in debauchery. Yet Sandwich, having fraudulently obtained a copy of the famous 'Essay on Woman' (an obscene parody of Pope's 'Essay on Man') which was said to have been composed by Wilkes,[4] had the audacity to read passages of it in the House of Lords on the grounds that it had been addressed to him (he had almost certainly been present at the first reading at Medmenham). This, he claimed, constituted a breach of his privilege as a peer.

It was too much. The general public, which had at least an inkling of the true state of affairs, resented what they regarded as the betrayal of a friend and when, at a performance of *The Beggar's Opera*, Macheath spoke the words 'That Jemmy Twitcher should 'peach me, I own surprised me', the house immediately, in a storm of applause, applied them to Sandwich. Henceforth he was known as Jemmy Twitcher.

Sandwich remained completely indifferent to public opinion, expressed inside or outside the House of Commons. Horace Walpole records that during a debate:

Colonel Barré . . . spoke too with extreme bitterness, which is almost new again; so civil have Parliaments been of late. He commended the present Secretaries of State, but foresaw it possible that, if one of them should die, his successor might be the most dissolute and abandoned sad dog in the kingdom. There sat Sandwich under the gallery, while the whole House applied the picture to him! Not a word was offered in his defence. You will ask if he was thunderstruck? Yes, say those who were near him. Yet so well did he recover the blow that at three in the morning, he commenced an intrigue with a coffee-girl, who attends in the Speaker's chambers.[5]

Sandwich's *maîtresse en titre* was Martha Ray, whom he had found behind the counter of a milliner's shop in Tavistock Street in London. He was so much taken with her charms that he had her educated in music and singing and established her not in an apartment in London but, with typical contempt for propriety, in his own house, Hinchinbrook, where his wife also resided. The liaison lasted for sixteen years and Miss Ray won golden opinions, even from those who disapproved of her equivocal position, for the beauty of her voice and the modesty of her behaviour. A certain lieutenant in the 68th Regiment of Foot, named James Hackman, on a visit to Hinchinbrook, fell violently in love with her and offered her marriage. She declined, saying that she did not wish to carry a knapsack. Incredible as it may seem, the young man resigned from the Army and entered the Church, becoming Vicar of Wyventon in Norfolk. But he continued to be infatuated with Miss Ray and she continued to reject him. So great was the force of his passion that he decided to commit suicide, if possible in sight of the lady. For this purpose he came to London, where Miss Ray was living with Sandwich at the Admiralty (he being at that time First Lord). He sought an interview with her, but she told him that she was engaged for that evening and refused to say where. He discovered, however, that she was going to see *Love in a Village* at Covent Garden. He followed her there and what happened afterwards is recorded in the *Morning Post* for 9 April 1779:

On Wednesday night, Miss Reay [*sic*] was coming out of the playhouse, accompanied by Signora Galli (one of the singers) and a gentleman who had politely offered to see her to her carriage, when she was followed by the resolute assassin. He stepped up to her just as she had her foot on the step of the coach, pulled her by her sleeve, which occasioned her to turn round, when, without the smallest previous menace or address, he put a pistol to her forehead and shot her instantly dead. He then fired at himself, which however did not prove equally effective. The ball grazed upon the upper part of the head, but did not penetrate sufficiently to produce any fatal effect.

He was tried at the Old Bailey for murder and duly executed at Tyburn on 19 April. The authorities certainly acted with despatch.

The whole affair caused a tremendous outcry. Sandwich, of course, was not in any way responsible but people were, or pretended to be, shocked to learn that she had been for sixteen years the mistress of a man old enough to be her father. Sandwich was much distressed. He had been genuinely devoted to her, though this had not prevented him from chasing after other women of all sizes, shapes – and colours. Among the most conspicuous of the 'Ladies of the Town' at this period was a Negress known as 'Black Harriot'. The anonymous author of a scurrilous book entitled *Nocturnal*

Revels tells us that she 'found it necessary to make the most of her jetty charms, and accordingly applied to Lovejoy. He dispatched immediately a messenger to Lord [Sandwich], who instantly quitted the arms of Miss R[ay] for this black beauty. The novelty so struck him ... that he visited her several successive evenings, and never failed giving her at least a twenty pound Bank-note.'[6]

We have noted that he was probably present at the first reading, at Medmenham, of the 'Essay on Woman'. He was certainly a member of the fraternity the history of which provides an example of that strange blend of debauchery and satanism so characteristic of the period. There had been several 'Hell-Fire Clubs' in the early years of the century, but the most famous was that established at Medmenham Abbey by Sir Francis Dashwood. According to Sir Nathaniel Wraxhall:

> He founded a society denominated from his own name 'the Franciscans', who, to the number of twelve, met at Medmenham Abbey, near Marlow in Buckinghamshire, on the banks of the Thames. Rites of a nature so subversive of all decency, and calculated by an imitation of the ceremonies and mysteries of the Catholic Church to render religion itself an object of contumely, were there celebrated as cannot be reflected on without astonishment. Sir Francis himself officiated as High Priest, habited in the dress of a Franciscan Monk,[7] pouring a libation from a Communion-cup to the mysterious object of their homage.[8]

The members were Sir Francis Dashwood, Sir John Dashwood King, Sir Thomas Stapleton, John Wilkes, Charles Churchill, Sir William Stanhope, Paul Whitehead, Robert Lloyd, Benjamin Bates, George Selwyn, Lord Sandwich and George Bubb-Dodington, afterwards Lord Melcombe. Dashwood rented the ruined Abbey of Medmenham and proceeded to fit up what rooms could still be used in luxurious fashion, with ample provision of wine and food in cellar and larder. There was a 'chapel' into which no servants were admitted, with mural paintings 'Pompeian in their audacity'.[9] And over the door was the motto *'Fay ce que tu voudra'* ('Do what you will') adopted from the Abbey of Thélème, described by Rabelais.

The Dashwoods were an old Dorset family, one of whom was, in the seventeenth century, a successful 'Turkey Merchant', trading with the Near East. One of his sons became Lord Mayor of London, and another, Francis, was made a baronet in 1707. Sir Francis married Lady Mary Fane, daughter of the Earl of Westmorland. Their child was the Francis with whom we are concerned, and he succeeded to the baronetcy on the death of his father in 1724. He was then sixteen years old, rich and well connected, and nothing was more natural than that he should almost immediately set off on the Grand Tour. It became for him a series of escapades in one capital after another. He had the originality to penetrate to Russia and the effrontery in St Petersburg to try to make love to the Empress at a masked ball.[10] In Florence he met Horace Walpole travelling with the poet Gray, and, it would seem, entered into a passing political intrigue with the Young Pretender, which was duly reported to the English Government by the British ambassador. Coming back to England Dashwood was returned to Parliament by the pocket borough of New Romney. He became Chancellor of the Exchequer in 1762 – an unlikely office, it would seem, to be given to so notoriously flighty a character.

Dashwood was a cultivated man, as is proved by his founding of the Dilettanti Society for encouraging the arts which, in spite of Walpole's sneer about 'a club of which the nominal qualification is having been to Italy, and the real one being drunk', it has continued to do ever since. But it is, of course, for the founding of the less worthy Hell-Fire Club that he is chiefly remembered.

Sir Francis lived at West Wycombe House standing above the Buckinghamshire village of that name. The house itself was not very large or splendid but, says Burgo Partridge, he 'made up for this in the elaboration of the gardens; and the statues and temples with which they were decorated. He had laid out one part of the garden in the shape of a woman, with most suggestive grouping of pillars and bushes, an expensive smutty joke which could not be appreciated fully until the invention of the aeroplane.'[11] John Wilkes described other parts of the garden, particularly a Temple of Venus, the door of which was in the shape of the 'entrance by which we all came into the world'. In a word, Dashwood had an obsession with sex which he had no compunction in displaying to the world, or at least to those who were his guests.

We can have a pretty good idea of the 'nameless rites' practised at Medmenham. None of the set seems to have been homosexual and so it was necessary to bring ladies from London to share in the orgies. They came for the most part from the London brothels, with which Dashwood was already well acquainted. Indeed, he is said to have had a financial interest in Mrs Stanhope's bawdy-house near Drury Lane. In this, as in similar establishments such as those of Molly King, Mrs Gould, Mrs Goudby or Mother Douglas, it was possible to give private parties. At these what might be called the serious part of the business was often preceded by a kind of strip-tease show. In an anonymous work of the period there is a detailed description of a performance by 'posture girls'. Having stripped naked and climbed on to a table, 'they each filled a Glass of Wine, and laying themselves in an extended Posture placed their Glasses on the Mount of Venus, every man in the Company drinking of the Bumper, as it stood on that tempting Eminence, while the Witches were not wanting in their lascivious Motions to heighten diversion. Then they went through the several Postures and Tricks made use of to raise debilitated Lust.'[12] The performance seems to have been merely a 'tease', for when the men present wished to take the affair to its logical conclusion 'this was a Step the Nymphs would not comply with, it being the maxim of those Damsels never to admit of the Embraces of the Men for fear of spoiling their Trade'. The men had to be content with the other women in the brothel.[13]

It seems to have been quite a usual thing for fine ladies to attend some of the brothel parties in search of excitement. A well-known 'Madame', Mrs Prendergast, actually advertised one such in the press and, says a contemporary account:

... intimated that on the Wednesday evening following, there would be a diversion quite out of the common routine, under the title of *Bal d'Amour*, where some of the finest Women in Europe would make their appearance, masked indeed, but in other respects in *puris naturalibus*. The evening of this Gala, Pall Mall was thronged with chairs and carriages; and everyone seemed emulous who should first enter the Paphian Temple. Lady G[rosveno]r and Lady L[igonie]r came in disguise. It is somewhat extraordinary that Lord G[rosveno]r and Lord L[igonie]r enjoyed their own wives without knowing it; and strange to tell, pronounced their imaginary Lais's most excellent pieces.[14]

Mother Douglas was an even more celebrated purveyor of such pleasures.

About the same period, Mother Douglas, well known by the name of Mother Cole, and so finely caricatured in Foote's [play, *The*] *Minor*,[15] was in all her glory. Her house was calculated for the superior ranks of Debauchees, Princes and Peers frequented it, and she fleeced them in proportion to their dignity.... Women of the first rank came here frequently *incog.*, the utmost secrecy being observed; and it frequently happened that while my Lord was enjoying Chloe in one room, in the adjacent compartment her Ladyship was cuckolding her *caro sposo* with a pair of the largest antlers she could procure. Demi-reps. of an inferior class also resorted hither. The celebrated Campioni and Peg Woffington have often sacrificed at the altar of Venus in this chapel; and it is said with some degree of authority, that it was owing to the detection of an intrigue between the last Lady and Sir Hanbury Will[ia]ms, that little Davy [David Garrick] escaped from being noosed in the connubial knot with Peggy.[16]

Those for whom even London provided insufficient scope could always go to Paris, already regarded as Europe's chief 'City of Pleasure'. Louis XIV, under the influence in the latter part of his reign of the prudish Mme de Maintenon, made some attempt to suppress the houses of prostitution in the French capital. He did not succeed; the Regent who ruled after his death did not even try; and Louis XV showed a similar indulgence. By means of spies and police agents he kept himself informed of what was going on, not in order to suppress it but in order to stimulate his own appetite with the salacious details. Two police reports have survived, one in the *Bibliothèque de l'Arsenal* and the other in the *Bibliothèque Nationale*, and they give a very clear picture of the moral climate of Paris in the second half of the eighteenth century.

The keeper of a house of ill-fame was known as the abbess, and one of the most successful of these women was the famous La Gourdan, known also as the 'little countess'. Her first house was in the Rue Sainte-Anne and here she worked in conjunction with du Barry, himself as we have seen a notable trader in female flesh. From time to time she was in trouble with the police, but always managed to escape punishment owing to powerful protectors at Court. She was far from being alone in her *métier*, but her career is so typical that we may perhaps dispense with recounting those of her numerous rivals.

We know a great deal of what went on in her establishment – she had several addresses in succession, always moving on to more commodious and luxurious premises – not only from the police reports already mentioned, but from a curious book published in 1783.[17] The editor recounts in his preface how, on a visit to Mme Gourdan's establishment, he was waiting in the salon for a woman to be brought to him and opened a small writing table which happened to be in the room. He found a quantity of letters to the mistress of the house and these seemed to him of such interest that he made off with a whole packet of them. These letters, provided with the initials but not the names of the senders, make up the volume. They cover a wide section of society from dukes to police officers, from physicians to *parfumiers*; there are even several from ecclesiastics.

One from the Bishop of C—— is not without its humorous side. 'You deserve,' he wrote, 'to be sent to prison. I received in your house *un fameux coup de pied de Vénus*[18] which obliged me to leave the capital and retire to my diocese in order to recover my health. It would seem that there is no probity any more and that one does not know whom to rely on.'

An abbé writes to say that he will be visiting the establishment – by the back door – that very evening, and asks to be supplied with a pretty girl *in the mirror room*. An English milord writes from London to say that on his arrival in Paris he wishes to be supplied with *une jolie maîtresse*, aged sixteen, blonde, five foot six inches in height, with a slender waist, blue and languorous eyes, pretty hands, shapely legs and a small foot. 'If you find me one such there will be fifty louis for you. Please reply to the *auberge de Dessaint* at Calais.'

The *parfumier* offers an astringent pomade guaranteed to 'give an air of novelty to things already used', i.e. to persuade the client that he has to do with an authentic virgin. And a rather sinister note is sounded by the police officer. He warns La Gourdan that she has been denounced to the authorities and that the new Lieutenant of Police arriving that very night will be inclined to take the matter up – unless of course La Gourdan cares to call upon him two hours before the Lieutenant's arrival. He mentions, *en passant*, that he is being dunned for a debt of twenty-five louis.

La Gourdan, like her competitors, not only kept a number of girls in her house, but had a long list of others who could be called upon when needed;

singers and dancers from the Opéra and the Comédie, florists and milliners, women dissatisfied with their husbands or keepers, and ladies of quality in search of a new sensation.

One of the letters is from a lady who explains that she has married, for his money, an 'old owl' aged sixty. She herself is nineteen and she offers her services. She is free to come any time, given a couple of hours' notice. But perhaps the most extraordinary letter of all is from the Marquise de G—— who complains that her husband has condemned her for four years to 'languish in the most frightful continence'. It is true that she has three lackeys, but one of them has a wife 'who does not sulk in bed' and so comes to his mistress exhausted; the second is suffering from a slight infirmity caught from a little *modiste* in the neighbourhood and the third, although furnished with *un instrument à faire envie*, becomes impotent at the very moment when he is about to make her happy. In consequence of all this she desires La Gourdan to find her a vigorous man 'devoted to the most violent passions' who will come to her on Sunday at ten o'clock in the morning. She promises that she will not only pay well but will respond with equal passion. The choice doesn't matter so long as he is healthy. A young butcher would do. She wants to be treated rough.

Some of the letters reflect quarrels among the prostitutes themselves. Violette complains that Justine, when at supper with clients, insists on stripping naked, thus compelling the writer of the letter to do the same or be called prudish. Justine replies that if she hears any more of it she will tear the other girl's eyes out. In another letter Rosalba explains that although, being thirty, she is past the age of love-making, she is still very handy with a birch rod for such gentlemen as require that kind of stimulation. And she gives her address: Rue d'Enfer, at the sign of Paradise Lost!

So the procession passes, pimps, grand seigneurs, homosexuals, lesbians, sadists, masochists, disappointed wives, girls on the make. There is something horrifying in the letters – so courteous, ceremonious and well-written – expressing the utmost readiness to take part in every variety of debauchery. No doubt prostitution is to be found in every age, and always will be, but it is reasonable to think that prostitution in the eighteenth century had a quality of cynicism almost unique in history.

It is perhaps not surprising that such a state of affairs did not pass without criticism. On the very eve of the Revolution a certain Laurent Pierre Béranger presented a memoir to the Deputies of the Third Estate calling for a radical reform in the mores of Paris. 'Let us denounce,' he said, 'with an obstinate courage these violations of public decency. Let us incite against the creators of scandal the wrath of all good citizens. The anger of fathers must be awakened and maternal fears reanimated, but most of all the magistrates must learn to blush for their lack of zeal.'[19]

He proceeds to suggest what might be done: forbidding pick-ups in the public gardens, obliging prostitutes to wear large feathers and rouge their faces, destroying obscene pictures in brothels, preventing the abduction of young girls for purposes of prostitution, closing the little theatres on the boulevards which offered nude spectacles, forbidding, in the larger theatres, curtains and grills in the boxes, as well as beds (!) and stoves, preventing actresses from wearing flesh-coloured tights, compelling every young woman living in furnished rooms to prove that she had a profession, other than the oldest one in the world, forbidding the exposure of indecent broadsheets and prints, flogging all pimps, especially those guilty of debauching girls younger than fifteen, condemning to life imprisonment all mothers who sold their daughters into a life of vice, closing the Luxembourg and Tuileries gardens at nightfall, compelling cabs to have plain glass in their windows, shaving the heads of women who exposed their breasts in public places . . .

Homosexuals could, of course, be catered for in Paris as in any other European city, but the English ones seem to have thought that Naples provided better opportunities. Certainly they flocked there in sufficient numbers for homosexuality to be known as the 'English vice'. It was, of course, well known in England also, a man like the actor Samuel Foote being particularly notorious; and Charles Churchill, the satirist, thought it worth while to devote almost a whole poem to the subject. Inevitably, in the way of satirists, he refuses to admit that Englishmen were *naturally* prone to unnatural vice:

> With our own island vices not content
> We rob our neighbours on the Continent;
> Dance Europe round, and visit every court,
> To ape their follies and their crimes import;
> To different lands for different sins we roam,
> And, richly freighted, bring our cargo home.
> Nobly industrious to make vice appear
> In her full state, and perfect only here.[20]

Then, working himself up into a fine frenzy, the poet apostrophizes Woman:

> Woman, the pride and happiness of man,
> Without whose soft endearments Nature's plan
> Had been a blank . . .

And laments that now:

> Women are kept for nothing but the breed,
> For pleasure we must have a Ganymede,
> A fine, fresh Hylas, a delicious boy
> To serve our purposes of beastly joy.

Satirists must ever be allowed the privilege of exaggeration. None the less it is evident that homosexuality *was* rife in Georgian England, and was well known to be so. It was only the Victorians who managed to persuade themselves that it did not exist – until the trial of Oscar Wilde shook them out of their complacency.

Second only to Paris in its opportunities for debauchery was mid-eighteenth-century Venice. Apart from its innumerable brothels, the attraction lay in the possibilities of amorous intrigue in a city where almost everybody went about masked for the greater part of the year. One of Goldoni's characters calls the mask 'the finest convenience in the world': convenient, that is, for intrigue; and, as every psychologist is aware, the very fact of anonymity leads to a loosening of moral control. During the Carnival many people were not only masked but in some kind of fancy dress; and the Carnival lasted from Twelfth Night until Lent and when Lent was over began again with the festival known as the Sensa, 'a kind of summer aftermath of the Carnival'. Molmenti, the social historian of Venice, describes the scene in the Piazza di San Marco:

It is a continual coming and going, a procession, an ant-heap of masked figures, a noise that is deafening. A harlequin murmurs sweet nothings into the ear of a young woman in a domino who laughs and takes refuge among the crowds. A mattucino in white with red garters and red shoes throws egg-shells filled with rose-water at patricians' windows. When night falls lanterns twisted with flowers are hung at the doors of the houses. Within there is feasting to the sound of pipe and viol. Everyone wears a mask, patricians and plebeians, rich and poor, are all disguised.[21]

This *dolce vita* was deliberately encouraged by the *Signori* who ruled Venice, anxious to turn the attention of its citizens from all political matters. The Venetians were, and are, markedly intelligent and lively minded even by Italian standards; and it is therefore not surprising that, excluded from politics, they devoted their talents to commerce (sometimes of a rather doubtful kind), to gambling – and to love. And if we are to select a typical mid-eighteenth-century figure whom can we choose but Casanova? Giacomo Girolamo Casanova (he added the 'di Seingalt' later) was born in Venice in 1725, the son of a travelling actor from Parma and a beautiful sixteen-year-old Venetian girl who, having given birth to Giacomo, also went on the stage. Casanova himself, however, preferred to believe that his actual father was Michele Grimani, scion of the patrician family which owned the San Samuele theatre where both his reputed parents performed.

As a child his existence seems to have been miserable enough. Neglected by his parents, he was forced to realize at an early age that if he was to survive at all he must do so by his own sharp wits. Somehow he managed to get a certain education at the University of Padua and in 1741 he was admitted to minor orders in the Catholic Church: not perhaps, in the eighteenth century, so strange a beginning to his career as it would have seemed in later epochs.

That career has been described in such detail by himself that it is unnecessary to do more than indicate its chief features. Casanova was a professional gambler, not disdaining the use of what he called 'correctors of fortune', i.e. marked cards and loaded dice. He was an astrologer and a cabalist. At one period of his life he was a police spy in Venice and may have acted as a government agent when he was abroad. For he travelled incessantly and was as much at home in Paris or London as in his native country. But, above all, he made love, incessantly and insatiably, and his famous memoirs are largely concerned with his amorous conquests; so much so indeed that his name has become synonymous with 'Great Lover'.

He has also been called a great liar, but it must be admitted that, when he is dealing with historical facts, subsequent research has tended to affirm his veracity. But was he, in spite of his innumerable adventures, a great lover in the accepted normal sense? Burgo Partridge, in an acute analysis of Casanova's erotic motivation, suggests that he was primarily an exhibitionist and a *voyeur*. Casanova had, he notes, 'a marked desire towards performing the sexual act with one woman in the presence of another,' or even in the presence of another man; and the purpose of the other man's presence was to humiliate him by a show of superior potency. Partridge concludes that 'Casanova, so far from being the healthy extroverted model of virile sexuality, begins to assume many of the characteristics of a neurotic pervert'.[22]

Be that as it may, Casanova does not seem to have pushed the desire to humiliate to the point of what we must call sadism, although the term had not yet been invented.[23] It was certainly known and widely practised in the eighteenth century and reaches its most psychotic expression in the actions and writings of the Marquis de Sade.

Donatien Alphonse François de Sade was a generation younger than Casanova, having been born in 1740. In his early twenties he had a *petite maison* at Arceuil near Paris which he used as a love-nest. But his methods of love-making were, to say the least, peculiar, and his penchants were soon so well known that, in 1764, we find the police inspector Marais writing to a procuress advising her not to supply any girls to the Marquis de Sade.

If he was already 'known to the police', he was shortly to attain a wider notoriety. He lured a young beggar woman named Rose Keller, first into his coach and then into his house where she was taken to a room, 'forced to undress, tied to a bed face downwards, mercilessly beaten several times with whips and sticks, cut about with a knife in various places, and had hot sealing wax dropped on her wounds'. She managed to escape, and the 'Keller case' caused such an outcry that the Marquis' family were compelled to buy off the complainants with 2,400 livres, a considerable sum in those days.

After this he was continually in trouble with the authorities. He was accused, with reason it would seem, of seduction, sodomy, flagellation (he liked being whipped as well as whipping) and of murder, two women having died from the effects of eating chocolates which contained a strong dose of the aphrodisiac drug cantharides. He fled to Italy but returned to Paris in 1777, and was arrested at his mother's request and imprisoned in the Bastille. Here he wrote the majority of his works, including *Le Philosophe dans le Boudoir*, a book which has had an extraordinary fascination for later generations.[24] To any normal person it is the work of a lunatic. The Marquis de Sade was indeed transferred from the Bastille to the Charenton lunatic asylum, where he died in 1814.

By then the climate of love (i.e. people's thoughts about love as opposed to their practice of it) had completely changed. The transformation had begun in the middle of the eighteenth century. Although Choderlos de Laclos and Samuel Richardson were contemporaries, nothing could be more different in tone than their two masterpieces, *Les Liaisons Dangereuses* and *Pamela*. The first is perhaps the most heartless and cynical book ever written, the other is all high moral sentiment. It was Richardson's great discovery that an exposition of such sentiments could be combined with 'a systematic dallying with seductive images'.

In *Pamela*, the virtuous servant girl who managed to combine her household duties with an extraordinarily voluminous literary output (how did she find time to write all those letters?) resists her employer's advances with such success, while still luring him on, that in the end he feels constrained to marry her. In certain circles cynicism was discarded and sentiment took its place, a process much aided by the writings of Rousseau, whose work had as much effect on the sensibility of the late eighteenth century as it had on its politics. And if the typical novel of the mid-eighteenth century was *Les Liaisons Dangereuses*, the typical novel of the end of the century was Bernardin de Saint-Pierre's *Paul et Virginie*, in which the heroine, far from being seduced by the hero, prefers to drown rather than that he should see her naked. But it is to be feared that the actual morals of the early nineteenth century were no better than those of the generations before. The eighteenth century was neither sentimental nor hypocritical; the nineteenth century was both.

7
FOOTNOTES

1 The authorship of the *Letters of Junius* long remained a mystery. They are now generally supposed to have been the work of Sir Philip Francis.
2 *Letters of Junius*.
3 Lord Glenbervie, *Diaries*, London 1928.

4 It is now generally thought to have been the work of John Potter, 'said to belong to the same family as John Potter, Archbishop of Canterbury' (*Dictionary of National Biography*).

5 Horace Walpole, *Letters*, ed. Mrs Paget Toynbee, Oxford 1914.

6 Anon., *Nocturnal Revels*, London 1779.

7 Strictly speaking, the Franciscans were not monks but friars.

8 Nathaniel Wraxall, *Historical and Posthumous Memoirs*, London 1884.

9 A description of some of these decorations is printed in *The New Foundling Hospital for Wit*.

10 The incident is recorded by Horace Walpole in his *Memoirs of the Last Ten Years of the Reign of George II*.

11 Burgo Partridge, *A History of Orgies*, London 1958.

12 *History of the Human Heart and of the Adventures of a Young Gentleman*, 1749.

13 The same distinction between the 'stripper' and the prostitute is maintained in modern Soho.

14 Anon., *Nocturnal Revels, op. cit.*

15 She also appears in three of Hogarth's pictures. Her house was at the north-east corner of Covent Garden piazza.

16 Anon., *Nocturnal Revels, op. cit.*

17 Anon., *Le Porte-Feuille de Madame Gourdan*, Paris 1783.

18 Presumably syphilis; gonorrhea would hardly have merited the adjective *fameux*. It is amusing that the disaster of contracting a venereal disease was necessary in order to induce the good bishop to reside in his diocese.

19 Laurent Pierre Béranger, *De la Prostitution. Cahier et Doléances d'un Ami des Mœurs*, Paris 1789.

20 The nineteenth-century editor of Charles Churchill's poem, W. Tooke, echoes these sentiments. Those accused by Churchill of homosexuality are indicated in *The Times* by an initial and a dash; Tooke refused to fill in the gaps on the ground that although 'a depraved few have occasionally imported from abroad crimes at the mention of which every good man must shudder . . . we should deem ourselves inexcusable were we . . . to gratify the curiosity of our readers'. This is all very well, but the duty of an editor is to elucidate his text; and the present author in his edition of *The Poems of Charles Churchill* (Kings Printers, London 1933) was able to fill in nearly all the names from scurrilous pamphlets, notably an attack on Foote entitled 'Sodom and Onan' in the Dyce Collection in the Victoria and Albert Museum.

21 P.G. Molmenti, *Storia di Venezia nella vita privata*, Turin 1880.

22 Burgo Partridge, *op. cit.*

23 It was used for the first time in this context by Kraft-Ebing at the end of the nineteenth century, in his great work *Psycopathia Sexualis*.

24 For its effect on the Romantic Movement, see Mario Praz, *The Romantic Agony*, London 1933.

8 Before the Deluge

Louis XV presided over the most corrupt court in Europe; the Empress Maria Theresa over the most respected and austere. On 21 November 1755 Maria Theresa gave birth to her fifteenth child, a girl who was christened Maria Antonia. The latter was therefore not yet fifteen when, early in 1770, she was married by proxy in Vienna to the grandson of the French King and set out on her long journey to Versailles.

There were many halts on the way with formal speeches, banquets and balls, and at Strasbourg Marie-Antoinette, as she was henceforth to be called, was received by a handsome young ecclesiastic, Prince Louis de Rohan, co-adjutor of the Archbishop of Strasbourg and shortly to become Archbishop himself. It throws a sharp light on the condition of the Catholic Church at this period that the Archbishopric, and the Cardinalate which almost inevitably went with it, was nearly always in the hands of a member of the princely House of Rohan, allied to the Bourbons by their common descent from a grandfather of Henry IV. Prince Louis was tall and well made with a face almost as refined as to be that of a beautiful woman. He made a complimentary speech which delighted Marie-Antoinette.

There was some talk about the possibility of his going to Vienna as French ambassador but Maria Theresa did not welcome this project. Her own ambassador in Paris had already sent her word that 'this ecclesiastic is entirely given up to the cabal of the Countess du Barry and of d'Aiguillon, and I fear that that is not the only disadvantage which may render him little fitted for the place he is destined to fill.' The Duc d'Aiguillon, supported by the ruling favourite, had just been made *premier ministre* at the French Court, and his policy was consistently hostile to Austrian interests.

However, Rohan did become French ambassador in Vienna. He arrived there on 10 January 1772 and soon gave reason for the pious and puritanical Empress to be shocked at his behaviour, so much more in keeping with the life of a feudal *seigneur* than of a dignitary of the Church. His life was a continuous round of hunting parties, dinner parties, balls and fêtes. The

85

Austrian aristocracy was delighted to be his guests on these occasions. With his charm, his wit and his lavish expenditure, he won all hearts – except that of the Empress herself. She continued to press for his recall and to inspire her daughter the Dauphiness with her own distrust and dislike. To some extent she succeeded, and this was to have the most unfortunate consequences in the years to come.

Marie-Antoinette's reception in France had been enthusiastic but her position at court was difficult from the beginning. Her husband was a well-meaning but rather lethargic and stupid young man. In temperament he resembled his father, that somewhat dim Dauphin who died in 1765 and whom history has forgotten, and he was not at all like his grandfather Louis XV, the old roué only interested in his pleasures. The ruling mistress was Madame du Barry who, as it has been noted, was very much inferior to her predecessor Madame de Pompadour in tact and common sense. Marie-Antoinette started, naturally enough, with a violent prejudice against Madame du Barry; but her mother, the Empress, was, in spite of her prudery, very anxious not to get on the wrong side of the favourite and instructed – nay, ordered – Marie-Antoinette to make up to her.

The unfortunate child – for she was still little more than a child – found herself surrounded by enemies. She was a gay and light-hearted girl, and everything she did was interpreted in a hostile sense. Her chief friends at court were the Princesse de Lamballe and the Comtesse de Polignac. Marie-Antoinette showered excessive favours upon the latter, and upon her family. 'During the last four years', says the Comte de Mercy d'Argenteau, 'it is reckoned that the Polignac family, without any claim upon the state, and by pure favour, has obtained through important public appointments and by other beneficial gifts, nearly five hundred thousand livres of annual revenue.'[1] Such favouritism made many enemies and the attacks on Marie-Antoinette, especially after she had become queen in 1774, grew steadily more envenomed. The fact that when her carriage broke a spring on the way to the Opéra she continued the journey in a hackney cab caused a wave of insinuations. Her unconventional behaviour at Versailles was interpreted as a sign of loose morals. Perhaps no queen, nor any woman ever, has had more to suffer and to fear from calumny. She was surrounded by men who asked for nothing so much as an intrigue, and who were not of the sort to allay suspicions, especially among those excluded from the private apartments of the Queen. Among those admitted were the Comte d'Artois, the King's brother, a noted debauchee, the Duc de Guines, a close friend of the Polignacs, the Duc de Guiche, the nephew of Polignac himself, Vaudreuil, famous for his success with women, and Beau Dillon, whom, it was said, none could resist. It is recorded that when he was first presented the Queen was plainly taken with his handsome face and figure.

The subsequent history of Marie-Antoinette is so tragic that it is difficult

The Pursuit of Pleasure

La Petite Morphil, Boucher's painting of Louise O'Murphy, who was one of the earliest occupants of Louis xv's Parc aux Cerfs

A view of the Trianon in the Park at Versailles in the eighteenth century

The sumptuous court of Louis XV at play in the Palace at Versailles

The Tactless Wife, from an engraving by N. de Launay

'Attracting custom' by Rowlandson; standards clearly fall the higher up the house one goes

Below The suppression of prostitutes in Paris in 1780

Above Masqueraders in Venice by Pietro Longhi

Casanova, the 'Great Lover', whose famous memoirs are largely concerned with his amorous conquests

Marie-Antionette at Versailles in 1775

The chief protagonists in 'The Affair of the Diamond Necklace': (*above left*) Cagliostro, a bust by Houdon; (*above right*) Prince Louis de Rohan; (*below*) Madame de la Motte on her way to the Bastille, after the discovery of her incredible deception

Above A masquerade at the Pantheon in London
Below A fête at night in the Trianon gardens at Versailles

not to regard her as a martyr. But it is easy to take the step from regarding someone as a martyr to regarding him, or her, as a saint. And if the martyr in question is a beautiful woman – and a queen – the tendency is even stronger. Chivalry alone inclines us to think that unhappy queens like Marie-Antoinette and Mary, Queen of Scots, were not only unfortunate but entirely innocent of any of the charges brought against them. People forget that Mary, Queen of Scots, was a Renaissance princess and a Guise; that is, a member of one of the most ruthless families in history. And if she was not an accessory 'before the fact' to Darnley's murder she was almost certainly – with whatever justification – an accessory 'after the fact'. People forget that Marie-Antoinette was at the centre of an extremely corrupt court and that she was married to a dull husband who, for some years, did not even manage to give her a child.

Naturally, when she did give birth, the gossips were busy on both sides of the Channel. Horace Walpole remarks, in a letter to the Countess of Upper Ossory:

The French mystery that you say is not tellable, I suppose implies that his Majesty's first surgeon has had a hand in the future Dauphin. Truly, I thought that any indecency relative to divinity or government might be told, if accompanied with proper gravity. I have heard the late Lord Lyttelton discuss points of mid-wifery with the solemnity of a Solon. I don't mean that I am curious for the particulars. Louis XIII was made to believe that he had begotten two sons, though he never knew how; and if his successor has been persuaded that the talisman is removed, I have no doubt but the Queen will convince him that she is as fruitful as the good of the monarchy requires. *En attendant*, and with all due respect for Lady Clermont's *intelligence*, I have little faith in conceptions that have been so long immaculate.[2]

This is mere scandal, but most of the memoirists of the period were con-vinced that there was one man who played an important part in the love life of Marie-Antoinette. Writing early in the nineteenth century, the Comtesse de Boigne remarks:

The Queen had only one grand passion and perhaps only one *faiblesse* [weakness]. The Comte de Fersen, Swedish, as beautiful as an angel, and distinguished in every way, came to Court. The Queen was coquettish with him as she was with all foreigners, for such was the fashion; he fell sincerely and passionately in love, she was certainly moved, but resisted and forced him to go away. He went to America, stayed there for two years and became so ill that he returned to Versailles looking ten years older and having almost lost his beauty. It is believed that the Queen was touched by the change in him; but, whatever the reason, there was not much doubt among her intimates that she yielded to the passion of M. de Fersen.[3]

Henry Fox, fourth Lord Holland, tells us of a visit he paid to Hortense, Queen of Holland, a generation later and records what she said to him:

Hortense speaks of the Bourbons with great respect, and always of Marie-Antoinette with much interest, owing, I conclude, to her education under Mme Campan.[4] The latter, she said, had formerly shewn her the Memoirs which were published some years ago, and had consulted her as to the propriety of acknowledging her suspicions as to the Queen's attachment to M. de Fersen. Hortense was then young and knew not the world. She therefore strongly advised her to state her real opinion, thinking that by owning one weakness the denial of all atrocities against that unfortunate woman would be more readily believed. Now, she says, having seen more of the injustice of the world, she thinks Mme Campan was right in not following her advice. Whatever is admitted against a friend is always imagined by the public as a faint acknowledgment of other delinquencies that are left untold. Monsieur de Fersen was the only man for whom, Mme Campan thought, the Queen had ever forgotten her duties. It was love at first sight. She was so struck at seeing him, that she quite started and caused all the ladies who were walking behind to halt.[5]

But the chief count against Marie-Antoinette was her wild extravagance. We have already noted her lavish gifts to her friends. Her personal expenditure was on a gigantic scale. In 1785 she spent 258,000 livres in her toilette and by 1787 her debts amounted to 487,000 livres.[6] Having a fancy to go to Fontainebleau by water, she had a yacht constructed costing 60,000 livres. She gambled heavily in spite of the King's disapproval, and frequently lost large sums.

The courtiers knew all this and many of them made it their business to spread rumours among a wider public by means of pamphlets hostile to the Queen. Perhaps no one in history has ever had a worse press, to such an extent that, in the end, people were willing to believe anything to her discredit.

The 'Affair of the Diamond Necklace' was the last straw. Nothing did more harm to her reputation; nothing made her fate more certain. We must try to disentangle the threads of this most complicated story. In spite of the fact that it is one of the most fully documented *causes célèbres* in history, some details are still obscure. Not only is the whole tale incredible but every detail of it is incredible. It reads like a rather bad film scenario, the script absurd, the actors hopelessly incompetent. The 'stars' themselves, if the word may be permitted, were the Queen and Rohan, the very man who had greeted her when she first arrived on French territory. As we have noted, the prejudices of Maria Theresa against him had strongly influenced her daughter, who refused to receive him. Anxious to regain her favour, he set about it in a most extraordinary fashion.

We must begin by accepting the fact that Prince Louis de Rohan was, in spite of his outward sophistication, extremely naive. He was completely taken in by a man who must surely be reckoned as one of the great impostors of all time. The eighteenth century, supposed to be the century of scepticism and enlightenment, was in fact the century of credulity about one thing:

magic. And there were a few clever and unscrupulous men who were able to exploit this to the utmost. Chief among these was Cagliostro.

Who exactly was Cagliostro? It is extremely difficult to say, in spite of all the contemporary pen-portraits that have come down to us.[7] Many people found Cagliostro impressive. The gossipy Mme d'Oberkirch found him fascinating. Casanova speaks of 'his boldness, his effrontery, his sarcasms and his roguery', and even he was rather awed. Rohan, with his passion for the occult, was completely captivated. Cagliostro professed to know all the secrets of universal medicine. He dispensed an 'extract of Saturn', one small phial of which effected miraculous cures. He had been initiated into Egyptian Freemasonry, and had actually, he claimed, conversed with the priests of Memphis. He also possessed the 'philosophers' stone', which could 'fix' quicksilver and turn all metals into gold. He could increase the size of diamonds and other precious stones.

Impressed by these claims, Rohan left his palace at Saverne and came to Strasbourg, where Cagliostro was then staying, and requested an interview with him. Cagliostro, who was, at least, a profound psychologist, refused. 'If the Cardinal is ill,' he said, 'let him come and I will cure him; if he is well, he has no need of me nor I of him.'

Such a reply merely whetted Rohan's appetite; he renewed his efforts and was at last received in the 'Sanctuary of Aesculapius'. The Abbé Georgel, the Cardinal's secretary, has left an account of his master's reactions, in Rohan's own words. 'I saw on the face of this man [Cagliostro] a dignity so imposing that I felt myself penetrated with religious emotion, so that my first words were addressed to him with the most submissive respect.'

It is a strange picture: on the one hand the impudent adventurer, coming from no one knew where, and on the other the Prince of the Church. There could be no doubt which of the two dominated the scene. Finally Cagliostro said: 'Your soul is worthy of mine, and you deserve to be the confidant of all my secrets.'

Cagliostro was installed in the archiepiscopal palace, with every facility for his work in alchemy, and with a suite of rooms at his disposal. It was here that Mme d'Oberkirch saw him in 1780. She was astonished at the ceremony with which he was treated, especially when a lackey flung open the double doors and announced, '*Son Excellence Monsieur le Comte de Cagliostro.*'

Rohan showed her the large solitaire diamond which he wore on a ring on his little finger and assured her that Cagliostro had made it. He also said that Cagliostro had made gold, in his presence, to the value of 25,000 livres.

These are not dreams, madame; they are things proved, and all his prophecies which have been verified, and all the cures that he has effected, and all the good he has done! I tell you that he is the most extraordinary, the most sublime of men, and that his knowledge is unequalled except by his kindness.

89

Naturally, Cagliostro was showered with gifts and, when he decided to shift the scene of his operations to Paris, he travelled thither with a train of couriers, lackeys, grooms, 'guards armed with battle-axes, and heralds draped in cloth of gold blowing clarions'. Arrived at the capital he rented a house from the Marquise d'Orvillers. He practised the same technique he had used at Strasbourg, refusing invitations to dine with the Comte d'Artois and other Princes of the Blood.

These tactics succeeded, and soon Cagliostro was the rage of Paris. His portrait was reproduced everywhere on ladies' fans and on men's snuff-boxes. The best sculptor of the period, Houdon, was commissioned to carve the bust which is to be seen in the Granet Museum, Aix-en-Provence. Cagliostro formed a Ladies' Lodge for the rites of Egyptian Freemasonry. It was called the Isis Lodge, with Cagliostro's wife presiding as Grand Mistress, and some of the noblest names of France among the adepts.

Returning to Strasbourg, Cagliostro continued to enjoy the favour of the Cardinal de Rohan, and it was under his auspices that he became acquainted with the woman who was to play such a disastrous part later in the life of Marie-Antoinette and of Cagliostro himself. This was Jeanne de Valois, Mme de la Motte, whose career is not the least incredible part of the fantastic story.

She was born in 1756 at the Château de Fontette near Bar-sur-Aube, the eldest daughter of Jacques de Saint-Rémy, Baron de Luge et de Valois. He was a genuine descendant of Henry II who had, by a certain Nicole de Savigny, a son whom he recognized and legitimized. The descendants of this boy, Henri de Saint-Rémy, had the genealogy certified by Hozier de Sérigny, Judge-at-Arms of the French nobility; but by the middle of the eighteenth century the family had fallen on evil days. The château which dated from the end of the sixteenth century had fallen almost completely into ruin, the surrounding land had been sold, and when Jacques de Saint-Rémy died in 1762 he left his family almost destitute.

Jeanne, then aged six, was sent out into the highroad to beg, half-naked and in rags. With her was her younger sister in a similar condition. The Marquise de Boulainvilliers who happened to be passing in her carriage was touched by the children's plight, stopped the vehicle and heard of their misfortunes. She did not at first believe Jeanne's account of her Valois descent but she befriended the two orphans and, having made inquiries, she decided to accept the story. She placed the two little girls in a school at Passy and then took them into her own house. She also, by having the genealogy authenticated, obtained a pension for them of eight hundred livres from the Privy Purse.

This hardly constituted a *dot* (dowry) in the accepted French sense, and young women without such an attraction did not easily find a husband. However, in 1780 Jeanne de Valois was married to a young officer in the

Royal Gendarmerie named Nicolas de la Motte. He was then twenty-six and Jeanne twenty-four. Unfortunately he had no money either, and for some years the young couple were in great straits.

Hearing that her benefactress, the Marquise de Boulainvilliers, was making a short stay in Strasbourg, Jeanne hastened thither and met there not only Cagliostro but Rohan himself. By this time he was Archbishop of Strasbourg and a Cardinal. He was also Prince of the Holy Roman Empire, Landgrave of Alsace, Abbot of several rich monasteries and Grand Almoner of France. He promised his protection to Jeanne and to her husband, for whom he obtained a captain's commission in a regiment of dragoons. In the relevant document he is entered as Comte de la Motte – 'an error', says Funck-Brentano tactfully, 'to which he himself contributed'.

The newly ennobled Comtesse de la Motte resolved to try her fortunes at court and with this in mind took a house at Versailles. Her method of attracting attention was to fall down in a faint as near as she possibly could to Marie-Antoinette. It is doubtful if the Queen ever noticed these fainting fits, but Jeanne was able to persuade people outside court circles that she had been befriended by Marie-Antoinette and had become quite intimate with her. She lived on the credit – in both senses of the term – which this enabled her to obtain. But she was aiming at higher game.

Her chance came when she learned that Rohan, who was still in disgrace at court, was most anxious to be received back into favour. Cagliostro promised to help him – by magic – and to this end produced a young girl as a clairvoyant who pretended to see pictures of the reconciliation which the Cardinal so ardently desired.

For her part, Jeanne persuaded Rohan that her influence with the Queen was now so great that she could induce Marie-Antoinette to receive him. She went further. Having obtained some letter paper embossed with the royal lilies, she forged letters purporting to come from the Queen. The 'Queen's letter' explained that she could not yet receive Rohan openly, but would meet him secretly at a lonely spot in the park of Versailles.

Rohan was overjoyed. And now (to adopt the language of melodrama which is the only one that seems suitable for this improbable story) the plot thickens. As it was obviously impossible to procure the Queen's presence at the suggested assignation, it was necessary to find a substitute – some woman who resembled the Queen in height and build; as the meeting was to take place at night facial resemblance was not so important.

One day de la Motte, walking in the gardens of the Palais-Royal, struck up an acquaintance with a young woman named Nicole Leguay. She was induced by the promise of a valuable present ('from the Queen herself!') to take part in the plot. The plan was that she should be dressed in clothes similar to those the Queen might be expected to wear on an informal occasion, and should be taken about midnight to a dark glade in the park of Versailles known as the Grove of Venus. There the Cardinal was to meet her. All this duly took place, although the stand-in for the Queen was too frightened to give him the letter which Jeanne de la Motte had forged in the Queen's name. The Cardinal on meeting her bowed to the ground and kissed the hem of her skirt. He persuaded himself that he had heard her murmur: 'You may hope that the past will be forgotten.'

The Cardinal was overwhelmed with gratitude to the woman who had made this reconciliation possible. He gave her 50,000 livres with the promise of more to come. She persuaded him to retire for a while to Alsace. She was now 'in the money' and she proceeded to invest most of it in house property. She bought clothes and jewels and began to entertain lavishly, explaining to her guests that her new-found wealth was due to the Queen's generosity. This had the effect not only of disarming suspicion but of increasing her prestige as a person influential at court.

Among those who were taken in was the jeweller Böhmer, who had spent years collecting the most beautiful diamonds he could find and making of them the most splendid necklace ever seen. He had hoped that Louis xv would buy it for Madame du Barry, but the King died before the purchase could be made. The jeweller then tried to induce Louis xvi to buy it for Marie-Antoinette, but the price – 1,600,000 livres – frightened them both. Böhmer, who had run deep into debt in purchasing the diamonds, was in despair. He tried again and again, even throwing himself at the feet of the Queen, sobbing and threatening to drown himself. Still he was refused. He then went to Mme de la Motte, showed her the dazzling treasure and entreated her to use her influence with the Queen. Of course Böhmer never guessed that Jeanne had virtually no influence; however, her agile and unscrupulous mind soon conceived a plan. She approached the Cardinal, who had now returned from Alsace, and told him that Marie-Antoinette wanted to buy the necklace without her husband's knowledge and that she was willing to pay the enormous price by instalments if only someone could be found to advance immediately the whole sum to the jeweller. A letter purporting to come from the Queen asked Rohan if he would be her intermediary in the matter; and he fell immediately into the trap.

Such a story would hardly seem acceptable in a work of fiction, for now (as if not to waste so picturesque a character in the working out of the plot) Cagliostro comes once more upon the scene. He staged a séance and the spirit invoked declared, in the words of the Abbé Georgel, 'that the negotiation was worthy of the Prince, that it would have entire success, and that it would put the seal on the Queen's good will'.

Meanwhile Mme de la Motte was arranging her own *mise-en-scène* for the comedy which was to be played out at her lodging. She had asked Rohan to come to her, bringing the necklace. She had also arranged for her accomplice, Rétaux de Villette, to arrive with a letter, supposed to come from the

Queen, asking for the necklace to be handed over to the messenger. The Cardinal did so, and Rétaux de Villette drove off.

When the Cardinal, completely satisfied, had left, Rétaux returned to Mme de la Motte's lodging and he and she and the Comte de la Motte gloated over the treasure which had come into their hands and began, there and then, to break it up, 'clumsily, with a knife'. If they had had as much sense as cunning they would immediately have left France for Holland which then, as now, was the centre of the diamond market. Instead, Rétaux de Villette began to offer the diamonds to various Paris dealers and at such low prices that they immediately suspected that the jewels had been stolen. On 15 February 1785 he was arrested – with his pockets full of diamonds.

Somehow he managed to convince the authorities that he had received the diamonds as a present from 'a lady of quality'. Naturally enough, they demanded the lady's name, and he said 'Mme de la Motte'. No move, however, was made against her and she was able to despatch her husband to England with the greater part of the necklace. He started for London on 10 or 12 April 1785 and, having arrived, contacted Robert and William Gray of New Bond Street and Nathaniel Jeffrys of Piccadilly. Once more the mistake was made of asking too low a price and the English jewellers became suspicious. However, they were informed by the French embassy that nothing was known in Paris of a theft of diamonds of this magnitude and they purchased from de la Motte brilliants to the value of 240,000 livres. Meanwhile his wife had managed to dispose of more diamonds in Paris to the tune of 36,000 livres. She was able to pay her debts and to set herself up in sumptuous style in a house in the Rue Saint-Gilles. She also had a house at Bar-sur-Aube and entered the little town in triumph in an English carriage drawn by four English mares and accompanied by several outriders. There she commenced to give fêtes and receptions and to keep open house – even when she was not in residence.

The Cardinal had been kept quiet by a note from the Queen (forged of course) asking him to absent himself from Paris for a while 'in view of the measures I am about to take in order to place you where you ought to be' (i.e. as *premier ministre*).

It is impossible in the compass of a single chapter to follow the affair in all its ramifications, the hesitations of Rohan, the wrigglings of Mme de la Motte. The Cardinal called in Cagliostro and showed him the letters he thought he had received from the Queen. Cagliostro pointed out that she never signed her letters 'Marie-Antoinette de France'; and he advised Rohan to go straight to the King and tell him everything he knew. What he did not know, of course, was that the Queen had never received the necklace. But she had received a visit from Böhmer pressing for the next instalment of the payment for the necklace. When she heard his story she went at once to the King. He hesitated, conscious of the importance and influence of the

Rohan family, but she insisted, and when Rohan came to Versailles on 15 August to celebrate a mass in the royal chapel in honour of the feast of the Assumption, he was confronted by Louis XVI and Marie-Antoinette and an explanation demanded of him. He agreed to write a statement and was left in the King's cabinet with pens and paper.

Meanwhile the brilliant crowd waiting for the mass was growing restive; the hour was already late. Suddenly the doors of the cabinet were flung open and Rohan appeared. A voice rang out, 'Arrest the Cardinal.' One can imagine the hubbub that broke out among the courtiers as Rohan, in his pontifical robes, passed through the state rooms and out of the palace of Versailles on his way to the Bastille.

This was not the end of the affair; indeed it was only the beginning: the beginning of a process which was to lead Marie-Antoinette to the scaffold. For, as Funck-Brentano admirably expresses it:

Marie-Antoinette reckoned without Rohan's partisans. In the first place, his immediate family, the Rohans, the Soubises, the Marsans, the Brionnes, the Prince de Condé, who had married a Rohan, and all his powerful house, around them all the malcontents of the Court, the whole of the French clergy, of whom Rohan was the head, from the most humble seminarist to the Prince Archbishop of Cambrai, who was himself a Rohan ... finally, the pamphleteers, paragraphists, gossip-mongers, tavern politicians, the orators of the Palais-Royal, who see in this conflict between the queen and the first dignitary of the church of France a struggle in which the throne and the altar, flung violently one against the other, will both be shattered. ...

In the Parliament, Fréteau de Saint-Just, one of the most popular of the counsellors, cried out, rubbing his hands when he heard of the scandal, 'Grand and joyful business! A cardinal in a swindle! The queen implicated in a forgery! Filth on the crook and on the sceptre. What a triumph for ideas of liberty!'[8]

A few days later, on 18 August, law officers arrived at the house of Mme de la Motte at Bar-sur-Aube and carried her off to the Bastille. They had not been ordered to arrest her husband and they allowed him to remove all the jewellery his wife was wearing: not only valuable in itself, but part of the evidence against her. When they had gone he broke the seals the officers had placed on the house and stripped it of everything. He then made off, via Belgium, to England where he tried once more to sell the diamonds to London jewellers.

Rohan's confinement was at first not onerous. He was allowed ample accommodation and service. He gave dinner parties, sometimes for as many as twenty guests, and he continued to administer his diocese. His innumerable visitors included some of the greatest nobles of France.[9] It is a remarkable example of the different treatment given to the victim of a *lettre de cachet*, depending on whether he were a man of Rohan's rank or just an ordinary mortal. Later, however, his custody having been established by a decree of Parliament, he was subjected to much more rigorous treatment.

And now Mme de la Motte, incarcerated since 20 August, had another brilliant idea. What if the whole charge against her could be diverted to Cagliostro? She succeeded at least to the point of inducing the authorities to arrest Cagliostro and his wife. Cagliostro, Rohan and Mme de la Motte were now lodged in the same fortress; but the Comte de la Motte and Rétaux de Villette were still at large. One other dangerous witness remained: the young woman who had impersonated the Queen in the garden of Versailles. Mme de la Motte managed to smuggle out a letter to her and, alarmed, she hastily departed for Brussels with her lover. However, both were arrested, returned to France and imprisoned in the Bastille.

England, however, had then no extradition treaty with France and so an attempt was made to kidnap the Comte de la Motte in Newcastle-upon-Tyne where he had taken refuge. He was clever enough to slip through the clutches of the men sent to capture him. But the Bastille was now crammed with all the other people except Villette who could be called as witnesses.

Louis XVI could have judged the case himself had he wished, but he decided, urged on by the Queen, to ask the *Parlement* to do so. This was a mistake as it was not only an abrogation of his own authority but gave the affair infinitely more publicity than it might otherwise have received. Napoleon at least thought so for, looking back on these events from his exile in St Helena, he remarked, according to the account of General Gourgand who visited him there: 'The queen was innocent and, to give greater publicity to her innocence, she desired the Parliament to judge the case. The result was that the queen was thought guilty, and that discredit was thrown on the Court.'

The trial was a sensation throughout Europe. It was also one of the best reported *causes célèbres* in history, for the documentation is immense. The Cardinal, Cagliostro and, of course, Mme de la Motte were the most important witnesses, and the last of these displayed the most extraordinary ingenuity in turning their questions against her accusers. Asked by Rohan how if, as she claimed, she had had nothing to do with the necklace, she had suddenly become so rich, she replied that he of all people should know, as she was his mistress. The young woman who had impersonated the Queen (she is referred to throughout the trial as Baroness d'Oliva, a title Mme de la Motte had conferred upon her) and Rétaux de Villette gave the same evidence about the scene in the Grove of Venus; and, compelled at last to accept their story, Mme de la Motte went into convulsions. At last, crushed by the evidence against her, she pretended to be mad.

Judgement was pronounced on 31 March 1785. The Cardinal was acquitted on every count; Cagliostro was dismissed from the case; Nicole received a verdict of 'out of court', the equivalent of the Scottish 'not proven'; Rétaux de Villette was exiled, the Comte de la Motte was condemned to the galleys for life, and the Comtesse de la Motte was sentenced to be whipped naked by the executioner, branded on the shoulder with the letter 'V' (for *voleuse* – thief), to lose all her property and to be confined for life in the Salpetrière prison.

Early in the morning of 21 June she was taken from prison to the place where the first part of her sentence was to be carried out. She fought like a tigress and, as she refused to undress, her clothes had to be cut from her body. After the first few strokes of the rod she fell to the ground and struggled so violently that the branding iron missed her shoulder and was implanted on her breast. She managed to bite one of her tormentors through the hand and then fainted. She was taken back to prison.

Böhmer was still waiting for his money and in December 1785 the Cardinal acknowledged a debt to him of 1,919,892 livres to be paid in instalments out of the revenue of the Abbey of Saint-Vast. The money continued to be paid until February 1790. Then came the sequestration of church property; there were no more rentals from Saint-Vast – and Böhmer was ruined.[10]

Such is the official story of the 'Affair of the Diamond Necklace', and most historians of the period have been content to accept it. The present writer is inclined to do the same. But is the case *quite* as simple as it seems? Was Marie-Antoinette as indifferent and as hostile to the Cardinal de Rohan as the official story makes out? Henri Rochefort did not think so. It is true that he wrote long after the event, and that he was a fervent republican, but he is usually given credit for veracity. He was himself of the aristocracy and based his account on the stories current in his own family circle. He records:

The Affair of the Diamond Necklace, of which all the Court and the King himself knew the other side, as I am now almost alone in knowing it, was the consequence of Antoinette's precocity in her passion for every kind of pleasure, even of the most doubtful sort. My grandfather first, as an *émigré*, and afterwards my father, in Paris, after the Restoration of 1815, were in close touch with a nobleman of great bravery and absolutely devoted to the Royalist cause, the Marquis d'Autichamp, who died in 1831 at the age of nearly ninety-two, and who at the Court of Louis XVI had been called: the handsome d'Autichamp.

Soon picked out by Marie-Antoinette, although he was by no means in his first youth when the Queen arrived in France, he was one of her earliest favourites and, in spite of her love of change, it was he to whom she appealed in those difficult situations in which she was always getting herself involved.

It was therefore he – as he told my father a score of times – to whom she appealed when there broke out that frightful scandal that suddenly revealed that the Queen of France was kept by a cardinal.

It will not be believed, nothing is nevertheless more certain: dazzled by the wild prodigalities, by the presence and the high breeding of the young Rohan, who had made several journeys to Vienna before being, in 1772, nominated French ambassador, the future Dauphine, neglected by the Empress, her mother, whose avarice caused her to lack for everything, allowed herself to be seduced by the audacious priest, who claimed that it was impossible to live under two million a year and that no woman could resist him.

With the consequence – I repeat that it was the Marquis d'Autichamp who told my father so many times – Louis XVI had the leavings – admitting that he ever had them – of him who was later to become the Grand Almoner of his Court . . .

I can add personally that the Princesse de Rohan-Rochefort, who was the fiancée of the Duc d'Enghien, and some of whose papers I still possess, had in the château of Ettenheim, belonging to her uncle the Cardinal, a very incriminating correspondence exchanged between him and the Queen. Unfortunately . . . after the arrest there of the Duke whom Bonaparte had shot without trial, the Princess was afraid to keep the papers and threw them in the fire.

These billet-doux Madame de Lamotte, who was later intimately connected with the Cardinal, had perhaps scanned, and certainly she knew of their existence. This scheming woman, exasperated by the Queen's ingratitude, tried to recon-struct them in her Memoirs, but she did it so clumsily that her idiocies served rather to defend Marie-Antoinette before the bar of history than to discredit her.

Only the people's credulity must have been without limit to allow them to be taken in by the organizers of the fraudulent 'Case of the Diamond Necklace'. The attack and the defence were equally prepared step by step between the alleged guilty ones and the Queen, their pretended accuser.

Rohan, to reconcile himself with the Queen (after quarrels which were not unjustified on both sides), had hastened to offer her the jewels which she could not bear to see purchased by some other sovereign. But at that time the fortune of the prodigal priest had been almost dissipated and, when the time came to pay the debt of nearly two millions, he pretended that he could not pay it just then without awakening the suspicions of the King.

When the jewellers Böhmer and Bossanger, preferring scandal to ruin, had let the public into the secret and all hope of avoiding a scandal was lost, the intimate entourage of the Queen tried desperately to concoct some story to save her reputation.

The Marquis d'Autichamp threw himself into this body and soul, more by loyalty to the Monarchy than through tenderness for a woman he loved no longer. It was Cagliostro, Madame de Lamotte and he who devised the comedy of the rose given to the Cardinal by a young girl mistaken by him for the Queen. The resemblance plea is always the first that occurs to the guilty:

'It wasn't I, but someone who looked like me.'

Cagliostro was entrusted with the task of finding a young lady who, against a promise of impunity and an indemnity proportionate to the danger she would have to run, agreed to dishonour her sovereign by substituting herself for her in an amorous rendez-vous; all of which constituted a crime of *lèse majesté* carrying with it the severest penalties.

It was to Madame de Lamotte's house that Balsamo [Cagliostro] brought the girl called Oliva. Marie-Antoinette was then nearly thirty-two and was beginning to put on weight. But, by an amusing piece of courtier's flattery, they had chosen as her substitute a person obviously younger and more slender than she. The Queen saw Mademoiselle Oliva and found her perfect for the rôle for which she had been destined.

Madame de Lamotte, in her Memoirs, which are full of lies, but certainly authentic, only designates the Marquis d'Autichamp by an initial letter. It was from him that my family had all these details. It was agreed that everything should end in a general absolution, easy enough to obtain from a tribunal without a jury. In the end everyone was acquitted – except Madame de Lamotte who, condemned to imprisonment, exposure in the pillory and branding, cried, and had reason to cry: 'Treachery!'

Thus the judgement of the court declared that the Cardinal de Rohan had been deceived, and that Cagliostro had been deceived also, a hypothesis difficult to digest, seeing that Rohan, as Grand Almoner of France, saw the Queen almost every day and those who organized the theft of the diamond necklace could not reasonably suppose for a moment that he would let himself be taken in by so clumsy a stratagem. . . .

Nonetheless, a considerable part of the French nation took this imbecile scenario seriously. It was only when it was learned that the girl Oliva had retired to the country with a good indemnity and that the Comtesse de Lamotte had suddenly escaped from the prison of the Salpetrière in broad daylight, after her husband, in England, had threatened to reveal everything, that the public began to see through this phenomenal imposture.

Madame de Lamotte, condemned for theft, had stolen nothing. The necklace had been delivered, complete, to the Queen, who, her caprice satisfied, understood that it would be quite impossible for her to wear in public a diamond *parure* [ornament] which the King had publicly refused to buy for her. She then decided to break up the necklace, giving some of the stones to the Comtesse for her services as an intermediary and selling most of the others to liquidate her gambling debts which sometimes amounted to as much as thirty thousand livres in an evening.

Madame de Lamotte and an obscure accomplice named Villette were delivered over to public vengeance. But the innocence of the convicted woman, to whom an acquittal had been promised in exchange for her scheme, was so notorious that the *émigré* nobles [after the Revolution] always considered her as the victim of a political intrigue.

The Comte de Lamotte, condemned in absence to forced labour for life for his part in the same affair, was received in London by the highest nobility at the Court of the exiled princes; and to such a point that, at the Restoration, Louis XVIII awarded him, as compensation for the iniquitous judgement that had been given against him, a pension of four thousand livres.[11]

Whatever truth there may be in this, the fact remains that the reputation of the Queen was, however unjustly, irredeemably tarnished. For Marie-Antoinette, the 'Affair of the Diamond Necklace' was the writing on the wall.

8

FOOTNOTES

1 Comte de Mercy-Argenteau, *Correspondence secrète entre Marie-Thérèse et le Comte de Mercy-Argenteau*, Paris 1776.
2 Horace Walpole, *Letters*, ed. Mrs Paget Toynbee, Oxford 1914.
3 Comtesse de Boigne, *Mémoires*, Paris 1921–2.
4 Madame Campan kept a school for young ladies and had a great admiration for the *ancien régime*, which she imparted to her pupils.
5 Henry Fox, fourth Lord Holland, *Journal*, ed. the Earl of Ilchester, London 1923.
6 There were twenty livres to the louis and the louis was, more or less, the equivalent of the English guinea.
7 The formidable documentation has been ably summarized by Frantz Funck-Brentano, *The Diamond Necklace*, authorized translation by H. Sutherland Edwards, London 1901.
8 Frantz Funck-Brentano, *op. cit.*
9 The list of his visitors for a single day (29 August 1785) is given in the Bibliothèque de l'Arsenal, MS. Bastille. 12,457, f.59.
10 However, the Rohan family has since done its best in the matter. The following letter appeared in *The Times*, 19 January 1959:

TO THE EDITOR OF *The Times*

Sir, – Whatever may have been the ultimate fate of the *Collier de la Reine* it will interest your correspondents to know that the cost of the necklace was paid off in instalments by the Rohan family over a period of nearly 100 years, the last payment being made in the early '90s of the last century.

It brought no material benefit to the family beyond the satisfaction of meeting a debt of honour.

Yours faithfully,
CHARLES DE ROHAN

Charmouth, Dorset.
11 Henri Rochefort, *Les Aventures de ma Vie*, Paris 1896.

9 The Broken Link

It is estimated that by the middle of the eighteenth century the number of people in the English colonies in America had risen to two million and that another half million were added by the 1770s. They were not all of English stock. In the early years of the century there had been a mass immigration of German farmers from the Rhineland and an even larger one of Scottish-Irish crofters from Ulster. There were also Scots, Welsh, Irish, Swedish, Italian and Dutch newcomers.

And of course there were the French. They had arrived in small numbers, in search of fish and furs, in the early years of the seventeenth century, and it was the fur trade which induced them to push further and further into the hinterland, following the main watercourses – the St Lawrence, the Great Lakes and the Mississippi. In the later years of the century La Salle had descended the Mississippi to its mouth. By the middle of the eighteenth century the French had established a series of forts and fur-trading posts in a huge crescent stretching from Quebec in the north, through Detroit and St Louis, to New Orleans in the south. Their object was to re-strict the British colonies to the narrow belt of land east of the Appalachian Mountains.

Some seventy years of bitter conflict was the result of this Franco–British rivalry. Both sides used Indians as allies and some frightful atrocities were committed. Battles were won and lost, settlements captured and recaptured, with British troops fighting side by side with the colonials. One of the results, as Allan Nevins and Henry Steele Commager astutely point out,[1] was to reduce the Americans' respect for the professional soldiers. For they dis-covered that the colonial troops, though ill-disciplined and badly equipped, fought just as well as the British regulars, and better when fighting in the wilderness. They also discovered that a young officer named George Washington was a much more competent soldier than the British com-mander, General Braddock. However, they still needed the British, and one of the ironies of history is that it was Wolfe's victory at Quebec which convinced them that the necessity of British protection was over. The French menace had been removed.

This was in 1759; four years later Great Britain and France ended the Seven Years' War by a treaty which gave England all Canada, all Florida (Spain having entered the conflict on the side of France) and all North America from the Atlantic to the Mississippi, with the exception of the city of New Orleans which remained French. The way was open for expansion westward; the prospects seemed limitless.

This situation, however, created new problems. The colonists began to feel themselves a nation, whereas to the British at home they were still the inhabitants of a British colony. Tensions were inevitable and the actions of the British Government did nothing to lessen them. The main cause of colonial discontent was the attempt by successive governments to control trade in favour of Great Britain. A generation before, in 1733, Parliament passed the Molasses Act restricting New England's trade with the West Indies. The Act was not rigorously enforced and smuggling was rife. Then in 1764 the Sugar Act, while reducing the rate of tax, made its collection more effective. In the same year the export tax on Continental goods shipped from the colonies to Great Britain was raised from two to three per cent.

In the South these considerations did not weigh so heavily, but there were other grievances. Products such as tobacco, hides and timber were exported direct to England, but the whole trade was financed from London, and was in the hands of the agents employed by the English commercial houses. The easy-going planters sold cheap, and bought dear the furniture, the carriages and the wines they needed to keep up their standard of living; many of them soon found themselves heavily in debt. The idea must have stirred in many of their minds that if only they could shake off the British yoke their debts would be cancelled. But these impulses had not yet taken any very definite shape or direction.

There was, however, a more fundamental reason for the irritations and misunderstandings between Great Britain and the colonies. America, in all essentials, was already democratic. Each colony elected its own House of Burgesses and, says C. Sheridan Jones, the biographer of Washington:

However rough-and-ready and imperfect the suffrage was, it served the American people well enough to get the views of all classes of the community considered in these small Home Rule Parliaments, with whom, as a rule, the Governor was on terms of social friendliness and whose members felt but lightly the chains that restricted their action, since those chains were not tightly drawn. There is no case on record, so far as I know, of the royal assent being refused to any of the measures that they passed.[2]

The Mother Country, in spite of all the talk of representative government, was in fact ruled by an oligarchy. Members of Parliament of both parties were, for the most part, country gentlemen, with a sprinkling of lawyers and merchants. The 'People' were hardly represented at all; and 'no taxation without representation' was not a maxim which had much reality for the greater part of the inhabitants of Great Britain.

Sir Robert Walpole was sagacious enough to refuse to tax America. 'It must be a bolder man than myself,' he said, 'and one less friendly to commerce who would venture on such an expedient. For my part I should encourage the trade of the Colonies to the utmost; one-half of the profits would be sure to come into the royal exchequer due to the increased demand for British manufactures.'

The Americans were, of course, subject to the Navigation Acts which forbade the colonists to trade with neighbouring nations except through British channels. This did not trouble the Americans very much until the law began to be more rigorously enforced. The war with France had involved a great expenditure, and in 1760 the politicians in London decided to tighten up the regulations. To do this they made all naval officers stationed on the Atlantic coast into Custom House officials.

There were some English statesmen who saw the folly of such proceedings. 'Men-of-war,' said Burke in a speech in the House of Commons, 'were for the first time armed with the regular commissions of Custom House officers. They infested the coasts and gave the collection of revenue the air of hostile contribution.' Customs officers were empowered to apply to the local authorities for 'Writs of Assistance', authorizing them to break open ships, stores, and private dwellings in quest of articles on which no duty had been paid, and to call in the assistance of others in the discharge of their task. All this caused great resentment, especially in Boston where the merchants opposed the execution of the writs on constitutional grounds. The case was argued in court and it was then and there that American independence was born.

In 1765 the English Parliament took another step which seemed to its members eminently reasonable. In England newspapers and certain legal documents were required to bear revenue stamps; the extension of this practice to America caused an uproar. It was regarded as a deliberate affront, and was taken so seriously that Benjamin Franklin was sent to London to protest against the Stamp Act. He told a committee of the House of Commons that if it were enforced America would revolt. He was not believed, and the British Government determined to pursue the policy it had laid down.

In America the clamour became more vehement. When the House of Burgesses in Virginia protested against the Act, the Governor took the unwise step of dissolving it and issuing writs for a new election. There were riots and tumults all over the country. In Boston the Stamp Distributor was hanged in effigy, and stamp offices were in some places burned to the ground. And there was another cause of resentment, for with the Stamp Act had been enacted a measure providing for the stationing in America of 10,000 soldiers, whom the colonists were required to furnish with billets, bedding, fuel and other requirements. In England all this may have seemed reasonable (since the troops were there to protect the colonies) but in America they were regarded almost as a foreign army of occupation.

The Parliament of London could not be entirely unaware of the irritation caused by their measures, but they underestimated its extent and importance. Parliament was concerned to uphold the principle of control from London, and in 1766 passed a Declaratory Act in which it was laid down that the colonies 'have been, are, and of right ought to be, subordinate unto and dependent upon the imperial Crown and Parliament of Great Britain'. It was further stated that the British Parliament had 'full power and authority to make laws and statutes of sufficient force and validity to bind the colonies and people of America . . . in all cases whatsoever'.

This was provocative enough, but the issue became more explosive still when the British Government proceeded to impose duties on glass, paint, pasteboard – and tea. At first the reaction was almost pedantic in its legalism. The General Court of Massachusetts petitioned the Crown for the abolition of the new taxes, and was promptly dissolved. Other State Assemblies, trying to follow the lead of Massachusetts, were also dissolved. It was as if the authorities were determined to *unite* the colonies in opposition, instead of dealing with the provincial assemblies one by one.

It was at this point that George Washington, by no means a prominent figure in the Virginian House of Assembly, came forward with a plan which was a refusal to deal in the taxed commodities. This was adopted all over the country with grave damage to British trade; and Lord North, who had succeeded the Duke of Grafton as Prime Minister, repealed all the taxes with the single exception of the tax on tea, which was retained in order to 'maintain the principle'.

But it was precisely 'the principle' that the Americans objected to. The tax itself was trifling: threepence in the pound, ninepence less than the people of England paid. Even at this stage the tax might have been accepted but, unfortunately, on the very day when Parliament was passing the bill to abolish the hated taxes (with the exception of the tax on tea) there was a clash in Boston between the soldiers of the garrison and a crowd of youths who were jeering at them. In answer to a shower of stones the troops opened fire and four civilians were killed. This was the 'Boston Massacre', the news of which spread rapidly all over the country, and inflamed opinion everywhere.

The 'massacre' made the men of Boston more than ever determined to boycott imported tea. When the tea ships arrived in Boston harbour the Town Council forbade their unloading; and during the night of 16 December 1773, a group of men, disguised as Indians, boarded the ships and threw the cargo overboard. This is the event which has gone down in history as the 'Boston Tea-Party', and has often been regarded as the spark which touched off the powder-keg of discontent, and indeed the Revolution itself.

Even Washington, conservative by nature and still hoping for a reconciliation with England, was beginning to lose patience. It is probable that his views were shared by a considerable proportion of Americans, who merely wished to get rid of what they regarded as an injustice but were by no means anxious to break entirely with the Mother Country. But there was a considerable body of men who had far more radical views, and they lost no opportunity of exploiting every grievance and exacerbating public feeling against England. They called themselves the Sons of Liberty. They were well versed in the ideology of 'natural rights', of which the late seventeenth-century exponent had been John Locke. In his essay *On Civil Government* he had laid it down that:

Every man has a 'property' in his own person; this nobody has any right to but himself. The labour of his body and the work of his hands, we may say, are properly his. Whatsoever then he removes out of the state that nature hath provided and left it in, he hath mixed his labour with it, and joined it to something that is his own, and thereby makes it his property. It being by him removed from the common state nature placed in it, hath by this labour something annexed to it that excludes the common right of other men.[3]

This was no Communist Manifesto; indeed, it joined the right to private property with the right to life and liberty. Such a doctrine had a natural appeal to all Americans. Indeed, it is no exaggeration to say, quoting Henry Bamford Parkes, that 'before the Revolution almost every literate American had learned the vocabulary of the natural rights philosophy and almost every American accepted its truth as self-evident.'[4]

Such convictions received a new impetus from the writings of Jean-Jacques Rousseau which were just beginning to make their way to America. Rousseau's *Contrat Social* was a restatement of Locke's views, but with an added intensity and passion. 'Man was born free but is now everywhere in chains' was a clarion call which found an echo in many hearts, and if the chains of Americans were as nothing compared with those of the French people under the *ancien régime*, they still chafed those who resented the dependence on England and the interference of the British Crown.

Men like Samuel Adams in Boston, Charles Thomson in Philadelphia, Samuel Chase in Baltimore, Christopher Gadsden in Charleston and Alexander McDougall in New York began to organize what were called 'Committees of Correspondence' all over the country. It was the men behind this movement who at the Continental Congress which met at Philadelphia in September 1774 carried, by a small majority, a resolution to impose an absolute boycott on trade with Great Britain, and to adopt measures to ensure that it was not violated.

One of the first military actions on the American side was taken by a man who was technically an outlaw and with his band known as the Green Mountain Boys, had occupied territory between the Hudson and Connecticut rivers and defied the New York and New Hampshire authorities to eject him. With his tough and picturesque companions, he now made a sudden swoop on Ticonderoga Fort and forced the British garrison to surrender.

Meanwhile the British general Burgoyne had arrived at Boston with considerable reinforcements. The town was surrounded by rebels who had taken up a strong position on Bunker's Hill. Burgoyne resolved to dislodge them and actually did so, but with such heavy losses that the 'victory' was almost as disastrous as a defeat.

Washington had with the utmost reluctance accepted the post of Commander-in-Chief of the American army now being gathered together, remarking to one of his friends: 'This will be the commencement of the decline of my reputation.' He alone, it would seem, saw the magnitude of the task before him. He had to work with jealous colleagues, incompetent officers and a raggle-taggle of inexperienced troops. And by no means all Americans were on his side. There were many loyalists all over the country, and it has been estimated that at least 25,000 Americans actually fought for the King.

The British had almost unlimited supplies and as, until 1778, they had command of the sea, they were able to bring these in without hindrance. They landed 30,000 German mercenaries, well officered and equipped, some of them veterans of the Seven Years' War in Europe. Howe, Burgoyne and Cornwallis were all competent commanders, and owed their subsequent misfortunes more to the bungling in London than to any incapacity of their own. There were times during the struggle when the fortunes of Washington and his army were at a very low ebb, and the cause of American independence seemed hopeless. It was then that there arrived in America a young French aristocrat: La Fayette.

He was a mere youth of eighteen when, in 1775, he had attended a dinner in Metz at which, rather surprisingly, the Duke of Gloucester was being entertained. The Duke spoke of the difficult situation in which the United Kingdom found itself in its struggle with the American colonists. He prophesied a British victory but admitted that the struggle would be a long one. La Fayette decided that the American cause was just and, overcoming his shyness, began to ask the Duke questions on the origin of the revolt and on the social conditions in the colonies, of which he knew absolutely nothing. However, he had heard of Benjamin Franklin who had already made several journeys to France and had impressed everybody by the elevation of both his morals and his mind. Here, La Fayette had thought, was a man who might lead his own country and the world to a life of noble simplicity, conforming in every way to the ideals of Rousseau.

Then the Duke of Gloucester made a dangerous admission. He said that the insurgents were badly organized and poorly equipped but that, if they ever received help from outside, the situation might become really difficult for England. La Fayette listened avidly and so did the Duc de Broglie, Governor of Metz, who was presiding at the dinner. He saw new possibilities open to his ambition and did not discourage the young captain who had asked so many questions of their English guest. Soon La Fayette was at work enlisting sympathy for the Americans and arranging for the shipment of goods. The Declaration of Independence exalted his imagination; even the word 'Republic' did not check his ardour; and, in spite of some discouragement from the more cautious members of the French Government, he resolved to go himself to America and take part in the struggle.

The French Government, although still smarting from the humiliation of the loss of Canada and anxious for revenge, was not yet ready to support this impetuous young man. He had already purchased a vessel and embarked in it at Bordeaux, but he was peremptorily ordered by the military authorities to go to Marseilles instead of crossing the Atlantic. He was even threatened with a *lettre de cachet*, which would have meant imprisonment in the Bastille. In defiance of all such orders and threats, he set sail and on 13 June 1777 arrived in America.

Landing at Georgetown in South Carolina, he took horse to Charleston where he was received with great enthusiasm. He for his part was charmed with the neat little town and its inhabitants, none of whom was very rich and none very poor. He was offered every hospitality and was immediately convinced that he had found in the New World the very type of community of which Rousseau and his disciples had dreamed. But he did not wish to linger in a region so far from the scene of battle. He ardently desired to reach Philadelphia.

The journey was long and arduous. Some nine hundred miles of very difficult country lay before him. The roads were rough or non-existent, settlements were few, and provisions for man and beast hard to come by. After thirty days' travel the little troupe reached the Quaker capital in rather poor shape on 27 July 1777. But La Fayette himself was full of gaiety and hope. He expected an even warmer welcome than he had received at Charleston.

He was sadly disappointed. No one seemed to pay any attention to him. And when on the following day he presented to Congress the letters of introduction which Franklin had given him, they were received with considerable suspicion. Many citizens found it difficult to believe that a young French aristocrat should wish to join them for any reason other than to further some deep-laid plan of his own. La Fayette's companions were much cast down and even accused him of having led them on a fool's errand. He, however, refused to be discouraged. 'I bring you,' he declared to Congress, 'no experience. I ask you for nothing. I offer you my zeal. My presence may be useful to you in America, my example may be useful to you in France. . . . The King will be forced to act.' He found himself accepted.

None the less, most of the officers who had accompanied him were sent back to Europe. It was still by no means certain that La Fayette himself would be given any part to play. However, at a dinner given in Philadelphia on 1 August in honour of Washington, he met the American Commander-in-Chief. Washington, who had himself been suspicious of the motives of the French in coming, was won over. He agreed that La Fayette should serve with the American armies but declined as yet to invest him with any command.

At the Battle of Brandywine La Fayette fought in the front rank, this being the very first time he had ever been in action, and behaved with such exemplary courage that he immediately won the confidence and the loyalty of those who fought with him. Washington sent a message to Congress praising his heroism.

It took La Fayette a month to recover from the wound he received at Brandywine, but as soon as possible he was back in the field. With two hundred riflemen he routed a troop of German mercenaries nearly twice as numerous. Washington once more commended him to Congress and on 1 December 1777 he was given the command of a division in the army of Virginia. He found his men in very poor shape, some without a shirt to their back, without breeches or boots. In fact it has been estimated that at Valley Forge, where Washington had gone into winter quarters, some four thousand men were unable to emerge from the cabins and huts in which they had been quartered because they had no clothes! The winter was severe, food scarce, and the soldiers were becoming demoralized. They might even have dispersed had it not been for the patience and determination of Washington and, one is tempted to add, for the irrepressible enthusiasm of the young Frenchman who had come to join their ranks.

He continued to distinguish himself and his fame and popularity grew daily. His notoriety even reached the British; they determined to try to capture him and on one occasion nearly succeeded. And then, on 14 July 1779, came the welcome news that his old friend, Comte Charles d'Estaing, had arrived at the mouth of the Delaware with a squadron of French men-of-war. The French Government had at last decided to come to the aid of the Americans. There could be no doubt that La Fayette had played an important part in bringing this about.

Congress granted him leave of absence in order that he might return to France; and after a voyage of twenty-five days he landed at Brest, and travelled on to Paris. He was received with enthusiasm everywhere, but the authorities thought it necessary, as he was a serving soldier who had left France in defiance of orders forbidding him to do so, to inflict on him a term of imprisonment. However, as this term of imprisonment was only a week and as he was allowed to reside in the Hôtel de Noailles, owned by his relations, it was seen to be a mere formality. The King received him in audience and gave him a free pardon.

While in France La Fayette exerted all his influence to induce the French Government to increase its commitment to the war; it was decided to send a formidable fleet to America, and on 30 August the Comte de Grasse, the most famous and competent French admiral of his time, arrived in Chesapeake Bay with twenty-eight ships of the line. General Cornwallis was besieged by the combined American and French forces in Yorktown and on 19 October he surrendered. The war was virtually over.

When La Fayette returned once more to France he was overwhelmed with congratulations and honours. He was made '*Maréchal du Camp au service du Roi*', and Louis XVI pinned on his breast the Cross of the Order of St Louis, the highest honour it was in the King's power to bestow. He had done what he set out to do, he had helped to found a nation, he had given the French the sweet taste of revenge. But he had also brought back with him in his baggage the seeds of Revolution.

9
FOOTNOTES

1 See Allan Nevins and Henry Steele Commager, *A Pocket History of the United States*, New York 1960.
2 C. Sheridan Jones, *A Short Life of Washington*, London 1920.
3 John Locke, *On Civil Government*, London 1690.
4 Henry Bamford Parkes, *The American People*, London 1949.

10 The Great Upheaval

The French Revolution was an event of such significance in the world that, until the end of history, its causes will be debated and its effects continue to be felt. Some economists point out that the French aristocracy, having thrown its patrimony to the wind in a wild orgy of extravagance, must, by the end of the eighteenth century, have lost its power also. Certainly, finance played a large part in the collapse of the *ancien régime*.

But there is something larger than all this. It is impossible to read the terrible story without feeling that there is something inexorable about it, like the progress of a Greek tragedy. An implacable destiny seems to be working itself out, as if the principal actors in the drama were *fated* to behave in a certain way and to perish as they did. The stars themselves fought against Louis XVI and Marie-Antoinette, as they fought against Sisera.

The stars themselves? No serious historian, one assumes, believes in astrology; and yet there are some very curious prophecies of the sixteenth century which disturb the mind even if they do not carry complete conviction. Pierre Turrel of Autun lived in the reign of Francis I, and was not only an astrologer but one of the greatest mathematicians of his time. In 1531, after his death, there was published a work of his entitled: *Le Période, c'est à dire la fin du monde; contenant la disposition des choses terristes par la vertu et influence des corps celestes;*[1] and in this work occurs the following curious passage:

Let us leave speaking of things accomplished ... and let us speak of ... the marvellous conjunction which astrologers say occurs about the year one thousand seven hundred and eighty and nine, with ten revolutions of Saturn, and moreover twenty-five years later will be the fourth and last station of the altitudinary firmament. All these things considered and calculated, the astrologers conclude that if the world lasts until then (which is known to God) very great and remarkable changes and altercations [*sic*] will be in the world, especially concerning sects and laws.

It will be seen that Turrel not only gives the date 1789 for the beginning of the upheaval, but indicates that it will reach its term twenty-five years afterwards, that is in 1814, the year of Napoleon's abdication.

The passage is quoted by Eugène Bareste in his work on the Provençal astrologer Nostradamus.[2] He claims to have had Turrel's volume in his hand, but a copy is not now to be found in any of the great libraries of France. It is, however, mentioned in the catalogue of the library of St Geneviève in Paris, the contents of which were dispersed at the Revolution; and the passage quoted above is reproduced *in extenso* in a work entitled *Le Livre de l'estat et mutations des temps* by Richard Roussat, canon of Langres, published in 1550, a copy of which is in the Bibliotheque Nationale. '*Ça épouvante et énerve l'imagination*,'[3] as Napoleon III said of the prophecies of Nostradamus. And Nostradamus himself, also writing in the mid-sixteenth century, had some very curious things to say about what he calls *le Commun Advènement*, which might be translated 'Advent of the Commons' or 'Rise of the Third Estate'. But let us extricate ourselves as best we can from these quaking quicksands and try to find some solid historical ground for our feet!

Historians are still arguing as to why, if the French Revolution had to happen, it happened precisely when it did. It is true that Voltaire, Diderot and the rest of the *Encyclopédistes* had undermined the old loyalties and the old pieties. Voltaire's ridicule of the Catholic Church had produced a climate of scepticism which affected many of the clergy themselves. But the *Encyclopédistes* were in general logical, dogmatic, cold. They appealed to the head; in contrast, Jean-Jacques Rousseau appealed to the heart. If influence is taken as the criterion, Jean-Jacques Rousseau was one of the greatest men who ever lived. The effect of his writings, especially *Emile* and *La Nouvelle Héloïse*, on his contemporaries was immense. Bernardin de Saint-Pierre, writing at the end of the eighteenth century, tells us that after reading these two books, 'queens began to suckle their own children, a king tried to learn a craft, rich men began to construct *jardins à l'Anglaise*. Rousseau softened the education of children to the point that the Empress of Russia banished corporal punishment from schools. Respected preachers quoted in their sermons his praise of Christianity.' And the author of a life of Rousseau, after quoting this remarkable passage, adds:

Thousands of letters, preserved by Rousseau, bear witness to the 'transports' and the 'inexpressible delight' experienced by his readers. Many of them tried to reform their lives in order to resemble the virtuous models presented by him. The taste for rustic life and for mountains, the feeling for Nature found expression; the taste also for virtue.

After his death *Le Contrat Social* [1762], rather neglected in his life-time, became the Bible of the Revolutionaries and promoted the growth of democracy. A crowd of writers, in France and abroad, was inspired by his writings. There is not today a single country where his thought has not produced some reform; there is no social, philosophic or literary doctrine which he has not encouraged; there is no human soul that he has not, directly or indirectly, influenced.[4]

And a modern historian of ideas of the stature of Charles Du Bos can divide his subject matter into '*générations Rousseauistes*'. We have now, apparently, reached the *huitième* (eighth).

Certainly he influenced Mirabeau, Robespierre, Saint-Just and Madame Roland, who was proud to be known as 'the daughter of Jean-Jacques'. In literature he had a marked effect on the work of Bernardin de Saint-Pierre, Madame de Staël, Chateaubriand, George Sand and all the French Romantics. He was admired in England by Goldsmith, Cowper, Wordsworth and Byron; in Germany by Kant, Fichter, Goethe and Schiller; his influence on Jefferson and the Founding Fathers of the United States is indisputable.

It is true that not every one, even of those we are accustomed to think of as virtuous and humanitarian men, approved of him. Readers of Boswell will remember that Dr Johnson did not think very highly of Rousseau. Boswell records that, on 15 February 1766, he was dining with Johnson at the Mitre:

I having mentioned that I had passed some time with Rousseau in his wild retreat, and having quoted some remark made by Mr Wilkes, with whom I had spent many pleasant hours in Italy, Johnson said (sarcastically), 'It seems, Sir, you have kept very good company abroad, Rousseau and Wilkes!' Thinking it enough to defend one at a time, I said nothing as to my gay friend, but answered with a smile, 'My dear Sir, you don't call Rousseau bad company. Do you really think *him* a bad man?' ... Johnson – 'Rousseau, Sir, is a very bad man. I would sooner sign a sentence for his transportation, than that of any felon who has gone from the Old Bailey, these many years. Yes, I should like to have him work in the plantations.' Boswell – 'Sir, do you think him as bad a man as Voltaire?' Johnson – 'Why, Sir, it is difficult to settle the proportion of iniquity between them.'[5]

One of Rousseau's fervent admirers was the Marquis René de Girardin. Early in life he was converted to the view that the only solution for the ills of mankind was a 'return to Nature'. He detested formal gardens of the kind which Le Nôtre had established at Versailles, and on his new estate at Ermenonville, on the road between Senlis and Meaux, he resolved to 'imitate nature'. To this end he brought in a number of Scottish gardeners who, for nearly ten years, planted woods, excavated lakes, and erected arbours, temples, monuments, ruins, grottoes and a hermitage. The columns of the principal temple bore the names of Isaac Newton, Voltaire, Montesquieu – and Rousseau.

It was here, in the domain of the Marquis de Girardin, that Rousseau decided to retire, and here he died. During the night of 4 July 1778 he was buried on the 'Island of Poplars' in a lake on the Ermenonville estate and a monument was erected over his grave. It immediately became a place of pilgrimage, visitors arriving from all over Europe. It is astonishing that these included the King and Marie-Antoinette, the Comte de Provence (the future

Louis XVIII) and his wife, and the Comte d'Artois (the future Charles X) and his; also the Emperor Joseph II and the King of Sweden.

Even the clergy came to pay homage. G. Lenôtre, the author of *En France Jadis*, quotes from the unpublished diary of a certain Abbé Brizard who visited the shrine (for it had become no less) with a nobleman named Baron Anacharsis de Clootz, and spent several days there:

> There was already a kind of Rousseau museum in the local inn, the Soleil d'Or, and here he admired the philosopher's snuff-box and sabots. He tried on the wooden shoes and was delighted to find that they fitted his own feet. He then put on the robe which Rousseau was wearing when he died. The two pilgrims crossed to the little island and, falling on their knees, pronounced a discourse which was really a prayer: '*O grand homme! Si tu n'es pas insensible.*' Then, taking everything out of their pockets they touched the stone of the tomb with each object in turn, so that virtue should pass into it. Catholic saints and sacred relics never received more ardent devotion, and all this from a Catholic priest.[6]

It is perhaps inevitable that high-minded leftists (if one may use a term which, in the eighteenth century, would have been incomprehensible) should be doomed to disappointment. The Marquis de Girardin welcomed with enthusiasm the French Revolution, with its promise of the 'sovereignty of the people'. He was nominated commandant of the National Guard at Ermenonville. He was a friend of the Jacobins, the extreme left-wing revolutionaries; all was going to be for the best in the best of all possible worlds. But the Revolution, once launched, pursued its inexorable way. The *sans-culottes*, the extreme republicans, invaded his domain. They ravaged his woods and overturned his statues. 'Who was Newton?' they demanded, for they had never heard of the philosopher. An Englishman, and probably a friend of William Pitt and the Coburgs considered by the French as the principal enemy of the Revolution. By order of the Committee of Public Safety, Citizen Girardin was arrested with the rest of his family. Only the fall of Robespierre saved him from the guillotine. The final blow was when the Government decided to remove Rousseau's remains from Ermenonville to the Panthéon in Paris.[7] Disgusted with philosophy he passed his later years in meditation and solitude. He died in 1808, in the arms of the Catholic Church.

Ideas like those of Rousseau will not alone cause a revolution unless they are accompanied and reinforced by a ground-swell of popular discontent. That there *was* considerable discontent among the peasantry cannot be denied, but the question is not a simple one; there are so many factors to be taken into consideration, and so many conflicting reports.[8]

English travellers like Arthur Young and Dr Rigby were struck by the way in which the peasant women in France shared the heaviest labours with the men. Whereas in England female labour was confined to milling, gleaning and haymaking, the French *paysannes* ploughed (and were sometimes yoked to the plough themselves) and bore immense burdens on their backs when they carried their produce to market. They grew old before their time, wrinkled and deformed. Young relates that, in July 1789, he rested his horse in a village in the Argonne. Hearing a woman groaning, he took pity on her and asked her questions. She told him that her husband owned a small strip of land, a cow and a little horse. He had not only to pay the King's taxes but to meet various charges to the *seigneurs du pays* (lords of the region): to one, forty-two pounds of wheat and three chickens; to another, a hundred and sixty pounds of oats. There was not enough milk for her seven children. Young asked her why her husband did not sell the horse and buy another cow. She replied that without the horse it would be impossible to transport produce to market; they were crushed with taxes and manorial dues. Seeing her bent back and wrinkled face, Young had judged her to be about sixty. He asked her age: it was twenty-eight.

Louis XVI had abolished forced labour on Crown lands, and in 1779 the enlightened minister Necker abolished the burden of mortmain (the perpetual ownership of land by institutions such as churches). This good example was not followed by the nobles in general who, it is said, grew every day more greedy and exigent. Taxes and dues were not only heavy but extremely complicated, and the system of collection and assessment was arbitrary and unjust. The peasant found it necessary to pretend to be even poorer than he was, as any appearance of prosperity merely placed on his back an additional fiscal burden. Several observers noted that it was on the most fertile lands that the inhabitants seemed most poverty-stricken.

Sir Nathaniel Wraxall, who travelled across France some dozen years before Arthur Young, noted that even on the banks of the Loire, where at first glance the countryside seemed an earthly paradise, the peasants were poorly clad and even more poorly housed. He grew indignant at the contrast between the luxury of the châteaux and the wretchedness of the huts by which they were surrounded.

Conditions varied widely from one part of France to another. Young admits that in Languedoc it was a very different picture and gives a delightful account of a threshing he had witnessed where men and women seemed to be enjoying their work. He describes the scene as extraordinarily animated and gay. And other travellers found the peasants of Provence happy and prosperous. In certain other provinces, notably Béarn, Limousin, Alsace and Lorraine, Young found the houses well-constructed and clean and their occupants eating three meals a day and drinking wine. In other regions it was black bread, cabbage soup and little else.

Yet the French Revolution was not like the Peasants' Revolt in Germany in the sixteenth century. It was essentially, at the beginning, an affair of the middle classes, the bourgeois intelligentsia, and of the more liberal nobles. These were all imbued with the ideas of Rousseau; it was they who had been most ardent in support of intervention in America; it was they who had applauded the Declaration of Independence and the proclamation of the Rights of Man. They had seen that a Revolution could be successful. It is impossible to overestimate the force of the American example. Moreover the renewed war with Great Britain, however pleasing to the *revanchisme* (revengeful spirit) of the French, had been very costly; it had pushed the French Government one step nearer bankruptcy. And now the combination of republican sentiment and an empty exchequer was to prove fatal to the *ancien régime*. The King was compelled to summon the States General, which had not met for more than a hundred years.

On 4 May 1789 a procession passed through the streets of Versailles, moving towards the palace. First came the representatives of the Third Estate, soberly dressed in black; next the nobles, splendid in embroidered coats, jewels and orders; then the delegates of the clergy, preceding the Holy Sacrament: forty-eight bishops, twenty-three abbots, canons and other Church dignitaries, and then more than two hundred curés providing, in their black cassocks, the same contrast between splendour and simplicity as that between the nobles and the Third Estate. All were on their way to acclaim the King, and how astonished they would have been, says Marie Henri Jette,[9] if any one had told them that they were about to start a process which was to destroy 'Throne and Altar' and make a clean sweep of ten centuries of history.

The vital factor at the beginning of the Revolution was the alliance between the two ends of the procession, the curés and the Third Estate. At the opening session of the States General there was a dispute as to the method of voting. Should it be by a simple counting of heads or should the three Estates vote separately? The lower clergy, who were mostly men of humble origin, elected to join the Third Estate. This decided the matter and the bishops, protesting, had none the less to give way. If the curés had had the gift of prophecy they would have realized that many of them were signing their own death warrants.

On 17 June the clergy and the Third Estate voting together, in the absence of the nobility, proclaimed itself the National Assembly. A royal decree excluded them from the room where the sittings were supposed to take place. They transferred themselves to an indoor tennis court and swore not to separate until they had given France a constitution. This incident is known to history as *le serment du Jeu de Paume* (the Tennis-Court Oath). A sitting which was to be presided over by the King was arranged to take place in the room known as *la salle des Menus Plaisirs*. This had two doors, and the Master of Ceremonies allowed the clergy and the nobility through the main door; the Third Estate was diverted to pass through a little door which required their queuing in the rain. After making a far from conciliatory speech, the King retired, followed by the nobles. The Third Estate remained, and when the Master of Ceremonies, the Marquis de Dreux-Brézé, ordered them to leave they refused to do so.

Mirabeau, although a noble, had been elected as a deputy of the Third Estate, and on this occasion made himself the spokesman of the rebels. 'Go tell the King,' he said, 'that we are here by the will of the people and only bayonets can get us out.' These words rang through Paris and Mirabeau became the hero of the hour.

His was a puzzling character. His conduct in early life was so disorderly that his father, the Comte de Mirabeau, made several attempts to have him imprisoned under a *lettre de cachet*. He had actually been confined for three years in the fortress of Vincennes and only released in 1780. He threw in his lot with the Duc d'Orléans in his campaign of implacable hostility against the King and Marie-Antoinette. He was certainly involved with the Duke in organizing the march on Versailles which was for the court a frightening presage of dangers to come. Later, however, he seemed to rally to the side of Louis XVI and defended the royal veto on acts of the Assembly. He began to be distrusted by his former friends and the newspapers accused him of having accepted a bribe. Mirabeau carried it off with superb effrontery, as Lord Glenbervie relates:

After Mirabeau had been gained by the Court, La Fayette one morning had paid him a thousand louis d'or as his price for carrying some great question in the Assembly. The question was carried and Mirabeau had the impudence, at the Hotel de la Rochefoucault, in the evening, to say to a company there, '*Savez-vous la nouvelle qu'on débite? On dit que je me suis vendu à la Cour et même qu'on m'a compté mille louis pour mon discours d'aujourdhui. Jugez comme les nouvellistes sont adroits et bien instruits.*' At that moment La Fayette came into the room and Mirabeau went on, '*Arrivez donc, Monsieur de la Fayette, que je vous dise aussi à vous la grande nouvelle. On sait pour sûr que la cour m'a acheté, moi, et qu'on m'a même payé ce matin mille louis. Mais qui sait? C'est peut-être vous qui me les avez payés?*'[10]

That he had actually received the money was confirmed, a generation later, by Talleyrand, then French ambassador in London, in a conversation with the diarist Greville:

I sat by Talleyrand at dinner the day before yesterday, who told me a good deal about Mirabeau, but as he had a bad cold, in addition to his usual mode of pumping up his words from the bottomest pit of his stomach, it was next to impossible to understand him. He said Mirabeau was really intimate with three people only – himself, Narbonne, and Lauzun; that Auguste d'Aremberg was the negotiator of the Court and medium of its communications with Mirabeau; that he had found [during the provisional Government] a receipt of Mirabeau's for a million [francs], which [receipt] he [Talleyrand] had given Louis XVIII.[11]

It is a small wonder that the court wished to buy him off, for his energetic intervention had rallied the Third Estate at a vital moment and the King was forced to give way all along the line. On 9 July 1789 the States General was recognized as the Constituent National Assembly. One of its first acts, promoted by certain young deputies of the liberal nobility, was to vote for the suppression of all class privileges and the abolition of feudal dues; and a few days later it produced a Declaration of Rights.

With an obvious echo of the American Declaration of Independence the first article reads: 'All men are born and remain free and equal,' and the third proclaims that 'the principle of all sovereignty resides essentially in the Nation.' When Louis XVI accepted this he ceased to be a King by Divine Right and became a Constitutional Monarch.

Article Five of the Declaration of Rights, guaranteeing the liberty of the press, was couched in the following terms: 'Every man is free to speak, to write, to print and to publish his thoughts without being subject to any censorship or inspection before publication.' This was to open the door wide and soon newspapers and pamphlets, some of them single sheets crudely printed on private presses, appeared all over Paris. Most of them were extremely left-wing, and abusive and libellous. Their very names indicate their tone: *Le Patriote Français*, *Les Révolutions de Paris*, *Les Révolutions de France et de Brabant*. The last was edited by Camille Desmoulins; Mirabeau's was the voice behind *Le Courrier de Provence*. The journalist Hébert wrote such violent and vile diatribes against the clergy that even Desmoulins was moved to protest. And then, of course, there was Marat, editor of *L'Ami du Peuple*, who demanded the guillotine for all enemies of the Republic. He put the figure, with curious exactitude, at 170,000, and estimated that it would need 800 guillotines in the garden of the Tuileries to carry out his programme. The idealists of 1789 little realized what forces they were unleashing.

The great majority of the deputies wanted to keep the Monarchy, albeit in a modified form, and, while working to reform abuses in the Church, was in no way hostile to Catholicism, which was, indeed, so intimately entwined with social life in France that even the *fêtes civiques* had a religious character. The festival of the Federation opened with a solemn mass celebrated at an altar built upon an immense platform in the Champ de Mars. The celebrant was assisted by three hundred priests wearing tricolour scarves. It is one of the surprises of history that the celebrant was none other than Talleyrand, Bishop of Autun and Abbot of Bec. Ida Saint-Elme, who was for a time the mistress of Napoleon, remarked:

The Bishop of Autun ... was chosen by Louis XVI to celebrate mass at the ceremony of the Federation. So much was known of his morals that one is tempted to ask if there was not a secret irony in this choice by the King. The spectacle was remarkable. Talleyrand as he was mounting the steps of the altar ... leaned towards La Fayette and said in a low voice: 'Don't make me laugh.'

The next day he wrote to his mistress, the Comtesse de Flahaut, a letter in which he ridiculed the ceremony at which he had officiated.[12]

The story is confirmed by the Chancellor Pasquier who had it from La Fayette himself:

M. de La Fayette recounted, a short time ago, that, when the Bishop of Autun was climbing the altar steps with the Host in his hands, he saw M. de La Fayette, the general commanding the National Guard, his sword held high, at the corner of the steps and passing as close to him as possible he whispered: 'Don't make me laugh.' Such a trait needs no commentary.[13]

Meanwhile the situation in Paris was getting out of hand. On 11 July 1789, the King, having concentrated a considerable number of troops at Versailles and around Paris, felt strong enough to dismiss Necker, the popular Controller General of the Finances, and replace him by Breteuil. This was known in the capital on the following day. The Stock Exchange, fearing national bankruptcy, closed its doors. On 14 July, the mob rose and Camille Desmoulins spoke in the Palais-Royal of 'a St Bartholomew of patriots'. It was decided to march on the Bastille in the east end of Paris. Originally a royal fortress built in the early Middle Ages, the Bastille had been made into a state prison by Richelieu in the mid-seventeenth century. It could accommodate forty-two prisoners and these were usually people of consequence rather than common criminals. They had their separate apartments and were allowed, in general, to see their friends and to bring in food and luxuries from outside.

The electors of the *Tiers* sounded the tocsin and the mob, armed with pikes and reinforced by the newly-formed *milice bourgeois* (the future *Garde Nationale*), marched on the Bastille and summoned the governor, de Launay, to surrender. He had only a force of thirty Swiss and some eighty old soldiers to defend the place and he made the mistake of ordering his men to fire on the assailants. A hundred men were killed and the mob went mad. Cannon were brought up and de Launay surrendered. He, together with three of his officers, three soldiers and the *Prévot des Marchands*, were massacred. The victors entered the building and found seven prisoners: four forgers, two lunatics and a young noble imprisoned for debt. The Bastille had long ceased to contain the 'victims of royal tyranny'.

The storming of the Bastille had a symbolic nature which has caused it to loom large in the perspective of history. But on the previous day something much more sinister had happened: the sack of Saint-Lazare. From early Christian times there had been in Paris, in the Faubourg Poissonnière, a hospital for lepers which, by the seventeenth century, had become the headquarters of all the charitable institutions inaugurated by St Vincent de Paul. The religious persons in charge were known as Lazarists, and their convent as Saint-Lazare.

The opening of the States General had taken place two months before; and the good fathers cannot have been unaware, in spite of the thick walls around them, that Paris was in a state of turmoil. There had already been serious riots and, on the previous day, the mob had armed itself by raiding the shops of the gunsmiths and by forcing their way into the Invalides and making off with all the weapons to be found in the museum. The only question was: against whom and against what institutions would the weapons be used?

The Lazarists were known for their charity; during the previous winter they had distributed bread and soup twice a day to eight hundred poor. It was essential that they should have a reserve of flour and other provisions, and it has been proved on the evidence of documents preserved in the Archives Nationales that they had, at this time, no more than was necessary. But the rumour had gone around that they were hoarding food. It is interesting to note that the famous revolutionary song, *Ça ira, ça ira, les aristocrats à la lanterne*, was in its original version:

> Ça ira, ça ira, les Lazaristes à la lanterne!
> Dansons la capucine,
> Ya pas de pain chez nous,
> Yen a chez eux,
> Ce qu'on n'donnera pas, on le prendra!...
> Ah! ça ira, ça ira, les Lazaristes à la lanterne![14]

The winter of 1788 had been a hard one and the poor of Paris were certainly hungry. To divert their anger against the Lazarists was all too easy, and as night was falling a wild procession formed and began to march on the convent. The leaders forced their way in, followed by a rabble of the kind of men who are only too delighted to use a popular movement for their own purposes of riot and pillage. They were given food and wine in the refectory, but this did not content them for long. They raged through the rest of the building, breaking down doors, smashing windows, destroying furniture and throwing books, pictures, vestments and altar vessels out of the windows. Having destroyed the bakehouse and even prised off the slates of the roof, they started fires in various parts of the building.

They surged into the garden, chopping down fruit trees in a fury of destruction. Fierce women (the future *tricoteuses* around the guillotine) raided the poultry farm, killing and carrying off the birds. When morning came the whole place was a ruin; and the town militia arrived only just in time to rescue two old priests who had already been put into a cart to be carried off and hanged from the nearest lamp-posts. A gruesome note was provided by a group of men, who, having decapitated the marble statue of St Vincent de Paul, stuck the head on a pike and paraded it through the streets.[15]

On 17 June 1790 the monastery of Saint-Lazare was declared national property, but it was not until the following year that, all religious congregations having been abolished, it passed definitely into government hands. The

The American Revolution

The Boston Massacre by Paul Revere; the killing of four civilians by soldiers from the garrison at
Boston inflamed opinion everywhere and hastened the outbreak of hostilities

Above One of the first actions in the War of Independence took place at Concord in April 1775 when the British commander sent troops to seize stores of gunpowder

Right A British political cartoon on the Battle of Bunker Hill; America (left), supported by Spain, fights Britainnia, while France stabs Britain in the back. The figures above are Lords Mansfield, Bute and North

A combined anti-recruiting poster and satire on the latest women's fashions in England. 'To Trenton' is a jibe at Washington's capture of Trenton in 1776

The impetuous young French aristocrat, La Fayette, who helped America in her struggle for freedom

The surrender of Cornwallis at Yorktown in October, 1781. La Fayette stands on Washington's right

The French Revolution

Storming the Bastille on 14 July, 1789 – an event of great symbolic significance although the
Bastille at the time housed only seven prisoners

The massacre of prisoners at the Abbaye of Saint-Germain-des-Prés at the height of the Terror

The arrest of Robespierre at the Convention in 1794; during the struggle Robespierre's jaw was broken and there was much dispute as to whether the wound was self-inflicted or not

Madame Tallien and the Empress Josephine dancing before Barras, while Napoleon peeps through the curtains. Gillray's famous cartoon is a biting comment on the immorality of the Directory

Napoleon's marriage to Marie-Louise, daughter of the Austrian Emperor, in 1810

Government had indeed found a use for it. The ordinary prisons of Paris had proved insufficient to accommodate all the prisoners of the State, whose numbers increased day by day. What could be more suitable as a prison than an abandoned convent? – the thick walls already built, the cells already provided. So Saint-Lazare, the Abbaye of Saint-Germain-des-Prés and other monasteries became places of detention for the enemies of the Republic.

Saint-Lazare soon had a prison population of six hundred persons, nearly all aristocrats, and at first the conditions were not too intolerable. The prisoners were allowed to bring in provisions from outside and even to furnish the quarters which had been assigned to them with furniture, linen, etc., from their own homes. We even hear of pianos and harps. Those detained were not confined to their cells but allowed to visit one another. This they did in the afternoon, the morning having been spent in the housekeeping tasks which most of the aristocratic ladies had never undertaken before. The tone was one of extreme good breeding, and many of the prisoners must have regarded Saint-Lazare as a kind of refuge from the storm raging outside its walls.

This comparatively happy state of affairs, however, did not last. The authorities decided to add to the political prisoners in Saint-Lazare some of the real criminals from prisons like Sainte-Pélagie and Bicêtre. These new arrivals were treated so badly, being herded into the refectory without food or fire or even a chair to sit on, that a rebellion was inevitable. This, indeed, was what the authorities were hoping for; when it broke out, they were able to claim that the aristocrats in the prison had revolted.

The number of prisoners swelled to about 1,400. Conditions grew steadily more harsh, and a new law was passed (the so-called 'Loi du 22 Prairial'[16] 1794), laying down that persons accused of treason should have no defending counsel and that there should be in future only one penalty: death. On the pretext of a fictitious conspiracy, the prisoners were transferred from Saint-Lazare to the Conciergerie, the last stage on their way to the guillotine. As they entered their new prison they were handed a slip of paper with the words: 'Take your death warrant.' The day after their arrival they appeared before the Tribunal with the inevitable result of being condemned to death. Among the victims was the great poet André Chénier. He is buried, with 1,300 other victims of the Terror, in the Cemetery of Picpus.

Those confined at the Abbaye of Saint-Germain-des-Prés were even less fortunate than those imprisoned in Saint-Lazare; for on 2 September 1792 they heard the noise of cannon and the sound of the tocsin and, looking out of the windows, saw approaching a wild mob of men armed with pikes and muskets. These men burst into the building and immediately set up a revolutionary tribunal to try the enemies of the State. One by one the prisoners were summoned to appear and, after a short pretence of questioning, heard the fatal words: 'Elargissez Monsieur' ('Release this gentleman').

I

As soon as they left the room they were cut to pieces by about fifty armed men with sabres. There was so much blood that the self-appointed president of the tribunal had to requisition forty-five bales of straw to mop it up.

Equally savage massacres took place in other prisons. At La Force they lasted five days and nights amid scenes of indescribable savagery; and among the victims was Marie-Antoinette's dearest friend, the Princesse de Lamballe. She was offered her life if she would swear hatred against the King and Queen, and when she refused to do so was run through the body with pikes. Her head was chopped off and by an extraordinary refinement of horror it was taken to a perruquier in order that the hair might be dressed and powdered in the fashionable mode. It was then stuck on a pike and paraded under the windows of the Temple where the Queen was confined.

At Saint-Firman there was no pretence of a trial, however perfunctory. The mob burst into the prison and massacred the eighty priests they found there. The same thing happened in what had been the monastery of the Carmelites. The clergy confined there included some of the highest rank in the Church: an archbishop, two bishops and the General of the Benedictines. All, and the priests with them, were despatched in less than two hours. Their murderers did not understand their calm behaviour. One of them, a man named Violette, Commissioner of the Section of Vaugirard, is reported to have said: 'I can't make it out. . . . They looked happy! They went to their deaths as to a wedding!'

Many of the nobles had already become *émigrés*, and armies were massing on the frontiers of France; for the despotic rulers of Europe saw clearly enough the threat the French Revolution created to their own position. Marie-Antoinette was certainly in correspondence with the Austrian Court, and Louis himself hoped that if he could escape from France and place himself at the head of an allied army he could become once more a King by Divine Right.

He had realized that he was a captive from the moment when, on 18 April 1791, he had prepared to leave Paris for St Cloud. It was Palm Sunday, and the royal party, with the bishops and courtiers, was already in the carriages and ready to set off. The crowd prevented their departure, the tocsin began to ring from the belfry of St Roch, and the cry rose from thousands of throats: 'The King is trying to run away.'

Louis, who was an excellent horseman, could easily have made his escape from the Tuileries disguised as a courier, but he was unwilling to leave the Queen and the children behind. A plan was therefore concocted by which they might all get away. Preparations were actively pushed forward but with an ineptitude and a refusal to face the plain facts of the case which make one wonder if Fate itself was not resolved upon the destruction of Louis and his family. To travel in a large *berline* with six horses (a privilege of royalty), to clothe the footmen in the livery of the Prince de Condé, who was already an *émigré*, to substitute for Monsieur d'Agout, a resolute man who knew the route, the governess of the royal children because her rank entitled her to precedence over him, to delay the departure twice when success depended upon an exact time-table: all this was to make the failure of the attempt inevitable. The King and Queen reached the frontier at Varennes only to be arrested and sent back to Paris. They had gambled and lost.

On 21 September 1792 a new Assembly met: the Convention. One of its first acts was to decree the abolition of the Monarchy. What, therefore, was to be done with the King? There is no doubt that the great majority of the deputies had no desire that he should be executed, but they were no longer masters of the situation. The Riding School where they met was open to the public, and the debates were constantly interrupted by shouts and menaces. The moderates were made to realize that their own fate depended on the condemnation of the King.

Meanwhile the Government itself, faced with war on its frontiers and a royalist insurrection in La Vendée and other provinces, moved rapidly to the left, and soon all power was in the hands of three committees: the Committee of Public Safety, the Committee of General Security and the Revolutionary Tribunal. In practice these three organs acted as one, and at the head of the Committee of Public Safety was Robespierre.

Maximilien Robespierre came from the provincial '*petite noblesse*'. At the college of Arras he proved a model pupil and impressed the Bishop of Arras so much that the latter obtained for him a *bourse* (scholarship) at the College of Louis le Grand in Paris. His private life was never subject to the least breath of scandal. Elected a deputy of the Third Estate in 1789, he became a member of the celebrated Club of the Jacobins; that is, he early identified himself with the extreme Left. He was, and was known to be, incorruptible, which was more than could be said for most of the Jacobins. On the Committee of Public Safety only Saint-Just and Carnot enjoyed an equal reputation for being disinterested. Men like Danton and Tallien enriched themselves without scruple; and if Danton was a patriot and, perhaps, a great man, Tallien was a cynical opportunist of the kind which always seems to emerge from a revolutionary movement. And yet the moralist is bound to ask himself: who did the more harm and caused the greater amount of human suffering, the 'sea-green incorruptible' or the shameless Tallien?

Certainly Tallien had shown himself, in the early days of the Revolution, ruthless enough, but he soon realized that, in a position of power in Paris, he could enjoy the sweets of life, especially with so charming a mistress as Thérèse Cabarrus. She was the daughter of a Spanish banker and at the age of sixteen, in 1789, was married to the Marquis de Fontenay. She was at Bordeaux with her husband when they were both arrested and thrown into prison. Tallien had been sent, as *Commissaire de la Convention*, to

Bordeaux to suppress the Moderates, which he did without mercy. He saw her and fell in love with her; and as Lord Glenbervie tells us:

Both Dupont, her first intended husband, and de Fontenay were then under confinement and in daily hazard of the guillotine. Madame de Fontenay made it an absolute condition of her consenting to live with Tallien that he should procure the liberty of both and furnish them with passports to enable them to come over to England, which he accordingly did, and they are now both in this country and indebted to her for their safety. A Madame de Gage, now in England, applied to her at Bordeaux for a passport. '*Vous êtes Aristocrate, Madame,*' said Madame de Fontenay to her. '*Je l'avoue,*' answered she. '*Hé bien! et moi aussi, mais j'aime Tallien.*'[17] She gave her a passport. Monsieur Tallien has since acknowledged her as his wife.[18]

The Chancellor Pasquier remarks that 'whatever may be thought or said of her private life, none of those who knew her well can fail to pay, apart from the homage due to her extraordinary beauty, a tribute of sincere esteem for the goodness of her heart and for the happy way in which she was of service in the most difficult and perilous times.'[19]

But of course Madame Tallien (she was married to Tallien in 1794) could only save a minute handful among the victims of the Terror, which raged on, counting more and more victims. Robespierre was implacable. And then he made a fatal mistake. He knew full well, through his spies, of the sympathies and activities of Madame Tallien, and suddenly she was *mise en accusation* before the Revolutionary Tribunal. Tallien realized that such an accusation was as good as a death sentence. Perhaps he was himself tired of the Terror; certainly he had no wish that his beautiful wife should fall a victim to it, and, at some risk to himself, he made the one gesture for which history still remembers him.

He and his friends finalized their plans during the night of 8 Thermidor (26 July) 1794, and on the following day he rose in the Convention and denounced Saint-Just and Robespierre. Their protests were shouted down and the assembly ordered their immediate arrest with that of a handful of their associates. They took refuge with the Commune at the Hôtel de Ville. The Convention then declared them outlaws and at two o'clock in the morning they were arrested by its troops. Robespierre turned a pistol on himself but only succeeded in breaking his jaw. He was hurried away and guillotined the same evening. And when Tallien and his wife appeared at the theatre they were enthusiastically acclaimed, Madame Tallien being hailed as 'Notre-Dame de Thermidor'.

The actors and actresses of the national theatre certainly had reason to be grateful. For them the events of Thermidor had happened just in time. In the early days of the Revolution they had been popular with the authorities, Mirabeau, Danton and Fabre d'Eglantine being among their chief admirers and friends. One of the principal actresses, Louise Contat, whom

Beaumarchais had chosen for the part of Suzanne in his *Mariage de Figaro*, achieved one of her greatest successes as late as December 1792. But the men of the Left who became all powerful looked upon the actors with dislike and distrust. Had not Louise Contat been the mistress of the Comte d'Artois (the future Charles X) and had she not manifested her dislike of the way the Revolution was going? In August 1793, the play *Paméla* was denounced to the Committee of Public Safety for its 'moderation'. Also, a 'patriot' had been thrown out of the theatre for disorderly conduct. The Committee of Public Safety issued the following announcement:

In view of the troubles which occurred at the last performance at the Théâtre-Français, when patriots were insulted, and in view of the fact that the actors and actresses at this theatre have, since the Revolution, given repeated proof of obstinate incivism, and produced anti-patriotic pieces,
Decrees:
1. That the Théâtre-Français shall be closed.
2. That the players attached to the Théâtre-Français, and the author of *Paméla*, François (de Neufchâteau), shall be arrested and imprisoned, and that all their papers shall be placed under seal.

They were hurried off to the prison of Sainte-Pélagie, a sure preliminary to the guillotine. Fortunately for them one of the clerks in the Public Prosecutor's office was a certain Labussière, a former clown, and he made a practice of mislaying and even destroying the papers prepared for their indictment, and so they never came up for trial. The story has been doubted, but Madame Dussane, in her biography *La Célimène de Thermidor, Louise Contat*, gives good reasons for believing it.

What is certainly true is that Fouquier-Tinville himself complained in an official letter that:

For the last two months there has been complete disorder in the documents presented by the Committee. Of thirty individuals whose names have been sent to me as those of persons who should be put on their trial, a half, two-thirds and sometimes more are always missing. Quite recently all Paris was expecting to hear of the trial of the Théâtre-Français players, and I have not yet received any papers bearing on this affair, of which Couthon and Collot had spoken to me. I await your instructions in this matter.
I cannot possibly place any prisoners on trial unless I am informed of their names and the prisons in which they are confined.

This letter was written on 6 Thermidor; on 9 Thermidor the Terrorists were overthrown; on 10 Thermidor, as we have seen, they were executed. The players were released on the fifteenth and re-entered their theatre in triumph on the twenty-ninth. It was a narrow escape.

The crowds in Paris had shouted, '*Le tyran est mort*' – the very words Robespierre had said of Louis XVI. Robespierre and Louis XVI! Perhaps we may suitably conclude the present chapter with a strange story which, if true, provides a final touch of irony, related by the memoirist Viel Castel:

The former deputy L'Herbette has just left me; we spoke at length of many things and ended by speaking of the great Revolution. He told me that he had seen in the hands of M. de Saint-Aubin the original Memoirs of Barras. . . .

The former *Directeur* records in them that he was present, after the death of Robespierre, at the opening of the grave of Louis XVI, and that he ordered a mass of quicklime to be thrown upon the bones of the unhappy King. Then, as an expiation [strange expiation] he buried in the open grave the body of Robespierre . . .

Barras spoke of this incredible fact [and said that] when what were believed to be the remains of Louis XVI were exhumed in order to deposit them in the Chapelle Expiatoire of the Rue d'Anjou, he advanced as proof of the truth of his assertion that there would be found shoe-buckles in silver and knee-buckles in gold, Robespierre wearing always the buckles of his shoes of a metal different from those of his breeches.

This was true, but he was asked to say nothing of the matter, and Robespierre lies still beneath the marble of the monument of Louis XVI.[20]

Side by side with Marie-Antoinette!

10
FOOTNOTES

1 'The period, i.e. the end of the world; containing the disposition of terrestrial things by the property and influence of celestial bodies.'

2 Eugène Bareste, *Nostradamus*, Paris 1840.

3 'It terrifies and staggers the imagination.'

4 René Guérin, *Jean-Jacques Rousseau*, Paris 1930.

5 James Boswell, *Life of Johnson*, London 1791.

6 G. Lenôtre, *En France Jadis*, Paris 1938.

7 That empty, cold, dead, disaffected church of St Genevieve in Paris contains the tombs of a most curious collection of French national heroes: Voltaire, Rousseau, Hugo, Zola!

8 These have been brilliantly summarized by Charles Kunstler, *La Vie Quotidienne sous Louis XVI*, Paris n.d.

9 See Marie Henri Jette, *France religieuse sous la Révolution et l'Empire*, Paris 1958.

10 'Do you know the news that is going round? It is said that I sold myself to the court and that I charged 1,000 louis for my speech today. Judge how the rumour-mongers are shrewd and well-informed. . . . Since you have arrived, Monsieur de La Fayette, I will tell you too the great news. Everyone knows for certain

that the court has bought me, and that they have paid me this morning 1,000 louis. But who knows? Perhaps it is you who has paid them to me?' Lord Glenbervie, *Diaries*, London 1928.

11 Charles Greville, *Diary*, ed. P.W.Wilson, London 1937.

12 Ida Sainte-Elme, *Mémoires d'une Contemporaine*, Paris 1897.

13 Chancellor Pasquier, *Mémoires*, Paris 1893.

14 'Come on, come on, string up the Lazarists!
   Dance the capucine,
   We have no bread,
   They have some,
We'll take whatever they don't give us! . . .
Come on, come on, string up the Lazarists!'

15 This vivid detail is vouched for in the well-documented study 'La Prison de Saint-Lazare sous la Révolution' by Dr Léon Bizard and Jane Chapon, *Les Œuvres Libres CLXXIII*, Paris 1935.

16 The Revolutionaries had invented new names for the months of the year.

17 'You are an aristocrat, Madame.' 'I admit it. Alas! but I love Tallien.'

18 Lord Glenbervie, *op. cit.*

19 Chancellor Pasquier, *op. cit.*

20 H. de Viel Castel, *Marie-Antoinette et la Révolution Française*, Paris 1859.

11 After the Deluge

One of the main counts against the *ancien régime* in the minds of the intellectuals and publicists of the Republic had been the deplorably low moral tone it was supposed (not without reason) to have encouraged. Men like Robespierre and Marat continued to contrast the vices of Royalty and Aristocracy with Republican Virtue. There is (to us) the sad story of the austere Evariste Fragonard tearing up his father's drawings because they seemed to him to reflect a frivolity which the Revolution had swept away. The new admired painter was Louis David who, apart from being an excellent portraitist, concocted a series of cold neo-classical pictures depicting the most noble moments in the history of the Ancients: *Leonidas and his Spartans*, the *Mother of the Gracchi*, the *Oath of the Horatii* and the rest.[1] It was all supposed to have a beneficial effect on public morals.

Perhaps we should be grateful for *l'homme moyen sensuel*[2] who, over and over again in history, has defeated the idealists, the fanatics and the cranks who would have created a hell on earth. The majority of Frenchmen – certainly the majority of Parisians – decided, once Robespierre was out of the way, that they had had quite enough of Republican Virtue. Those who had survived the Terror were determined to enjoy themselves come what might. The Directory period was probably one of the most dissipated in French history.

As always happens after a great social upheaval, there was a dance mania. Private dances were thronged and *bals publics* sprang up all over Paris. All classes danced but the most blatantly extravagant were those young aristocrats who had ventured back and who had come into their inheritance rather sooner than they would have done if their fathers had not been guillotined. Some of them pushed cynicism to the point of wearing round their necks a thin red ribbon, *à la victime* as it was called.

Prominent in this new society were a number of women, some of aristocratic descent or connections, some mere adventuresses who had become the mistresses of men who had enriched themselves during the upheaval. Such men formed a group of which Barras and Tallien were the leading figures. Tallien, who had now lost any trace of republican idealism, and was popular in Paris for having defied Robespierre, was, as we have noted, already married to Thérèse Cabarrus; Barras was living with Josephine de Beauharnais.

Josephine Tascher de la Pagerie was a creole from Martinique (which, of course, does not imply any admixture of Negro blood) and had been married at an early age to the Comte de Beauharnais. He had died, leaving her with a son, Eugène, and a daughter, Hortense, both of whom were destined to play a certain part in history, one as a Napoleonic general, the other as Queen of Holland.

The Chancellor Pasquier records in his memoirs that Josephine, having survived the Terror, was living in the early years of the Directory in a little house at Croissy, near Saint-Germain; at least she rented it once a week in order to receive Barras. From early morning baskets of provisions would begin to arrive containing poultry and game (this in a period of the utmost scarcity) to be followed by the young Director on horseback, accompanied by an escort of mounted police. The house, says Pasquier, had every luxury but no comfort, the most necessary things such as glasses and plates being lacking, and he comments, 'as is the custom among the creoles'. It is alleged that Madame Tallien was also the mistress of Barras and that the two women danced naked before him while he ate his dinner. This rumour became the subject of a famous caricature by Gillray which depicts this scene with a lean and hungry-looking Bonaparte peeping through the curtains.[3]

Why did Barras decide to pass his mistress on to this ambitious but as yet not very important young soldier? It is true that Bonaparte had distinguished himself as an artillery officer during the siege of Toulon and that he had made himself useful to Barras in suppressing (when no one else would take on the job) a tumult in the streets of Paris. He had dispersed them with the famous 'whiff of grape-shot', the bullet marks of which can still be seen on the façade of the Church of St Roch. His reward was the command of the army which was about to invade Italy – and Josephine de Beauharnais. Madame de Rémusat comments in her memoirs:

Josephine had often assured me that at this time Bonaparte was really in love with her. She hesitated between him, General Hoche and Monsieur de Caulaincourt, who also loved her. Bonaparte prevailed. I know that my mother, then living in retirement in the country, was much surprised on learning that the widow of Monsieur de Beauharnais was about to marry a man so little known as Bonaparte.[4]

Josephine herself was a little doubtful about the wisdom of what she was doing; for she is said to have remarked to a friend: 'My most beautiful dream has vanished. It was foretold to me [Josephine was a great frequenter of fortune tellers] that I should be Queen of France. How can that be, since I am marrying the least important of the generals of the Republic?'[5]

In any case they were duly married by a civil ceremony in the *Mairie* of the *premier arrondissement*.[6] Bonaparte departed for Italy (some people thought that Barras had given him the command in order to get rid of him) and Josephine remained in Paris. A curious light is thrown on her conduct during this period, and on her attitude to her husband, by a discovery made three-quarters of a century later by Henri Rochefort:

On 5 September 1870, having been delegated as member of the Government of National Defence to go to the Tuileries to make an inventory of the Emperor's papers . . . I went straight to a green file in a pigeon-hole above the Emperor's desk on which he had written with his own hand 'To be preserved'. We were all sufficiently surprised to find that the first paper that he wanted so particularly to be preserved was a letter from Josephine to Barras' secretary beginning with these words:

'My dear —— (I have forgotten the name)

Tell Barras that I can't have supper with him this evening. Bonaparte comes back tonight.'

It was signed 'La Pagerie'.

Thus not only did Josephine reassume her maiden name when writing to her lover, leaving aside as a negligible quantity the name of her new husband, but she took into the confidence of her adultery the very servants of the President of the Directory. It was prostitution in all its nakedness. . . .

This letter from his grandmother to her lover was a very strange one for Napoleon III to preserve. It is quite plain from it that even after her marriage to the commander-in-chief of the Army of Italy, she continued, in the absence of her young, new husband, to consecrate her nights to Barras.[7]

Josephine's indiscretions while her husband was away first in Italy and then in Egypt provoked considerable comment. Bourrienne, Napoleon's valet, tells us how the gossip reached Bonaparte himself:

One day [in Egypt, in 1799] I saw Bonaparte walking alone with Junot [one of his most able generals] as he often did. I was some little distance away and I do not know why my eyes were fixed upon him during that conversation. The general's face, always very pale, had become more so than usual, I knew not why. There was something convulsive in his visage and strange in his look, and several times he beat his head. After a quarter of an hour's talk he quitted Junot and came towards me. . . . 'If you were really attached to me,' he said in a brusque and severe tone, 'you would have told me of all that I have just learned from Junot: he is a real friend. Josephine! . . . and I am six hundred leagues away . . . you ought to have told me! Josephine! to have deceived me thus. . . . If Josephine is guilty, a divorce must separate us for ever. I am not going to be the laughing stock of all the idle people in Paris. I will write to Joseph. He will announce the divorce.'

I represented to him how imprudent it would be, on probably false information, to write to his brother. 'The letter might be intercepted,' I told him. . . . 'As for the divorce it will be time enough to think of it later.' . . . He became quite calm and listened to me as if eager for these consoling words, and after this conversation he spoke no more of the subject. But, a fortnight later, before Acre, he expressed great discontent with Junot, complained of the pain he had given him by his indiscreet revelations, which he was beginning to regard as malignant inventions. I noticed later that he had not forgiven him for this *faux pas*; and I can say almost with certainty, that it was one of the reasons why Junot never became a Marshal of France. Although Bonaparte did not tell me so, I have many reasons for thinking that Murat's name as well as that of Charles was mentioned by Junot in the course of his indiscretions. . . .

It is permissible to think that Madame Bonaparte in seeking to captivate the mind of Murat, and promoting his advancement, had chiefly in view to raise one partisan more to oppose to the brothers and the whole family of Bonaparte. . . . Convinced that she had attached Murat to her by the ties of friendship and gratitude, she ardently favoured with all her wishes and all her influence his union with Caroline [Napoleon's sister]. She could not be unaware that there had already been between Caroline and Murat a beginning of intimacy which made their marriage very desirable, and it was she who first proposed it to Murat.[8]

Joachim Murat was a man of strikingly handsome appearance, very attractive to women, and much attracted by them. The diarist Croker gives us an unexpected glimpse of his humble beginnings:

When Huskisson was attached to Lord Stafford's embassy in 1792, he and Mr Fergusson, since a barrister at Calcutta, and now MP, used to dine at Beauvilliers', where there was a smart young waiter, whom, however, these two Englishmen used to *row* exceedingly. At last Beauvilliers told them one day that they had driven the *pauvre garçon au désespoir*,[9] and he had gone and enlisted. It was a lucky persecution for him. The young waiter made rapid advances in his new profession – he was Joachim Murat, King of Naples. This Huskisson told us.[10]

Murat's marriage to Caroline made him a man of consequence in the Bonaparte circle. He was, in spite of his impetuosity, a good general and Bonaparte valued his services. Also he was not a possible rival, which General Moreau was. There was a time when Moreau seemed as important a man as Bonaparte himself. The son of a guillotined aristocrat, Moreau became a general in 1793 and was extremely successful in the campaigns in Germany and the Netherlands. Napoleon might well have lost Italy if Moreau had not crushed the Austrians at Hohenlinden in 1800. Suspected of monarchist intrigues, he was condemned to death, a sentence later commuted to exile in America. He returned to Europe and was killed, fighting against Napoleon, at the Battle of Dresden.

But Napoleon's dislike of Moreau and his family was not only the result of military and political rivalry. Moreau's mother, when visiting Josephine's favourite residence, Malmaison, had been indiscreet enough to jest about the suspected scandalous intimacy between Bonaparte and his sister Caroline, then newly married to Murat. Bonaparte never forgave these remarks. Whether he ever had an incestuous relationship with his own sister may well be doubted, but the rumour indicates clearly enough the general opinion of the morals of the whole family, the most notorious of whose members was, perhaps, Pauline, married first to General Leclerc and then to Prince Borghese.

She was certainly the most beautiful of the Bonaparte sisters, and she was so proud of her beauty that she allowed herself to be sculpted, nude, by Canova. As Madame Junot (who became the Duchesse d'Abrantès) tells us:

The Princess Borghese was a graceful nymph. Her statue, made by Canova and which was *moulded on her body*, reveals a ravishing creature. It has been said that the artist corrected some faults in the limbs and in the bust. I know that I *have seen* the limbs of the Princess Borghese, like all who knew her at all intimately, and that I never perceived these faults.[11]

Pauline was married to Prince Borghese in 1803, but they soon separated and she, like her sisters, considered herself free to follow her fancy. She was Napoleon's favourite; he created her Grand Duchess of Berg and refused to believe the current gossip about her. He may even have been unaware of it in the beginning.

His secret police, however, headed by Fouché, knew all about the broad-mindedness of Napoleon's sisters, one or other of whom had been involved with the Comte de Flahaut and others, including Fouché himself. That perhaps was the reason why, according to the Duchesse d'Abrantès, 'these ladies had never yet been betrayed by the secret police.' But Napoleon heard from other sources that his sister Pauline was being compromised by Junot, whose liveried coachmen were seen at most unsuitable hours in the courtyard of the Elysée Palace.

Pauline was indeed the most flighty of all the sisters, the 'minister to her pleasures' being the notorious Montrond. He had a post at Pauline's court, where he lived openly with her principal lady-in-waiting. He admitted selecting lovers for Pauline and made no secret of her appetite for amorous adventure. The diarist Creevey comments: 'It was for such like offences that the moralist Bonaparte whipped Master Montron [*sic*] into prison one fine day, and kept him there, saying he *would* put an end to the debauchery of his sister's establishment.'[12]

Napoleon was a great stickler for morality – in everyone's behaviour except his own. His motto was like that adopted by Marshal Pétain more than a century later: *Patrie, Famille, Travail*. All he required of men was that they should be ready to serve their country as soldiers and of women that they should breed more soldiers. But he regarded himself as entitled to act entirely as he wished.

He was sufficiently taken with Madame de Mathis, one of the Ladies of the Household of Pauline, to write to her every day and, says the Duchesse d'Abrantès, 'it was at the period when he had just given proofs of his attachment to Madame Grassini and Madame Gazani'.[13] In addition to the three ladies mentioned, Napoleon's other mistresses were, according to Fleischman,[14] Pauline Fourès, Mme Bronchu, Eleanore Denuelle de la Plaigne, Mlle de Vaudey, Mlle Lacoste, Mlle Guillebeau, Mme Walewska and Mlle George. The last-named was a young and beautiful actress destined not only to become the mistress of the First Consul but, in later life, to create all the principal tragic roles of the French Romantic Drama. Her interest for us is that she left an account of the *affaire* which throws a somewhat unexpected light on Bonaparte. The discovery of the manuscript is itself a romantic story.

In the year 1903 Paul Chéramy attended a sale in Paris. He was then an old man and had recently retired from the profession of the law which he had followed for half a century. But in his youth he had known Alexandre Dumas *fils*, by whom he had been introduced to the theatrical world of the early Second Empire, at a time when Frédéric Lemaître and Rachel were at the height of their fame; and now, in the twentieth century, it was his abiding passion for the stage and everything connected with it that brought him to the sale-room. There were being dispersed certain theatrical properties which had once belonged to Mademoiselle George: the tinsel crowns of Mary Tudor, Marguerite de Burgoyne, Rodogune and Semiramis, together with a few books – early editions of the dramas of Dumas and Victor Hugo. In addition to all this was a packet of manuscript, and Chéramy bought it without knowing very clearly what it was. When he had sorted the scattered leaves, he found himself in possession of the authentic memoirs of Mademoiselle George.

Marguerite Josephine Weimer, called Mademoiselle George, made her first appearance on the stage at the height of the French Revolution. It was true that she was only five years old, having been born in 1787 during a performance of *Tartuffe* in the theatre at Bayeux. Here her father, George Weimer, filled the difficult double role of manager and *chef d'orchestre*, while her mother played all the soubrette parts required by the repertoire.

In 1801, George Weimer was at Amiens struggling to make a living and only too happy to let his theatre to any more celebrated actors who might take a fancy to play there. Such actors and actresses were not lacking, for the Comédie-Française itself did not disdain to go on tour; and towards the end of the year arrived a real 'star', no less a person than the celebrated Mademoiselle Raucourt, one of the most famous actresses of her day (which, indeed, was almost over). She wished to play the part of a tragic queen, but she had no one to take the part of the young girl playing opposite to her. George Weimer suggested his daughter, who was then aged fourteen but looked considerably older, and Raucourt, rather reluctantly, consented to hear her recite.

Tremblingly, the girl began, and, before she had finished, the old actress had recognized the real tragic note and the promise of a career as glorious as her own. She not only gave the girl the part but, when she left, carried off both mother and daughter to Paris. She even bestowed upon them a small pension which had been entrusted to her by the Minister of the Interior for just such a purpose. The humble provincial players found their lives transformed by the magic of Raucourt's favour.

Mademoiselle George made her *début* at the Comédie-Française in November 1802, in the part of Clytemnestra. It seems a strange choice for a young girl but, physically, she was already mature and she had the sculptural shoulders, the firm, full breasts. Gérard's portrait, painted some years afterwards, does something to explain the enthusiasm of theatrical Paris when this goddess first burst upon its gaze.

More than that, Mademoiselle George could act. The presence on the same boards as Talma, the thunder-god of French tragedy, the rivalry of actresses as famous as Fleury and Vanhove, did not intimidate the *débutante*. Nor did the presence in a box of the First Consul and Madame Bonaparte. But in the middle of one of her scenes, suddenly there was a hiss. It actually came from the enemies of the actor Talma, but Mademoiselle George did not know this and, for a moment, she faltered. From her box Raucourt cried: 'Begin again.' Again she faltered, but, mastering herself, spoke the line a third time, and with so much conviction that the whole theatre rose in acclamation; and the next day she was famous.

Soon afterwards (the exact date is in dispute) Bonaparte went once more to the theatre to see Mademoiselle George; when she returned home, she found his valet, Constant, waiting with an invitation from the First Consul to visit Saint-Cloud the next evening at eight o'clock in order that she might be congratulated on her success. It seemed an odd place and hour for such congratulation, and the young and beautiful actress cannot have been under any illusion as to what the message implied. Nevertheless, as she says in her memoirs, 'curiosity settled it, or self-love.' She agreed to be fetched the following evening, not from her house but from the theatre: 'I suppose to compromise myself at once.'

According to her account of their first meeting, Bonaparte showed himself very tender, although she admits that he tore off her veil and, when he learned that it had been given to her by Prince Sapieha, rent it into a thousand pieces. Perhaps every man has his own way of being tender, and this was Bonaparte's way. But Mademoiselle George asks her readers to believe that nothing happened on the first visit or the second.

All the gossips of Paris knew of the two trips to Saint-Cloud and had already drawn their own conclusions. On the third evening, when Mademoiselle George was on the stage, an extraordinary event revealed the public's participation in the liaison. Bonaparte was not in his box when the curtain rose, and the play – the tragedy of *Cinna* – opened slowly. Suddenly he arrived. '*Recommencez!*' was the cry, and the actors began again. The whole theatre was full of excitement and when Mademoiselle George came to the line, '*Si j'ai séduit Cinna, j'en séduirai bien d'autres,*'[15] there was a tumult of applause. The entire audience rose to its feet and turned towards the First Consul clapping their hands. It was that night, according to Mademoiselle George, that she yielded. 'He undressed me little by little, and acted as my *femme de chambre* with so much gaiety, grace and decency, that there was no resisting him.' And before she left the palace at seven o'clock next morning he insisted on helping her to make the bed, 'witness of so much tenderness'. It was a side of Bonaparte that did not usually emerge in his relationships with women.

The liaison did not last very long. 'He left me to become Emperor,' says Mademoiselle George. Stendhal says they were together on sixteen occasions. Mademoiselle George claims more, sometimes at Saint-Cloud and sometimes at the Tuileries, and it is at the latter place that we catch a glimpse of Josephine's attitude. Madame de Rémusat describes in her memoirs how Josephine – whose lady-in-waiting she was – compelled her to accompany her in an attempt to surprise Napoleon in the arms of his beloved. On a dark staircase Madame de Rémusat took fright and fled, and Josephine did not persist. But wife and mistress were, according to other memoirists, on one occasion brought face to face. In the middle of his love-making Napoleon fainted. Mademoiselle George jumped out of bed and pulled the bell. The whole palace was roused and, when the cause of all the tumult came to his senses, he found himself supported by Josephine *en peignoir* and Mademoiselle George without any clothes on at all. His fury was frightening, and perhaps it was this incident which brought the *affaire* to an end.

Madame de Rémusat tells us that Josephine's discovery of the liaison 'caused her extreme distress':

> She told me of it with great emotion, and shed more tears than I thought such a temporary affair called for. I represented to her that gentleness and patience were the only remedies for a grief which time would certainly cure; and it was during the conversations we had on this subject that she gave me a notion of her husband which I would not otherwise have formed. According to her account, he had no moral principles whatever, and only concealed his vicious inclinations at that time because he feared they might harm him; but when he could give himself up to them without any risk, he would abandon himself to the most shameful passions. Had he not seduced his own sisters one after the other? Did he not hold that his position entitled him to gratify all his inclinations?[16]

The liaison lasted from 1802 until 1808, after which the memoirs,[17] which were written in 1857 when Mademoiselle George was seventy, contain only isolated jottings. She certainly had an astonishing career for her lovers included – besides Napoleon – Talleyrand, Murat, Lucien Bonaparte, Jerome Bonaparte, Count Benckendorf, the Emperor Alexander I of

Russia, the Prince of Würtemberg, and, later, Jules Janin and Alexandre Dumas *père*. It is sad to relate that in her old age she was reduced to keeping the *chalets de necessité* at the Paris Exhibition of 1855. She died at Passy on 11 January 1867 at the age of eighty, and Napoleon III defrayed the expenses of her funeral. Well he might, for Mademoiselle George had never wavered in her Bonapartism. But, for her, there was only one Napoleon. 'Ah,' she exclaimed, as in her old age she watched the mounting of the guard at the Tuileries, 'I have seen that very often – in former times – under the *other*.'

Josephine certainly had need of all her patience not only because of her husband's infidelities but because of the hostile attitude of his entire family. His sisters hated her and took every opportunity to show their dislike. That Josephine should be the wife of the First Consul was bad enough, but when she was elevated to the rank of Empress they bitterly resented her new dignity. The sharp-eyed Madame de Rémusat tells us that during the Coronation 'when she had to walk from the altar to the throne, there was a slight altercation with her sisters-in-law, who carried her mantle[18] with such ill grace that I observed at one moment the new-made Empress could not advance a step. The Emperor perceived this and spoke a few sharp words to his sisters which speedily brought them to reason.'[19]

Napoleon was certainly not impotent, but he had a nagging fear that he was unable to beget a child: the son he so much desired to carry on his dynasty. Since Josephine already had two children (by Beauharnais), the fact that she had been childless since her marriage to him disturbed him greatly. When Henry Fox, fourth Lord Holland, visited ex-Queen Hortense, daughter of Josephine, in Rome in 1828, she told him a curious story:

She told me of Napoleon's having encouraged the idea that her eldest son was by him, as meaning to make him his heir; he thought it would make him popular with the army.[20] She says Napoleon always doubted his own powers of begetting a child, and that he confided his fear to his sister Caroline, who (obliging lady) procured for him a *jeune personne*, who soon became with child, but as Napoleon discovered Murat had visited her he would not believe the child was his.[21]

The lady who finally set his mind at rest was Marie Walewska. Napoleon, when about to visit Poland for the first time, sent Murat ahead of him to Warsaw with instructions to find him a young and pretty mistress to entertain him during his stay. The lady he found was the young wife of Count Walewski who had behaved until now with the utmost propriety. But the Poles hoped that Napoleon would revive the Kingdom of Poland, now partitioned among Russia, Austria and Prussia. Appeals were made to the patriotism of the ardent young woman. It is easy to imagine the arguments which were brought forward, and at last she agreed to go to the castle near Warsaw where the Emperor was lodged.

She arrived, according to her own account, in a state of considerable agitation. Her arrival was announced to the Emperor who was in his study. He sent word that she was to be offered supper and a bath and was free to retire to rest afterwards if she so wished. Napoleon went on writing until a late hour. He then made his way to the apartment set aside for Marie Walewska, but to her surprise he did not launch into the preliminaries of love-making. Instead he plunged into a discussion of the political situation in Poland, questioning the young woman about the Polish nobles, their opinions and their interests as if he had been a police agent, and it was only when he realized that she had no more to tell him that he got down to the business of the night.

This rather strange behaviour did not prevent Marie Walewska from falling in love with him and, to some extent at least, he with her. It was perhaps the only real love-affair that Napoleon ever had. They met again in Warsaw during several subsequent campaigns. Madame de Rémusat recalls:

Afterwards the fair Pole came to Paris, where a son was born,[22] who became the object of the hopes of Poland, the rallying point of Polish dreams of independence.

I saw his mother when she was presented at the Imperial Court, where she at first excited the jealousy of Madame Bonaparte; but after the divorce she became the intimate friend of the repudiated Empress at Malmaison, whither she often brought her son. It is said that she was faithful to the Emperor in his misfortunes, and that she visited him more than once at the Isle of Elba. He found her again in France, when he made his last and fatal appearance there. But, after his second fall (I do not know at what time she became a widow), she married again, and she died in Paris this year [1818]. I had these details from Monsieur de Talleyrand.[23]

The importance of the liaison for Napoleon was that it convinced him that the childlessness of Josephine was not his fault, and from that moment he pushed forward plans for a divorce. Negotiations were begun for the hand of Marie-Louise, daughter of the Austrian Emperor. Finally, all was arranged and the young Princess, like Marie-Antoinette before her, set out from Vienna on the long journey to Paris. The Chancellor Pasquier tells us what happened when she met the man she had been brought up to think of as an ogre:

The Emperor went out to welcome her; met her two leagues from Compiègne, got into her carriage and returned with her to the palace. It is said that that very evening he behaved as Henry IV did at Lyons with Marie de Médici, and she must have lent herself the more easily to his will because the event had been foreseen, and at Vienna, where they forget nothing, they had been careful to warn her to regard herself as married already. The civil marriage took place at Saint-Cloud on 1 April [1810] and the religious ceremony was celebrated next day in one of the great rooms of the Louvre arranged as a chapel.

When the Emperor passed before us we were struck with the air of triumph which radiated from him. His face, naturally serious, was shining with happiness and joy. The ceremony, celebrated by Cardinal Fesch as Grand Almoner, was not

K

long, and what was our astonishment when we saw on his return that his face, lately so radiant, had become sombre and menacing. What could have happened in so short an interval?

Places of honour for the religious ceremony were reserved in the Louvre for the Cardinals who, since the Pope had been transferred to Savone, lived in Paris. The first thing that struck Napoleon when he entered the chapel was that some of these places were vacant, thirteen Cardinals having ignored his invitation. No insult could have affected him more; it was the more grave because it appeared a sort of protestation against his new marriage and seemed to accuse it of illegality.'[24]

Was the marriage valid? Plainly the thirteen absent Cardinals did not think so. It is true that Napoleon's original marriage to Josephine had been a civil one, but the Pope had declined to crown Josephine Empress at the same time as the Emperor unless the pair were married according to the rites of the Church. Napoleon was furious, says Chancellor Pasquier:

... either because he regarded it as a condemnation of his past life or because he did not wish to make indissoluble an engagement which political considerations might one day make him wish to break. Perhaps also he suspected that Josephine herself had influenced the Pope's demand. However that may be, he had to yield, and I am certain that, the night before the Coronation, he was married by Cardinal Fesch in his own study, without witnesses. The Cardinal assured the Pope of this, and I cannot have any doubt of the details, for I received them from Monsieur Portalis, the Younger, whose father, then Minister for Religious Affairs, served as intermediary in all the negotiations with His Holiness.[25]

When M. de Rémusat, who was not only Grand Chamberlain but also Keeper of the Wardrobe, went to see Josephine two days before the Coronation in order to show her the superb diadem which had been made especially for the occasion, he found her radiant with delight. She must have felt that she was an 'honest woman' at last. For after the marriage ceremony she had procured from Cardinal Fesch a written certificate which she carefully preserved, in spite of all the Emperor's efforts to obtain it from her.

Nevertheless Napoleon was duly married to Marie-Louise in 1810 and in 1811 she gave birth to a son, created by his father King of Rome. In 1814, after the Emperor's abdication, she took the boy to Vienna and, on her father's orders, broke off all correspondence with Napoleon. It was certainly not she who visited him on Elba; she would not have been allowed to do so. Indeed the Austrian Court treated her with complete indifference to her own feelings. She had been a pawn in the political game and she was a pawn still. Metternich, who was all powerful in Austria, had no tenderness either for her or for her son. He was no longer King of Rome but merely Duc de Reichstadt; he was dressed in an Austrian uniform, and no effort was spared to make him forget any connection with France. Metternich realized how dangerous he could be if he became the rallying point for Napoleonic revival.

As Marie-Louise herself was also a danger, it was resolved to discredit her and even to suggest that her child's father had not been Napoleon. It was decided to make her first the mistress and then the wife of the Austrian General Neipperg. Jerome Bonaparte, ex-King of Westphalia, told Lord Holland that:

... he *knew* beyond any doubt the details of Monsieur Neipperg's first success with Marie-Louise; that it is totally false she had ever seen him before her marriage; that he was introduced by Schwarzenberg to her at Paris; that they hardly saw each other; and that it was only at the Congress of Vienna that her mother-in-law by the assistance of her *confessor*! contrived to ease her conscience and forced her to yield to Neipperg, which she did at first unwillingly, by actually being shut up in the room with him.[26]

Marie-Louise was created Grand Duchess of Parma and died there in 1847, having long outlived her Imperial husband and his son, and being one of the last survivors of *l'épopée napoléonienne*.

She was not, however, the only survivor into the new epoch. The indestructible Talleyrand, having survived the Revolution of 1789, the Directory, the Consulate, the Empire, the Restoration of the Bourbons and the Revolution of 1830, was King Louis-Philippe's ambassador at the Court of St James's. He had met every person of importance in the preceding half century. As Bishop of Autun he had officiated, as we have seen, at the mass attended by Louis XVI as France's first constitutional king.

He had no scruples and no morals. But, just as everything is forgiven to Charles II because of his wit, so everything is forgiven to Talleyrand. As a young man, limping along the corridors of Versailles, he encountered a malicious old lady of the court who, fixing her gaze on his game leg, said: '*Comment allez-vous, M. de Talleyrand?*' He looked up, saw that she squinted, and instantly replied: '*Comme vous voyez, Madame.*'[27]

Such wit was usefully employed later. Napoleon never trusted him but could not do without him. He once asked him, rather sarcastically, how he came to be so rich. Talleyrand's reply could not have been more witty – or more flattering. 'Nothing could be simpler,' he said; 'I bought stock on the 17th Brumaire, and I sold it again on the 19th.'[28] Somehow, he always managed to feather his own nest:

Public business did not prevent M. de Talleyrand from looking after his private affairs. A week after becoming a Minister he was already the possessor of five or six hundred thousand francs. This talent for making money never left him, he exercised it with equal good fortune on every occasion and such occasions were provided by every one of the treaties with which he was concerned. The Peace of Lunéville, in which it was stipulated that Austria should honour the bonds she had issued in Belgium, gave him the chance of enormous profits by buying up such bonds before any one else knew of the stipulation.[29]

What everyone found difficult to understand was why so astute a man saddled himself, first as his mistress and then as his wife, with a woman like Madame Grand. She was the divorced wife of an Englishman in the employment of the British authorities in Calcutta, and the mistress of another. The divorce, which took place when she was sixteen, cost her lover fifty thousand rupees (almost ten thousand pounds). She lived for a while under his protection but left India before him. Talleyrand met her at Hamburg and took her to Paris in 1796. In 1803, having been secularized by a papal brief (he wrote it into the Concordat with the Vatican), he married her. The secularization was necessary because Talleyrand had been, and in the eyes of the Catholic Church still was, Bishop of Autun. People wondered why he had troubled to legitimize the liaison at all. Chancellor Pasquier thought that she was 'the possessor of some secret of high importance' and had blackmailed him into marriage.

Certainly in her youth she had been beautiful; her luxuriant hair was particularly admired. The Comtesse de Boigne retails a piquant episode in her career:

My uncle Edouard Dillon, known in his youth as Beau Dillon, had had all the conquests that such a title might suggest. Madame de Talleyrand, then Madame Grant [*sic*] had made eyes at him, but, occupied elsewhere, he had paid little attention. The rupture of a liaison . . . decided him to leave Paris and undertake a journey in the Levant. . . . Madame Grant redoubled her efforts to captivate him. Finally, on the eve of his departure, Edouard agreed to have supper with her after the Opera. They found a charming apartment, supper laid for two and all the refinements of Madame Grant's *métier*. She had the most beautiful hair in the world. Edouard admired it and she assured him that he did not yet know all its beauty. She passed into the *cabinet de toilette* and came back with her hair down so as to be completely covered by it. But it was Eve, before any clothing had been invented, and with less innocence, *naked and not ashamed*.[30] Supper was continued in this primitive costume.

Edouard left the next day for Egypt. This happened in 1787.

In 1814 the same Edouard, returning from exile, was in a carriage with me on our way to the Princesse de Talleyrand's. . . . 'There is such an amusing contrast,' he said, 'between this visit and the previous one I made to Madame de Talleyrand, that I cannot resist telling you of my last and only interview with her.'

He then told me the story. We were both very much amused and curious to know what attitude she would take up with him. She received him most kindly and simply. But after some minutes she began to examine my coiffure and to praise my hair and calculate its length, and turning suddenly towards my uncle, who was behind my chair, she said: 'Monsieur Dillon, you are fond of beautiful hair!' Luckily our eyes could not meet: otherwise it would have been impossible to keep our faces straight.[31]

Certainly the morals of the Napoleonic epoch were no better than those of the *ancien régime*, and its manners not nearly so good.

11

FOOTNOTES

1 He usually depicted his heroes naked except for their helmets and, as these resembled those worn by firemen, the style, when it had degenerated into a *salon* convention, was known as *le style pompier*.

2 'the average sensual man'.

3 It is said that the caricaturist James Gillray was the only man of whom Napoleon was really afraid. Certainly this particular cartoon threw him into a paroxysm of rage.

4 Mme de Rémusat, *Memoirs*, tr. Mrs Cashel Doey and John Lillie, 4th ed., London 1880.

5 Quoted by Théodore Gosselin, *Histoire anecdotique des Salons de Peinture depuis 1673*, Paris 1881.

6 This was a hotel formerly belonging to a *fermier général* which had been taken over at the Revolution. The room in which the ceremony took place can still be seen imbedded in a modern building now owned by the Banque de Paris et des Pays-Bas.

7 Henri Rochefort, *Les Aventures de ma Vie*, Paris 1896.

8 Louis-Antoine Fauvelet de Bourrienne, *Mémoires*, Paris 1910.

9 'poor waiter to despair'.

10 J.W. Croker, *Papers*, ed. L.J. Jennings, London 1882.

11 Duchesse d'Abrantès, *Mémoires*, Paris 1893.

12 Thomas Creevey, *Memoirs, Diaries and Correspondence*, ed. Sir Herberth Maxwell, London 1903.

13 Duchesse d'Abrantès, *op. cit.*

14 See Hector Fleischman, *Une Maîtresse de Napoléon*, Paris 1908.

15 'If I have seduced Cinna, I will seduce many others.'

16 Mme de Rémusat, *op. cit.*

17 *A Favourite of Napoleon, Memoirs of Mademoiselle George*, edited, from the original manuscript, by Paul Chéramy, London 1909.

18 It is probable that her train is meant. The Bonaparte sisters can be seen in position in the painting by Louis David of the coronation ceremony.

19 Mme de Rémusat, *op. cit.*

20 There was, of course, no blood-relationship between Napoleon and his wife's daughter by her first marriage. Still an *affaire* between them would have been incestuous in the eyes of the Church. Hortense's first child died young but her second son, Louis Napoleon, afterwards Napoleon III, also encouraged the rumour that he was actually the son of Napoleon I and not of Napoleon's brother, Louis, King of Holland.

21 Henry Fox, fourth Lord Holland, *Journal*, London 1923.

22 This was the Count Walewski who was to play such an important part at the court of Napoleon III.

23 Mme de Rémusat, *op. cit.*

24 Chancellor Pasquier, *Mémoires*, Paris 1893.

25 *Ibid.*

26 Henry Fox, fourth Lord Holland, *op. cit.*

27 'How are you, M. Talleyrand?' 'As you see, Madame.'
28 It will be recalled that Napoleon seized power on 18 Brumaire.
29 Chancellor Pasquier, *op. cit.*
30 These words are in English in the original.
31 Comtesse de Boigne, *Mémoires*, Paris 1907.

12 The Regency

'The Regency' is a convenient term for a period of English history which had a recognizable character of its own. For the purposes of this chapter we shall allow ourselves, following the example of the dealers in antique furniture and silver, to stretch it a little, say, from about 1795 to the accession of King William IV in 1830, or even to that of Queen Victoria in 1837. It is true that George, Prince of Wales, was not Regent continuously from 1795, for old King George III recovered from his fits of madness several times, and in 1820 Prinny became King. Nonetheless there is a kind of unity in the period which perhaps justifies the use of the word in this extended sense.

The Regency had a curious flavour of its own; raffish, full-blooded, boisterous and philistine. It was as if the naturally barbarous male had escaped from the salon and had not yet been imprisoned in the drawing-room. One has the sensation of living in the open air: on the racecourse, following the hounds, on the great coaching roads which had just come into existence. The dandies walked about London in a tightened and smartened version of 'country' clothes: cutaway coat, breeches and riding boots.

It was a period of tremendous historical events on the other side of the Channel: the Revolution and the long war with Napoleon. Yet both these made very little impact on the life and the pleasures of the English upper classes. The diarists and the memoir writers of the period leave little doubt about the frenzied pursuit of pleasure in which all who could afford it indulged. And leading the rout was the already portly figure of the Prince of Wales.

He was born in 1762, and grew up to be a handsome young man who early evinced what Dr Johnson would have called 'amorous propensities'. His first *romantic* attachment was to the famous Mrs Robinson, known as 'Perdita' from her most successful stage part. She was born Mary Darby in 1758 and her chief protector before she took to the stage was Lord Lyttelton. The Prince of Wales saw her and fell in love – genuinely, it would seem. The go-between was the Earl of Essex who, according to the Reverend William Beloe:

... so far forgot ... the dignity of his elevated station, as to play the part of Pandarus to one greater than himself. The beauty, however, of the lovely object in question proved so irresistible, that he fell a victim to it himself, and betrayed the trust reposed in him. The circumstances have since been partially related by the lady herself, and the whole would involve sufficient materials for a most curious novel.[1]

We obtain a glimpse of her, at the height of her favour, from John Thomas Smith. He was a pupil in the studio of John Sherwin,[2] and tells us:

It fell to my turn that morning, as a pupil, to attend the visitors, and Mrs Robinson came into the room singing. She asked to see a drawing which Mr Sherwin had made of her, which he had placed in an upper room. When I assured her that Mr Sherwin was not at home, 'Do try to find the drawing of me, and I will reward you, my little fellow,' said she. I, who had seen Rosetta, in *Love in a Village*, the preceding evening, hummed to myself, as I went upstairs, 'With a kiss, a kiss, and I'll reward him with a kiss.'

I had no sooner entered the room with the drawing in my hand than she imprinted a kiss on my cheek, and said, 'There, you little rogue.' I remember that Mrs Darby, her mother, accompanied her, and had brought a miniature, painted by Cosway, set in diamonds, presented by a high personage, of whom Mrs Robinson spoke with the highest respect to the hour of her dissolution. The colour of her carriage was a light blue, and upon the centre of each panel a basket of flowers was so artfully painted, that as she drove along it was mistaken for a coronet.[3]

Mrs Robinson did not retain the favour of the Prince for very long. Robert Huish tells us how he transferred his affections to another lady and of the rather sinister part in the matter played by Charles James Fox:

At the time when the Prince had satiated himself with the charms of Mrs Robinson, a lady appeared in the hemisphere of fashion, whose beauty was the theme of general admiration, and whose mental endowments were little inferior, if any, to those of the ill-fated *Perdita*. That a meteor of this kind should be blazing in the world, and the Prince of Wales not desire to behold it, could not be expected by those who were in the least aware of his propensities. Of the early life of this lady it becomes us not to speak; it is only when she appears as one of the characters in the scenes of the eventful drama which we are portraying, that she becomes an object of our notice. At the period, however, when her beauty became the theme of general conversation, she was living secretly under the protection of Mr Fox, although, to all outward appearance, her conduct was regulated by the strictest rules of propriety and decorum. She was received into the first circles, caressed by all the libertines of rank and fashion, although the doors of the royal drawing-room were closed against her on account of some little stain which was supposed to attach to her character, and which she could not wipe off to the entire satisfaction of the rigidly virtuous and illustrious female who then presided over the British court.[4] Moving, therefore, in a sphere different to that of his Royal Highness, he had no opportunity of obtaining a view of her in public, and he therefore applied to one of his immediate and confidential associates to effect an interview – and this associate was no other person than Mr Fox himself. It was rather a startling commission for him, but at this period Mr Fox so completely compromised his honour as to become the most active pander to the passions of the Prince, and Mrs Armstead was one evening introduced by him to the Prince of Windsor. The secret must now be told: from that moment Mrs Robinson declined in his affections. She declares in her narrative that she found herself surrounded by enemies, and subject to attacks, but from what quarter they came she knew not; she was assailed by pamphlets, but of the authors of them she was ignorant; she was libelled, caricatured, insulted, and abused, and all on account of falsehoods which were propagated to her injury by individuals, who, like the bat, kept themselves in the dark, that their hideous forms might not be seen. And from what quarter did all these annoyances in reality proceed? – from a set of unprincipled and dishonourable men, who saw that as long as his Royal Highness was under the influence of a lady in no measure connected with their party, and whom they could not make subservient to their own personal views, their plans could not be carried on with that prospect of ultimate success, as if that lady were supplanted, and one substituted for her, who would fall into all their views, and through the medium of whom they could obtain the requisite information of the proceedings of the opposite party, who were endeavouring to obtain the ascendancy in the councils of the Prince. Mr Fox and his party beheld in Mrs Armstead the very individual who was to accomplish this task, and every instrument was now set in motion, in the first instance, by base and insidious reports to defame the character of Mrs Robinson, to undermine the attachment of the Prince for her; and, in the second, by a continued course of annoyance and persecution, to induce her to leave the country. Mr Fox undertook to effect the latter, and the successful manner in which he executed his dastardly commission has been already described.

Mrs Armstead now became the companion of the Prince, and Mr Fox consoled himself for the temporary loss of her edifying society by the benefit which her influence over his Royal Highness obtained for his party, personally and politically. In a short time, however, Mrs Armstead shared the fate of her exiled predecessor, when Mr Fox kindly and *honourably* accepted of her again; and we shall, in the sequel, find, when the question of the Regency came to be discussed, that he was travelling on the continent with her, pointing out to her the beauties of southern France and Italy, and recruiting himself from his career of profligate dissipation in the contemplation of her faded charms.[5]

We obtain a final glimpse of Perdita from the memoirs of the Duc de Lauzun:

I met in Paris [in 1781] Mrs Robinson, first flame of the Prince of Wales, of whom the English papers have talked so much under the name of Perdita. She was gay, lively, frank and friendly; she did not speak French. I was an object of interest to her; a man who had brought great news [of the Lord Cornwallis's surrender], who had returned from the wars, who was about to return; a man who had suffered and would suffer more. She thought she could not do too much for me; so I had Perdita.[6]

The amorous propensities of the Prince of Wales were exercised in every rank of society, including what we would call the 'ladies of the lighter stage':

It was behind the scenes of the theatre that the Prince first became acquainted with Mrs Billington,[7] and at that time she appeared to be his chief inducement for visiting the theatre. Those who like ourselves are aware of some particular traits in the character of Mrs Billington, and of the peculiar penchant, which was her ruling passion in her intercourse with her favourites, must be well aware that the Prince of Wales was, notwithstanding his exalted rank and high personal endowments, not exactly the individual who could long enchain her affections. The vicinity of her dwelling to the Thames, it being situate at Fulham, and immediately on the banks of the river, offered many facilities to the Prince to partake of the society of the fascinating syren and to enjoy the delight of her musical conversaziones, which were held almost every night that her presence was not required at the theatre. This connexion of the Prince was not, however, of long duration; the coarseness of her manners soon disgusted him, and he declared at last, that the only satisfaction he enjoyed in her society, was when he shut his eyes and opened his ears. We shall briefly state another amour which followed that of Mrs Billington, and that was with Mrs Crouch,[8] also an actress, who was then in the zenith of her beauty. On this lady the Prince expended considerable sums, in one instance to the amount of £10,000 independently of a profusion of jewels and trinkets, which were purchased at Gray's, to the amount of £5,000 and which, when in a short time afterwards, a schedule of his Royal Highness' debts was laid before his Royal Parent, excited so strongly his disapprobation and resentment, that the King refused to interfere in the liquidation of his debts. Kelly, in his Reminiscences, when treating of the life of Mrs Crouch, studiously avoids making any mention of the impression which her charms made upon his Royal Highness; but it is melancholy to relate, that after having squandered immense sums of money, and exposed himself to the ridicule of his associates, he found that he had selected an individual, who, although her person and form were beauteous, was so addicted to intoxication, that her breath became disgustingly tainted, which gave rise to the well-known simile of George Hanger, comparing her throat to a smoky chimney – foul and stinking.[9]

The man who served as go-between for the Prince and his loves was Sir John M'Mahon:

We could point to two ladies now living, the mothers of families, and moving in a most respectable station of life, who, but for the intriguing skill of John M'Mahon, would never have reposed in the arms of his Royal Highness; and we could point to another lady, in the person of Mrs M'Mahon herself, to the effect of whose charms on the heart of the present most illustrious personage in the kingdom was solely owing the aggrandizement and elevation of her pliant and accommodating husband. . . . John M'Mahon was the principal agent in procuring Mrs Jordan from Mr Ford for the Duke of Clarence.[10]

M'Mahon's services came in very useful in the case of Louise Hillisberg about whom very little is known except what Robert Huish tells us:

Hillisberg was a woman fit to be wooed and won by royalty; and the Prince of Wales no sooner saw her than the abilities of John M'Mahon were called into action to commence the negotiation. She was, however, one of those women who, although yielding to the weakness of their nature, pay great deference to the opinion of the world; and although the Prince acquired a decided ascendancy over her heart, yet she so veiled her partiality, as to conceal her connexion from the eyes of the public; and this secret amour was so well managed at Carlton House [the residence of the Regent] by M'Mahon, who was in the confidence of both parties, that Hillisberg stood in the estimation of the public as an exemplary pattern of female virtue. A stronger proof of the secrecy with which this amour was carried on and con-summated, cannot be deduced than the circumstance that, at the very time when she was the secret nocturnal guest of Carlton House, the late Duke of York was making every exertion in his power to make an impression upon her apparently obdurate heart, little suspecting, at the time, that that same heart was vivified by an ardent attachment for his own brother.[11]

Another woman mentioned by the same author was Lucy Howard:

We will not transcribe the scenes which led to the fall of this earthly angel, but the visitants of Brighton may recollect a comfortable mansion, which stands about three miles from the town, at the foot of a wood, on the right hand of the road leading from London, and to this place was Lucy Howard conveyed, the secret love of the Prince of Wales. It has been mentioned as rather a remarkable circum-stance, that no issue was ever known to emanate from any of the amours of either the Prince of Wales, or the late Duke of York: we have it, however, in our power to contradict that statement, as far as concerns the former illustrious personage, for in this retreat at Brighton, Lucy Howard became the mother of a child, which, however, lived but to its second year, and was buried in Brighton churchyard, under the name of George Howard.[12]

Among the aristocratic ladies favoured by the Prince's attentions were Lady Jersey, Lady Melbourne and the Duchess of Devonshire. A generation later Creevey, in a letter to Miss Ord dated 18 August 1821, tells what happened to the correspondence between the Prince and the first of these:

The other day Lord Jersey received a letter from Lord Clarendon begging him to come to him, which he did. He [Lord Clarendon] then told him that he was going as executor to open his [Lord Jersey's] mother's papers. The seal was then taken off, and letters from the Monarch to his former sweetheart caught Jersey's eye in great abundance. Lord Clarendon then proceeded to put them all in the fire, saying that he had merely wished Lord Jersey to be present at their destruction, and as a witness that they had never been seen by any one. Very genteel, this, on Lord

Clarendon's part to the living Monarch and memory of his mistress, but damned provoking to think that such capital materials for the instruction and improvement of men and womankind should be eternally lost.[13]

That Lady Melbourne was the Prince's mistress for a time was well known, and Sir Nathaniel Wraxall tells us that:

To Lady Melbourne succeeded, after a short interval which I shall not fill up, the Duchess of Devonshire, but of what nature was that attachment, and what limits were affixed to it by the Duchess, must remain matter of conjecture. I know, however, that during her pregnancy in 1785, his Royal Highness manifested so much anxiety, and made such frequent morning visits on horseback to Wimbledon, where she repaired for a short time, as to give umbrage to her brother, Lord Spencer, and even it was supposed to excite some emotion in the phlegmatic bosom of the Duke, her husband.[14]

It is ironical that it was the Duchess of Devonshire who was largely responsible for introducing the Prince to a lady who was probably the most sincere, and certainly the most lasting, love of his life, Mrs Fitzherbert. Maria Anne Fitzherbert was a widow twice over when she first met the Prince of Wales. He is said to have fallen in love with her at first sight and he tried to stab himself when she rejected his advances. The Duchess of Devonshire induced her to visit Carlton House but, says the *Dictionary of National Biography*, rather primly, she 'soon after went abroad to escape further solicitations'. Then, while she was still on the Continent, she received the Prince's offer of marriage and accepted it, albeit, it is said, reluctantly. They were married on 21 December 1785 in her own drawing-room at Richmond, by an Anglican clergyman.

It was a curious affair. By the Royal Marriage Act of 1772 any marriage contracted by a member of the Royal Family under twenty-five, without the King's consent, was invalid. Also, as Mrs Fitzherbert was a Roman Catholic, the Prince, by marrying her, forfeited his right to the Crown under the Act of Settlement. She on her part might be expected to regard *any* Protestant marriage as invalid. The fact remains that she was always regarded with the highest respect and was always treated by the Prince as his wife. And even after his marriage to Caroline of Brunswick, her own (Catholic) Church advised her that it was lawful to live with him. She continued to do so (except for a short interval after his marriage to Caroline) for the rest of his life. George iv died with her portrait round his neck. She survived him by seven years, dying in the year of Queen Victoria's accession.

In the perspective of history we are at last able to do justice to 'Prinny'. In contrast to his brothers, the Prince of Wales had a certain sense of style and taste. He made a collection of Dutch seventeenth-century pictures at a time when they were completely out of fashion, and even his Pavilion at Brighton, after more than a century of ridicule and abuse, has come in our own day to be recognized as a remarkable architectural achievement. He was passionately fond of music, although it was perhaps unfortunate that he liked to join in. Henry Fox, fourth Lord Holland, gives us a vivid picture of him after he became King:

One evening I was suddenly sent for to the Pavilion. My dismay was not small at finding myself ushered into a room where the K. and Rossini were alone. I found that I was the only person honoured with an invitation to hear this great composer's performances. A more unworthy object than I am could not have been selected. H.M. was not much pleased with his manner, which was careless and indifferent to all the civilities shown him. The K. himself made a fool of himself by joining in the choruses and the Hallelujah Anthem, stamping his foot and overpowering all with the loudness of his Royal voice.[15]

One thinks of the Emperor Nero competing with his own musicians. Indeed Prinny was rather like Nero – minus the cruelty. He was essentially an actor throughout his life. The diarist Croker reports a conversation he had with the Duke of Wellington:

The Duke told me that when he went with the Chancellor on the ninth of January to the King to accept the Government, His Majesty was in bed, and when they first went in was groaning and appeared very miserable and unhappy, but as the conversation went on he grew better, sat up in the bed, and began to tell all his communications with his late Ministers, mimicking them all to the life, and exhibiting such a drama, so lively, so exact, and so amusing, that the D. never saw anything like it – Goderich, Lansdowne, and, above all, Anglesey, whom he positively made himself look like. I myself had seen many similar exhibitions, and though I have seen better mimics than the King as to the mere voice and manner, I never saw any who exhibited the niceties of character with so much discrimination. As a mere imitator the King has some superiors, but I have never seen his equal for a combination of personal imitation, with the power of exhibiting the mental character.[16]

He had excellent manners when he chose to make himself agreeable; and a certain kindness of heart, when his own vanity or interests were not involved. We get a rather pleasing impression of him from Captain Gronow's account of his first meeting with George Brummell:

At the small entrance of the Green Park, opposite Clarges Street, and close to the reservoir, there stood some years back a neat cottage surrounded by a court-yard, with stables for cows. The exterior of the cottage betokened no small degree of comfort and modest affluence; nor did the interior disappoint those who formed that opinion. Its inmates were two old ladies, dressed in the style of Louis xv, with high, lace caps and dresses of brocaded silk.

In the autumn of 1814 I happened to stroll into the Park to see these cows, which were famed for their colour and symmetry. It was the hour for milking them, and one of the old ladies, observing my curiosity to see that operation performed, came up to the palings and begged me to walk in. I readily complied, and remaining some time, then, thanking her for the honour she had done me, I took my leave, having accepted her invitation to pay her a visit the next evening; which I did. After saluting Mrs Searle and inquiring after her health, I led her on to talk on divers matters. She had an excellent memory, was replete with *esprit*, and appeared to possess a knowledge of everything and everybody. I soon discovered that the old lady was proud of her blood, and she told me that she was aunt to George Brummell, the Beau; that George III had placed her as gate-keeper of the Green Park, and that the Princess Mary had kindly furnished her little cottage. Her description of the Royal Family was somewhat interesting. She said that one day the Prince of Wales, accompanied by the beautiful Marchioness of Salisbury, called upon her, and as it was a beautiful summer's evening, stopped to see her cows milked. Her nephew George Brummell, who had only a day or two before left Eton, happened to be present. The Prince, attracted by his nice manners, entered into conversation with him, and before he left said, 'As I find you intend to be a soldier, I will give you a commission in my own regiment.' Tears of gratitude filled the youth's eyes, and he fell on his knees and kissed the royal hand. Shortly after, George Brummell's commission in the 10th Hussars was made out, and he was soon quartered with his regiment at Brighton. Mrs Searle added, 'But what is most singular, a striking change took place in my nephew's behaviour; for so soon as he began to mix in society with the Prince, his visits to me became less and less frequent, and now he hardly ever calls to see his old aunt.'[17]

Charles MacFarlane met Brummell in exile and reports his opinion of the Prince:

He did not speak harshly of his *çi-devant* friend the Regent, by this time His Majesty George IV; on the contrary, he related several clever and two or three kind things of him, and gave him credit for a great deal of natural ability and *esprit*. He confirmed what Raikes and others have said of the Prince's extraordinary powers of mimicry. 'If his lot had fallen that way,' said he, 'he would have been the best comic actor in Europe.' Brummell confessed to the story of the 'stout friend',[18] and to his threat, after his quarrel with the Prince, to go down to Windsor and make the old people fashionable; but he emphatically denied that other common tale, 'George, ring the bell!'[19] 'I knew the Prince too well,' said he, 'ever to take any kind of liberty with him! Drunk or sober, he would have resented it, with a vengeance! His vindictive spirit – and he could be vindictive about trifles – was the worst part of him; and where he once took a spite he never forgave.'[20]

The Prince was extremely sensitive on the subject of his own corpulence. He was already putting on weight at the beginning of the century and by the end of his reign, especially when he had discarded his stays, he was grotesque. His remedy for all his ills was the rather drastic one of blood-letting. Sir Nathaniel Wraxall tells us that:

After those bacchanalian festivals which frequently took place at Carlton House or at Brighton, in order to obtain relief when attacked by fever, he very early in life had recourse to a fatal expedient – the lancet; long before he reached his thirtieth year he had been bled above a hundred times. Elliot, who was then his principal physician, often refused to authorize or to permit of the operation, against which he remonstrated as only a palliative affording momentary relief, but producing eventually the worst consequences. It is a fact that when the Prince found himself thus debarred of professional aid, he has frequently opened a vein for himself.[21]

The real remedy would have been to go on a diet but the Prince could never forgo the pleasure of eating gargantuan meals and swallowing enormous quantities of brandy.

He remains, nevertheless, the most likeable, and certainly the most intelligent, of the royal brothers. All of them – York, Clarence, Cumberland and Kent – ate and drank prodigiously and openly kept mistresses. The Duke of Cumberland was perhaps the most uncouth. Frederick Locker-Lampson tells us that 'the sons of George III all of them swore lustily; but I think the Duke of Cumberland was the only scion of royalty who habitually swore when conversing with the Archbishop of Canterbury!'

All of them found it difficult to maintain their illegitimate establishments and were perpetually in debt. The old King disapproved of their way of life, but there was little that he could do about it. Lord Glenbervie records that:

At the Duke of Portland's dinner Wednesday last (the Queen's birthday) Lord Liverpool, who sat next Charles Townshend, told him that the Duke of Clarence had got Bushey Park. Mr Townshend said he thought the King was prudish on the point of kept mistresses living in his houses. That had been the ground held out for taking the Deputy Rangership of Richmond Park from Meadows, and he would have made Brummell give up his apartments in Hampton Court Palace if he had not removed the objection by marrying his mistress. Lord Liverpool said, 'Things are altered, and the Duke of Clarence has managed so well that the King jokes with him about Mrs Jordan.'[22]

Mrs Jordan was a very popular and, for a time, successful actress, and it is said that her royal lover was sometimes so out of funds that he used to wait at the stage door to collect her share of the box office takings.

The Duke of York had an even better method of exploiting the talents of his mistress, Mary Anne Clarke. The lady set up an office for the sale of commissions in the Army, of which the Duke was Commander-in-Chief; and this became such a scandal that Parliament was compelled to institute an inquiry into the matter. To quote once more from the writings of Robert Huish:

It was, indeed, alleged, by the advocates of the Duke of York, that no instance had been adduced, by any of the witnesses examined at the bar of the House of Commons, of his Royal Highness having participated, even in a remote degree, in any of the emoluments derived by his mistress from her traffic in the sale of places and commissions. This was, however, completely blinking the question, for he could not but be regarded, relatively speaking, as a considerable gainer by the concern; in fact, he might, with the greatest propriety, have been considered as the *sleeping* partner, whilst Mrs Clarke took upon herself the active part of the business. The resources of the Duke were at the lowest ebb. The demands of his mistress were extravagant and boundless; her establishment partook of the splendour of royalty itself; at the same time that the Duke was supporting another lady at a beautiful cottage at Fulham, whose habits, although not so extravagant nor profuse as those of Mrs Clarke, subjected his Royal Highness to many heavy drains on his finances, which, added to his gambling speculations, kept him in a continual state of the deepest embarrassment. To supply the pecuniary necessities of the establishment of Mrs Clarke from his own immediate resources, was found to be an impossibility; and therefore the influence of the Duke, and his exalted patronage as commander-in-chief, were called into action, as the sources from which the pressing exigences of his mistress could be supplied. Her price for a majority was 900 l. [i.e. pounds], a captaincy 700 l., a lieutenancy 400 l. and an ensigncy 200 l., to be paid to her by Colonel French, who, in 1804, was appointed to a commission for raising new levies; and Mrs Clarke was not only to enjoy a certain patronage in the appointment of the officers, but a certain sum out of the bounty to every recruit that was raised. This influx of emolument stifled the clamours of Mrs Clarke for any supply from the immediate resources of the Duke; and thus, although he could not be styled an actual participator in the profits, yet, he was a considerable gainer, inasmuch as, if those resources had not been made available, the supply must have been produced from his own immediate income.

Whilst, however, Mrs Clarke was carrying on this traffic at the west end of the town, a public office was opened in the city of London, under the auspices of Mrs Carey, the fair resident of the cottage at Fulham, where commissions in the army were offered to purchasers at reduced prices, and where the clerks openly and unequivocally stated that they were employed by the before-mentioned lady, and that, in addition to commissions in the army, they were employed to dispose of places in every department of church and state.[23]

There were many devious ways in which advancement or preferment could be obtained – not excluding the use of blackmail. The irrepressible Creevey relates an attempt on William Lamb, afterwards Viscount Melbourne:

Do you know of Wm Lamb's crim. con.[24] case? The facts are these. Lord Brandon, who is a divine as well as a peer, got possession of a correspondence between his lady and Mr Secretary Lamb, which left no doubt to him or anyone else as to the nature of the connection between these young people. So he writes a letter to the lady announcing his discovery, as well as the conclusion he naturally draws from it; but he adds, if she will exert her influence with Mr Lamb to procure him a bishopric he will overlook her offence and restore her the letters. To which my lady replies, she shall neither degrade herself nor Mr Lamb by making any such application; *but* that she is very grateful to my Lord for the letter he has written her, which she shall put immediately into Mr Lamb's possession.[25]

Perhaps there was never another period in English history when so many people seem to have been keeping diaries or writing memoirs. We have drawn largely upon them because, without doubt, it is they who give us,

The Regency

'The Dandy Club' by Richard Dighton; the flamboyance of the dandies in Regency London provided the caricaturists of the period with an endless source of amusing material

'Dandies and Monstrosities of 1818' by Cruikshank

MONSTROSITIES of 1818

A vicious caricature by Cruikshank of the Prince Regent, whose vulgarity and extravagance brought the monarchy into great disrepute

The Prince Regent at Brighton in 1804 before the reconstruction of the Brighton Pavillion which was to be the most lasting monument to his excesses

The notorious Harriet Wilson, whose memoirs provide a vivid picture of the immorality of Regency London

'Morning promenade on the cliffs of Brighton', by Gillray

The Inner Man

Above 'A voluptuary under the horrors of digestion', Gillray's caricature of the gross eating habits of the Prince Regent

Below Members of the French aristocracy enjoying an elegant mid-day meal

The GIN Shop.

" — now Oh dear, how shocking the thought is
They makes the gin from aquafortis :

They do it on purpose folks lives to shorten
And tickets it up at two-pence a quartern. "

New Ballad.

Designed Etched & Pub.d by Geo.e Cruikshank — November 1.st 182(?)

The poor in England drunk large quantities of cheap gin with disastrous results – as contemporary moralists and philanthropists frequently pointed out

The Revolution of 1830

Barricades in the streets of Paris during the 1830 revolution which resulted in the abdication of the king, Charles X

The 'Captain Swing' riots in England in 1830; an illustration from a contemporary pamphlet shows an evicted peasant explaining to a clergyman the causes of rick-burning

The Irish potato famine was the worst of the famines and starvation which afflicted the European poor in the 1840s

most convincingly, the form and pressure of the time. But among them all there is none that does so more effectively than the notorious Harriet Wilson, who has placed all subsequent social historians in her debt by the liveliness of her recollections. Other *grandes cocottes* have written memoirs but they are either insufferably dull, like those of George Anne Bellamy in the mid-eighteenth century, or plainly unauthentic, like those of Cora Pearl. They are also, for the most part, badly written, probably by some hack employed for the purpose, whereas the memoirs of Harriet Wilson[26] are full of excellent descriptions, vivid pen-portraits and happy turns of phrase. Did she write them herself, or were they written for her by her publisher Stockdale? If so, he never wrote, under his own name, anything half as good.

The opening paragraph gives a taste of her quality. 'I shall not say why and how I became, at the age of fifteen, the mistress of the Earl of Craven.' He set her up in a house on the Marine Parade, Brighton; but she soon grew tired of him (he was forever talking of his campaigns in the West Indies) and decided to try for higher game. She even wrote to the Prince Regent and received a reply (not, of course, in the Prince's own hand) inviting her to come to London. She declined as she was already being 'visited' by the Honourable Frederick Lamb, one of the handsomest men of his time, and although 'the idea of the possibility of deceiving Lord Craven, while I was under his roof, never once entered my head', she was plainly attracted by Lamb.

It is an astonishing comment on the manners of the time that Lord Melbourne, Frederick Lamb's father, was most indignant at his son's lack of success and personally intervened to induce her to yield to his son's wishes. She consented, broke with Lord Craven and joined Frederick Lamb in Hull where he was acting as aide-de-camp to General Mackenzie. However, she soon tired of garrison life and, back in London, wrote with the utmost coolness to the Marquis of Lorne, 'merely to say that, if he would walk up to Duke's Row, Somerstown, he would meet a most lovely girl'. The pair met and the Marquis (soon to become the Duke of Argyle) invited her to supper at Argyle House, with the inevitable consequence that she became his mistress. Harriet had, at one bound, reached the highest levels of her profession. This was in the year of Trafalgar, or thereabouts, when Harriet was nineteen or twenty.

She was born Harriette Dubochet on 22 February 1786, at 2 Carrington Street, Mayfair, where her father, a Swiss named John Dubochet, kept a shop as a clockmaker. He had fifteen children, several of whom obtained no small notoriety. He was a man of stern and taciturn disposition and his daughters soon tired of their cramped and unexciting life. Harriet's sister Amy was the first to abandon the path of virtue for that broader highway which led so temptingly to Brighton – and beyond; and so far from terrifying her sisters by her 'ruin', she found her new life so much more agreeable than

L

the one she had abandoned, that they all resolved to follow her example as soon as possible. In this, as we have noted, Harriet soon succeeded, and she was quickly followed by her younger sister Fanny.

Amy, already launched in London, seems to have regarded the advent of her two sisters with no very friendly eyes. She felt, no doubt, that her prestige was lowered by the presence in town of two such notorious relations, and she and Harriet exchanged many a sisterly scratch (Fanny was too good-natured). However, they refrained from open war, and were seen much in one another's society.

Amy had a box at the opera, and Harriet had a share in another. The London season a hundred and sixty years ago began much earlier than it does at present. But it was unfashionable to care for the opera for the first six weeks or so, and Harriet and Amy, following the usual custom, lent their boxes to their creditors, or to their *femmes de chambre*, till about March or April. Then they shone forth as rival suns, each with her own circle of attendant planets.

Their satellites included some of the most fashionable and notable men of the day: Lord Alvanley, Lord Lowther, the Marquis of Hertford (then Lord Yarmouth), later to be immortalized by Thackeray as the Marquis of Steyne, John Wilson Croker, and the great Brummell himself, with his broken nose and elaborate cravats.

After the theatre they would all repair to Amy's, and eat a tray supper of cold chicken and other delicacies, 'with plenty of champagne and claret'. Amy, indeed, presided over a *salon de courtisane* where men of the very highest fashion congregated, secure in the knowledge that they would meet only ladies who, if of the highest fashion, were also of the *demi-monde*. There were those who preferred such society to that of their own class, and they were always welcome. Others who tried to compromise (Palmerston looked in one evening, coming from Lady Castlereagh's) were received more coldly.

Harriet's younger sister Sophia, who although scarcely thirteen years of age had allowed herself to be seduced by Lord Deerhurst, was the hardest-headed member of the family. She had no great opinion of any of her sisters, and seems to have resolved at a very early age to follow their example only so far as might lead to fortune, or at least to a comfortable settlement. Deerhurst was soon abandoned for a more promising lover, in the person of Lord Berwick, and even with him the young lady was careful not to compromise herself too completely in the eyes of the world.

Lord Berwick took a comfortable house for her in Montagu Square, but the lady was still unsatisfied, and shortly afterwards he married her (on 8 February 1812) and the happy pair settled down in the family mansion in Grosvenor Square. There Her Ladyship, the sole member of the family to bring her adventures to a triumphant conclusion, began to be conscious of her dignity, and, with her husband's approval, to cut herself off from her former acquaint-ance. 'I had always wished,' laments Harriet, 'to love my sisters dearly. It was very hard on me that they would not let me.'

Amy was less fortunate, for she married, not a peer of the realm, but Robert Nicolas Charles Bochsa, a musician of somewhat irregular life. Fanny, whether by law or by courtesy, became Mrs Parker, and owed what comfort she enjoyed in her closing days to the kindness of Lord Hertford. That irregular nobleman, who has become almost proverbial for dissolute be-haviour, certainly emerged from his relations with the Dubochet family with considerable credit.

Perhaps it was not to be expected that Lady Berwick should recall with any satisfaction the events of her past life, but how did it come about that Harriet, and not Amy or Fanny, became the mouthpiece of the family fortunes? The facts are simple.

Lord Worcester, while still a minor, had become fascinated by her charms, and even for a time considered her as his future wife. His family, and in particular his father, the Duke of Beaufort, were naturally enough opposed to the match. The liaison, however, lasted three years and Harriet only aban-doned her prize in return for an annuity of £500. One of the conditions of this yearly payment was that she should live abroad, and this to Harriet, with her perfect knowledge of French and her still considerable personal attractions, was perhaps no great hardship. Unfortunately the Duke grew weary of the continual drain on his finances, and proposed to compound the promised income by a single payment of £1,200. This action, although it excited the unbounded indignation of Harriet, was of benefit to humanity, for it produced the memoirs.

It was, therefore, no creative impulse that inspired her book, nor even a Casanova-like desire to live over again the scene of former triumphs. It was a very understandable wish to extract money from the public by a *chronique scandaleuse*, and from the Duke by blackmail.

She took up her residence in Paris, and seated in an easy chair, as she tells us, at No. 111 Rue du Faubourg St Honoré, she wrote down the history of her life in a free, conversational style, which a hundred years has not robbed of its piquancy. She had considerable talents for such a task, for although her education had been somewhat neglected, she was far from being unable to express herself on paper. Events which had passed before her own eyes she could describe vividly enough, and there was little need of imagination after such a life as hers. She shows, in an account of a coach journey to Oxford, a real power of seizing upon the characteristic remarks of her fellow passengers – in particular the London tradesman who says, 'Sink the shop, and let's have a little genteel conversation' – which foreshadows the method of Dickens. Her gift of sarcastic phrase was considerable, as in her delicious description of Viscount Berwick driving down to Brighton in a

coach and four, with Sophia following at a decent interval in a little chariot –
'*parce que Mademoiselle Sophie voulait faire paraître les beaux restes de sa vertu
chancelante*'.[27]

Her book was published by J. J. Stockdale of No. 24 Opera Colonnade,
London, and the nature of his wares may be guessed from the titles of several
other of his publications: *The New Art of Love; Marriage Ceremonies and
Intercourse of the Sexes, in all Nations*, and *Dr Robertson's Anatomy and
Physiology*. Harriet's work appeared in 1825 and was instantly a success.
Harriet had hoped for twenty editions. Stockdale sold thirty within the year;
and a French version in six volumes carried the notoriety of the authoress to
her new place of residence. The happy publisher was compelled to erect a
barricade in front of his premises to prevent the public from storming the
shop. He was, however, not without his troubles. Frederick Lamb called to
threaten prosecution, and two of Harriet's victims did prosecute, and
involved Stockdale in considerable expense. But as he and the authoress
between them 'fingered' £10,000 of the public's money, they had little reason
to complain.

She had no hesitation in printing the names of her former lovers, however
distinguished they might be. She remarks that 'Wellington was now my
constant visitor – a most unentertaining one, Heaven knows! and, in
the evenings, when he wore his broad red ribbon, he looked very like a
rat-catcher.'

She tells an amusing story of his attempt to visit her when the Duke of
Argyle was already in possession of the field:

Wellington was really said to have won a mighty battle, and was hourly expected.
Canons were fired, and much tallow consumed in illumination. His Grace of
Argyle came to me earlier than usual on that memorable evening; but, being
unwell and love-sick, he found me in my bed-chamber, when, catching me in his
arms, he swore, by his brown whiskers, that this night, at least, he would be a
match for mighty Wellington.

'*Quelle bizarre idée vous passe par la tête?*'[28] said I. 'Surely you have forgotten
the amiable duchess, his bride, and all the fatigue his Grace has encountered,
enough to damp the ardour of any mighty hero or plenipotentiary, for one evening,
at any rate; therefore, trust me, Wellington will not disturb us tonight.'

At this very moment, a thundering rap at the door was heard.

'*Vive l'amour! Vive la guerre!*' said Argyle: '*Le voilà!*'[29] And hastily throwing my
dressing gown over his shoulders, and putting on one of my old nightcaps, having
previously desired 'the most particlerst man as is' not to let anybody in, hastily
put his head out of my bed-room window, which was on the second floor, and soon
recognized the noble chieftain, Wellington! Endeavouring to imitate the voice of
an old duenna, Argyle begged to know who was at the door?

'Come down, I say,' roared this modern Blue Beard, 'and don't keep me here in
the rain, you old blockhead.'

'Sir,' answered Argyle, in a shrill voice, 'you must please to call out your name, or I don't dare to come down, robberies are so frequent in London just at this season, and all the sojers, you see, coming home from Spain, that it's quite alarming to poor lone women.'

Wellington took off his hat, and held up, towards the lamp, a visage which late fatigue and present vexation had rendered no bad representation of that of the knight of the woeful figure. While the rain was trickling down his nose, his voice, trembling with rage and impatience, cried out, 'You old idiot, do you know me now?'

'Lord, sir,' answered Argyle, anxious to prolong this ridiculous scene, 'I can't give no guess; and, do you know, sir, the thieves have stolen a new water-butt out of our airy, not a week since, and my missis is more timbersome than ever!'

'The devil!' vociferated Wellington, who could endure no more, and, muttering bitter imprecations between his closed teeth, against all the duennas and old women that had ever existed, returned home to his neglected wife and family duties.[30]

She is not much more complimentary about the Duke of Argyle himself:

I will not say in what particular year of his life the Duke of Argyle succeeded with me. Ladies scorn dates! Dates make ladies nervous and stories dry. Be it only known then, that it was just at the end of his Lorne shifts, and his lawn shirts.[31] It was at that critical period of his life, when his whole and sole possessions appeared to consist in three dozen of ragged lawn shirts, with embroidered collars, well fringed in his service; a threadbare suit of snuff colour, a little old hat with very little binding left, an old horse, an old groom, an old carriage, and an old château. It was to console himself for all this antiquity, I suppose, that he fixed upon so very young a mistress as myself.[32]

Her comments on the contemporary scene do not lack acerbity:

A man is a gentleman, according to Berkeley Craven's definition of the word, who has no visible means of gaining his livelihood; others have called Lord Deerhurst and Lord Barrymore, and Lord Stair, gentlemen; because they are Lords: and the system, at White's Club, the members of which are all choice gentlemen, of course, is, and ever has been, never to blackball any man, who ties a good knot in his handkerchief, keeps his hands out of his breeches-pockets, and says nothing. For my part, I confess I like a man who can talk, and contribute to the amusement of whatever society he may be placed in; and that is the reason I am always glad to find myself in the company of Lord Hertford, notwithstanding he is so often blackballed at White's.[33]

The fashionable world was in great agitation, especially as further instalments of the damaging record were threatened. Meetings were held at White's, Brooks' and the United Services clubs in order to decide what could be done. It is probable that the action brought by Blore, the stone-mason of Piccadilly, was financed from these aristocratic institutions, as a kind of *ballon d'essai*. Harriet had held the unfortunate Blore up to ridicule for the boorishness of his alleged advances, and the stone-mason, now married and father of a family, claimed damages. In spite of the eloquence of Stockdale he won his case, and was awarded £300. Another plaintiff, one Hugh Evans Fisher, received even more, but although both actions were successful, Harriet's former wealthy admirers decided that it would be safer to go no further. They seem to have bought her silence, and Harriet troubled them no more.

Her life in Paris was not disagreeable. She had had, since her emigration in about 1820, a considerable amount of good society. She was allowed to send her letters (a startling commentary this!) in the Foreign Office bag, and no less a person than Henry Brougham, MP, took her to see the great Talma in *Racine*. She even claims to have written to Byron in Ravenna, and to have received from him fifty pounds. But all this was probably before she threw her bombshell into the midst of the polite world.

With the earnings of the book she had written, and the probably greater earnings of the one she had refrained from writing, she settled down and married a Monsieur Rochfort who, it may be feared, belonged essentially to that middle class in society which Harriet so cordially despised. She returned to England a pious widow, and died in 1846, in a world which had already felt the salutary moral influence of the young Queen.

12

FOOTNOTES

1 Rev. William Beloe, *The Sexagenarian, or the Recollections of a Literary Life*, London 1817.

2 John Keyse Sherwin (*c*. 1751–90) was a draughtsman adept at producing chic female portraits which caused his studio to be much frequented by fashionable ladies.

3 John Thomas Smith, *A Book for a Rainy Day, or Recollections of the Events of the Years 1766–1833*, London 1905.

4 Queen Charlotte, wife of George III.

5 Robert Huish (1777–1850) was a miscellaneous writer whose output included novels, 'A Treatise on Bees' and memoirs of the reigns of George III and George IV. His gossip should be treated with caution here owing to his bitter hostility to Charles James Fox.

6 Duc de Lauzun, *Mémoires*, 2nd ed., Paris 1858.

7 Mrs Billington was perhaps the most celebrated vocalist of her day. She was born in Soho, the illegitimate child of a singer at Vauxhall and a German musician named Weichsel. In 1783 she married the double bass player at Drury Lane. Some years later, driven from England by a scandalous pamphlet, she had a great success in Italy.

8 Anna Maria Phillips, later Mrs Crouch, was the daughter of a lawyer. She appeared at Drury Lane in 1790 and had much success both in opera and drama. She played Ophelia to the Hamlet of John Philip Kemble. She died in 1805.

9 R. Huish, *Memoirs of George IV*, London 1821

10 *Ibid.*

11 *Ibid.*

12 *Ibid.*

13 Thomas Creevey, *Memoirs, Diaries and Correspondence*, ed. Sir Herbert Maxwell, London 1903.

14 Sir Nathaniel Wraxall, *Historical and Posthumous Memoirs*, London 1884.

15 Henry Fox, fourth Lord Holland, *Journal*, London 1923.

16 J.W. Croker, *Papers*, ed. L.J. Jennings, London 1882.

17 Captain R.H. Gronow, *Reminiscences*, London 1847.

18 This was the story that Brummell, strolling down Bond Street with a friend, came face to face with the Prince. His Royal Highness stopped to talk to Brummell's companion but pointedly ignored Brummell himself. As they parted Brummell was heard to murmur: 'Who's your fat friend?'

19 The story denied by Brummell was that, being alone with the Prince, and the services of a footman being required, he drawled: 'George, ring the bell.' The Prince did so and, when the footman appeared, said: 'Call Mr Brummell's carriage.'

20 Charles MacFarlane, *Reminiscences of a Literary Life*, London 1917.

21 Sir Nathaniel Wraxall, *op. cit.*

22 Lord Glenbervie, *Diaries*, London 1928.

23 Robert Huish, *op. cit.*

24 Short for 'criminal conversation', i.e. adultery.

25 Thomas Creevey, *op. cit.*

26 Harriet Wilson, *Memoirs*, London 1825.

27 'because Mademoiselle Sophie wished to display to the world the last beautiful shreds of her vacillating virtue.'

28 'What bizarre idea is passing through your head?'

29 'Long live love! Long live war! There he is!'

30 Harriet Wilson, *op. cit.*

31 Lord Lorne was a somewhat shifty character and was not famous for the cleanliness of his linen.

32 Harriet Wilson, *op. cit.*

33 *Ibid.*

13 The Inner Man

The French rightly enjoy such a reputation for skill in the arts of the table that it is somewhat surprising to discover how comparatively recent such fame is. Certainly in the sixteenth century they were surpassed by the Italians, for it was Catherine de Medici who introduced some refinement into French cuisine. Even a hundred years later, at the court of Louis XIV, the method of serving food was still medieval: fish, flesh and sweet things served pell-mell.

The King himself always dined alone, at a table set up in his bed-chamber, and we know from contemporary accounts the dishes which were set before him: for example, four or five different kinds of soup, a joint of veal, a pigeon tart, six chickens *fricassé*, a minced partridge, two turkeys, nine roasted chickens, four tarts, two baskets of fruit and two dishes of sweet-meats. All this might be dismissed as mere ostentation, but it was not. Louis was a voracious eater, and even contemporaries were astonished at his appetite. His personal physician, Fagon, has left it on record that on one occasion, when the King was dieting, he yet managed to put away 'four wings, four legs and four breasts of chicken'.

The Regent, the Duc d'Orléans, was a great gourmet and brought some refinement into French cooking, but Frenchmen continued to eat prodigiously. The famous Chevalier d'Eon, for example, who prided himself on his frugality, consumed at a single sitting melon, stewed eels, a carp, two chickens, a rabbit, a joint of beef, a tart and dessert.

In England things were very much the same. Charles II had brought with him from his exile many French notions including ideas for the improvement of English cooking, hitherto somewhat crude. Soon cookery books began to appear, the most notable being *The Accomplisht Cook, or The Art and Mystery of Cookery*, by Robert May, who assured his readers that 'God and his own conscience would not permit him to bury his experience with his silver hairs in the grave'.

On the whole, however, the English continued to prefer simply dressed meats, so long as they were in sufficient quantity. Readers of Pepys will remember that, in the very year of the King's return, he gave a party for some friends and says: 'I had a pretty dinner for them, viz.: a brace of stewed carps, six roasted chickens, and a jowle of salmon hot for the first course; a tansy, a kind of sweet dish made with eggs, cream etc., flavoured with the juice of tansy; and two neat's tongues and cheese, the second. We had a man cook to dress dinner today.'[1]

We do not know how many sat down to this repast, but on another occasion his wife presented him with a meal, presumably for two, which she had cooked with her own hands. He describes it, as well he might, as 'a very fine dinner, viz.: a dish of marrow-bones, a leg of mutton, a loin of veal, a dish of fowl, three pullets, and a dozen of larks all in a dish, a great tart, a neat's tongue, a dish of anchovies, a dish of prawns, and cheese.'[2]

It all seems an unconscionable amount of animal protein, but presumably there were some vegetables in addition. To the modern mind, also, the order of service seems odd, flesh and fowl all mingled together and the 'good red herring', or its equivalent, bringing up the rear.

Cookery books continued to pour from the press. George H. Ellwanger lists more than twenty of them published between the Restoration and the end of the eighteenth century, but very justly remarks:

Here are manuals enough in all conscience to have produced a progressive cuisine, were not the majority a repetition of all the crudities and barbarisms of their antecedents, where one heresy was passed on to be augmented by another author, and by him transmitted to his successors. Essentially differing from France, England was unblessed with originality, and not until the influence of the splendid restaurants of the Parisian capital had extended across the Channel did the Briton awake from his lethargy and cease to see through Mrs Glasse darkly.[3]

Mrs Hannah Glasse, the reputed author of *The Art of Cookery Made Plain and Easy*, first printed in 1747, achieved the same kind of reputation in the eighteenth century as Mrs Beeton enjoyed in the nineteenth. Both ladies have been credited with the phrase 'First catch your hare', but this seems without foundation in both cases. But Mrs Glasse *does* say: 'Stick your pig just above the breast-bone, and run your knife to the heart,' an injunction which few modern housewives would be willing to follow. What strikes the modern reader most forcibly when turning over her recipes is the excessive amount of spices: cinnamon, mace, nutmeg, cloves. Perhaps we should remember that in the days before refrigeration meat was very often tainted.

We have to remind ourselves also that many of the things which we take for granted, especially vegetables, were not yet available. Dried peas and beans were staple diet, but cauliflowers, aubergines and even potatoes were unknown before the seventeenth century, and tomatoes and beetroots before the eighteenth. Bread was of poor quality and butter scarce; even the olive oil which took the place of butter in the south of France was unrefined and unpalatable. Most of the fish eaten was fresh-water fish; sea-fish, owing to transport difficulties, was either salted or pickled. Meat tended to be tough, for it was not until the end of the eighteenth century that the cattle raisers in England and Holland began to breed animals especially for the table.

In the matter of service the great were much worse off than those in humbler walks of life. In the houses of the aristocracy comfort and efficiency were sacrificed to grandeur and display. Most servants wore the livery of their master and, naturally, the grander the master the grander the livery – and in general the more useless the servant. In the servants' hall the servant of a duke took precedence over the servant of a mere earl, and protocol was strictly observed.[4]

In France in the eighteenth century the hierarchy of servants was even more rigidly observed; the various ranks ate at different tables, the *valet de chambre* being excluded from that of the *intendant* and the *maîtres d'hôtel*, the lackeys from the table of the valets, and the kitchen boys from the table of the lackeys. The various kinds of work to be done were as rigidly laid down as in a modern trade union. It is related of the Duchesse de Rohan that when she came back hungry from a ride and ordered a lackey to bring her something to eat he refused point-blank, and as the *maître d'hôtel* could not be found the hunger of the Duchess remained unappeased.

The number of servants employed in a great house was prodigious. Cardinal de Rohan in his palace at Saverne employed fourteen *maîtres d'hôtel*, twenty-five *valets de chambre* and two hundred other servants, and he was always complaining of their inadequacy. Royalty itself fared no better, in spite of the fact that at Versailles Louis xv had nearly four thousand persons in his employment, and the Queen two thousand. The Duc de Luynes records that one day in 1747 the Queen noticed that the woodwork at the end of her bed was covered with dust. Her lady-in-waiting sent for the *valet de chambre-tapissier* who declined to touch it, maintaining that he and his aides were responsible for making the Queen's bed but not for polishing the furniture or even for dusting it. That was the work of another body of servants known as the *garde-meuble*. The Queen's bed remained undusted.

The process of dining was equally complicated. If, for example, the King wished for a cup of bouillon, word was sent to the far-away kitchens and a procession formed escorted by soldiers. The cup of soup was placed on a marble table in the Council Chamber under the eye of the first *maître d'hôtel*; the first taster tasted it and the chief doctor did likewise, a footman then announced in a loud voice 'The King's soup,' the door opened, the procession entered, the first gentleman-in-waiting received it and passed it to the King. It must by this time have been cold. Louis xv had at least the sense to light his own fire in the morning, and he needed to, for his room in winter was icy. When he wished to relieve nature a noble in a velvet suit with a sword at his side supervised the bringing in of a commode. This was the noble's only duty and for it he received an annual salary of twenty thousand livres.

We learn of the type of food eaten by people who were neither very poor nor very rich from the diary of Parson Woodforde.[5] He had a comfortable country living and nothing very much happened to him: country matters, visiting neighbours, preaching and dispensing charity; but his diary is fascinating because he was so meticulous in setting down what he ate. He certainly consumed plenty: good wholesome fare in what seems to the modern mind and modern stomach to be prodigious amounts. 'Dinner today a Loin of Veal rosted, a boiled Rabbitt and Onion Sauce, some Beef Stakes, a fine Pheasant rosted, Apple Pudding, some Cheese-cakes.' This seems to have been for six people.

At a friend's house at Castle-Cary to which he had driven in a 'Bruton Chaise' arriving at two o'clock, he and seven other people consumed 'a very handsome dinner, very fine Soals nicely fried, boiled Ham and three boiled Chickens, a large Piece of Beef rosted, a very fine fat Goose rosted, Apple Pye, Barberry Pye, and Custard. After Coffee and Tea we returned . . . and got home by seven in the Evening.'

On a visit to Oxford he dined in the Hall of New College where 'we had for dinner a Rump of Beef boiled, a Jigget of Mutton alias Haunch rosted with sweet Sauce etc. etc.'. One would like to know more about the *et cetera* as this seems a rather modest meal for the High Table. However, after dinner he was entertained in the Senior Common Room and would presumably be given fruit, nuts and wine.

That seems to have been the kind of dessert he provided in his own home, for when two friends came to dine 'we gave them for dinner, Hashed Calf's Head, a boiled Chicken etc., some Bacon, a Leg of Mutton rosted, and a Norfolk batter Pudding and drippings, after that we had Duck rosted, Maccaroni and Tarts. By way of Desert, we had white Currants, Pears, Apples and Filberts.'

He does not often tell us what he drank but it was probably beer for the most part. 'Brewed a Barrel of Table-Beer today,' he tells us in one of his entries. But on his 'Tithe Audit Day' he entertained at his house a score of farmers who had come to pay him their 'respective Composition'. Most of them did not leave 'till after 2. in the Morn', three of them 'very much disguised in liquor'. They had consumed, in addition to an ample repast which included beef, mutton, salt fish, rabbits etc., plum and plain puddings in plenty, 'Small Beer and strong, Punch and Wine as much as they pleased to make use of – Strong Beer amazingly liked and drank in great Quantity, six Bottles of Rum made into Punch, one Dozen of Lemons, and about five Bottles of Port drunk today. They were all extremely well pleased with their

Entertainment and very harmonious.' The port wine cost him twenty-nine shillings a dozen and the rum sixteen shillings a gallon.

Coming a little lower down in the social scale, we find that a small farmer of the same period – the closing years of the eighteenth century – ate much more sparingly:

I was accustomed to eat what may be termed black bread, for which the small wheat called hinder ends, or light wheat taken out of the best sent to market, is used and kept for family use. . . . Yeast not being then in general use, a piece of dough was kept out of the last baking and salted; which before the time of using it for the next batch, becoming sour, this sort of bread acquired the same quality. Very fat bacon was the chief of our diet, garden stuff not being in such general use at this time, excepting the large Windsor beans in summer, and potatoes occasionally in the winter, with pease-puddings. I know no greater dainty to me than these beans and fat bacon, or pease-pudding, to the offal of pig's flesh in the winter, or some of the black bread and fat bacon.[6]

The poor, and even the lower middle classes in the towns, were even worse off, as they had no means of growing vegetables, still less of keeping a pig. A clerk working in London in 1767 drew up a budget to prove that wages were too low and that he fed 'even worse than a day labourer feeds himself'.[7] He earned about ten shillings a week and his food alone cost him nearly that amount.

Breakfast:	Bread and cheese and small beer	2d.
Dinner:	Chuck of beef or scrag of mutton or sheep's trotters or pig's ear soused; cabbage or potatoes or parsnips, bread and small beer with half a pint of porter	7d.
Supper:	Bread and cheese with radishes or cucumber or	3d.
	onions small beer and half a pint of porter	1½d.
		1s. 1½d.
	Per week	7s. 10½d.
	An additional repast of Sunday	4d.
		8s. 2½d.

Towards the end of the century, prices rose steeply owing to the war with France, and, in the winter of 1795, there was something like famine in London and other cities. George III was hissed and hooted at as he rode in the state coach from the Houses of Parliament to St James's Palace. In the Park a huge crowd had gathered, estimated by Parson Woodforde, who was present, at two hundred thousand people. Those near the royal coach shouted: 'No King! Give us peace and bread.'

Political considerations played a large part in the drinking habits of

England in the eighteenth century. Wine had been imported from France and other European countries from medieval times. Brandy had been made in France at least since the fourteenth century and was known in England under the Tudors. Considerable amounts were brought in during the seventeenth century when the upper classes began to acquire a taste for 'strong waters'. But the men who made the 'Glorious Revolution' of 1688 disliked brandy not because it was strong but because it was French. Accordingly, in the following year, they prohibited the importation of spirits from all foreign countries and allowed anyone in England to set up a distillery on giving ten days' notice to the Excise.

This cannot have been very pleasing to the Dutch King William III, especially as the English were very soon able to produce a very tolerable imitation of the 'geneva' made in the Netherlands.[8] They gave it a name which very soon became all too familiar. Mandeville in his *Fable of the Bees*, published in 1714, refers to 'the infamous Liquor, the name of which, deriv'd from Juniper-berries in Dutch, is now by frequent use . . . from a word of middling length shrunk to a monosyllable . . . Gin.'

All historians are agreed that the effects of cheap gin, especially on the poorer people in England, were disastrous. Between 1684 and 1727 the annual production rose from a mere half million gallons to more than three and a half million. The story has often been told that retailers were accustomed to hang out a board which read: 'Drunk for a penny; dead-drunk for twopence; clean straw for nothing.'

Moralists and philanthropists denounced the habit of dram-drinking, and Hogarth brought out two of his most successful prints, entitled *Gin Lane* and *Beer Street*, to drive home the different effects of the two beverages. But so fond had the populace become of gin that when the Gin Act of 1736 sought to restrain the sale of 'brandy, rum, arrack, usquebaugh, geneva, acqua vitae, or any other distilled spirituous liquors, mixed or unmixed', there was an outbreak of rioting in most of the larger cities. Mock funeral processions were organized to lament the 'death of Madame Gin'. The Act was a failure. The consumption of spirits rose from 13·5 million gallons in 1734 to 19 million gallons in 1742.

The hostility of the Whigs to anything French had a striking effect on the wine-drinking habits of the English. After 1688 the duty on French wines was progressively raised by four hundred per cent and when, in 1703, the Government signed what is known as the Methuen Treaty with Portugal, England bound herself to receive Portuguese produce at a rate of one-third less duty than on the produce of France. From that date until 1931 the differential rate against French wines was never less than thirty per cent. The result was that Englishmen took to drinking the wine from Oporto, which they called Port. Old wine labels are inscribed 'Red Port', 'White Port' and the now forgotten 'Lisbon'.

It would seem that the change was not at first welcomed by everybody. In the anonymous poem 'Farewell to Wine', published in 1693, we read:

'Some claret, boy!'
'Indeed, sir, we have none.
Claret, Sir? Lord! there's not a drop in town.
But we have the best red Port.
'What's that you call Red Port?'
'A wine, sir, comes from Portugal.
I'll fetch a pint, sir.'

A century later an English father who found his son drinking burgundy could remark: 'I'll not have these foreign wines in the house, sir! Port was good enough for me and my father. It is good enough for you.' So English a thing had port become. So English a thing? History, it is said, has been written by Whigs and therefore we are apt to forget that quite a number of people in England in the eighteenth century, and more in Scotland, disapproved of the Hanoverian Succession, and were ready to do anything, short of actual rebellion, to oppose it. Some of them would have been glad enough, in theory at least, to see the German Georges go. Bonnie Prince Charlie had many sympathizers, both before his landing and after his defeat, and it was their custom to drink to 'the King over the Water'. In hostile surroundings they did so silently, signifying their sentiments merely by holding their glasses over a jug of water as if by accident when they toasted 'the King'. But much glass was manufactured, both in Scotland and in the neighbourhood of Newcastle, which was actually engraved with Jacobite emblems. And what was drunk from such glasses was not port but claret, which continued to be consumed in spite of all the difficulties which had been put in the way of its importation. To drink claret was to show sympathy with France and the exiled Stuarts, just as to drink port was to show sympathy with the Whigs and their trading policy. It is not often in history that a choice between two drinks has had so much political significance. That Dr Johnson, in spite of his Toryism, did not altogether share these views is shown by his famous remark: 'Claret for boys, port for men, brandy for heroes.'

Perhaps the change from French wine would not have mattered so much if the wines of Portugal drunk in England had not been so heavily fortified. 'When first introduced into this country,' says the anonymous author of *A Brief Discourse on Wine*, 'the Oporto wines were received in a pure state, but about this time [i.e. the early years of the eighteenth century] the custom commenced of mingling brandy with the shipments for English use, and to such an extent that in later imports no less than from sixteen to eighteen gallons of spirit per pipe [a wine cask holding 126 gallons] was infused, and that often of execrable quality.' Perhaps it is not surprising in view of the enormous quantities of port consumed as a beverage (we hear of 'three-bottle men' and even of 'six-bottle men') that the prevalent disease of the upper classes in the late eighteenth century was gout.

Nothing is more puzzling to the modern reader than the times at which meals were consumed in the eighteenth century. Mackay, the author of *A Journey through England*, published in London in 1724, gives two o'clock as the hour for dinner. Twenty years later Fielding in *Joseph Andrews* suggests that the man of fashion dined at four, but this was not universal, for we find Lord Holland writing to George Selwyn in 1764: 'We dine exactly at two, so you will have full time to go to Canterbury after your coffee if that is what you choose.'

In France conditions were very similar under the *ancien régime*, but one of the curious side-effects of the French Revolution was to alter the traditional hours of meal times, especially in Paris. The sittings of the National Assembly began at ten o'clock in the morning and ended between four and five in the afternoon. The morning meal therefore had to be taken at nine, and dinner, instead of being at half past two was put off until five. The theatres were compelled to open later and the performances did not now begin until eight, which pushed the hour for supper to eleven. At this hour even the man and woman of the eighteenth century could not stomach the heavy evening meals which had formerly been customary. Also, during the Terror food was scarce and extremely expensive; currency had been devalued and prices rose enormously.

During the wars of the Empire soldiers who had been accustomed to eat rapidly during the campaigns were unwilling to sit down to the old leisurely meals. Napoleon himself was no gourmet; he simply ate everything within reach of his hand: fish, flesh or sweet dishes indiscriminately, and the moment his appetite was satisfied he rose from the table and those who were dining with him were compelled to do likewise. It was, however, under Napoleon that French gastronomy really became established. Napoleon's gastronomic austerity – not to say eccentricity – was not shared by all the prominent men of the Revolutionary period. Barras in particular was a great gourmet and entertained lavishly during the Directory. Many of his menus have survived, annotated by his own hand. The following may serve as a specimen:

CARTE DINATOIRE

Pour La Table Du Citoyen Directeur et Général Barras
Le Decadi 30 Floréal

Douze personnes

1 potage	2 plats de rôt
1 relevé	6 entremets [side-dishes]
6 entrées	1 salade

24 plats de dessert

Le potage aux petits oignons à la çi-devant minime [onion soup]
Le relevé, un tronçon d'esturgeon à la broche [sturgeon]

Les Six Entrées

1 d'un sauté de filets de turbot à l'homme de confiance [turbot fillets)
1 d'anguilles à la tartare [eels]
1 de concombres farcis à la moëlle [cucumber stuffed with marrow]
1 vol-au-vent de blanc de volaille à la Béchamel [chicken vol-au-vent]
1 d'un çi-devant St Pierre sauce aux capres [John Dory fish]
1 de filets de perdrix en anneaux [partridge fillets]

Les Deux Plats de Rôt

1 de goujons du département [gudgeon]
1 d'une carpe au court-bouillon [carp]

Les Six Entremets

1 d'œufs à la neige [eggs]
1 betteraves blanches sauté au jambon [beetroot with ham]
1 d'une gelée au vin de Madère [jelly made from Madeira wine]
1 de beignets de crème à la fleur d'oranges [cream fritters]
1 de lentilles à la çi-devant reine à la crème au blond de veau [lentils]
1 de culs d'artichauts à la ravigote [artichoke hearts]
1 salade céleri en remoulade

Barras comments: 'There is too much fish. Leave out the gudgeons; the rest is all right. Do not forget to place cushions on the chairs of the *citoyennes* Tallien, Talma, Beauharnais, Hainguerlot and Mirande. And for five o'clock precisely. Have the ices sent from Veloni's; I don't want any others.'

The list of the ladies present, including as it does Madame Tallien, the wife of the great actor Talma, and the future Empress Josephine, is as fascinating as the menu itself.

A few years later the tables of Talleyrand and Cambacérès were the most renowned in Paris. Talleyrand's chef was the famous Carême who served him for twelve years. Later he was employed in England by the Prince Regent. Another great culinary artist to come to England was Louis Eustache Ude who had been chef to Louis XVI. He became chef to the Duke of York and, after the Duke's death, went to Crockford's.

Much of the credit for refining French cookery in the early nineteenth century has gone to Brillat-Savarin, whose *Physiologie du Goût* was published in 1825, a year before his death. A lawyer by profession, he took refuge first in Switzerland and then in America during the Revolution; returning to France, he became a judge of the *cour de cassation* (the Supreme Court of Appeal). His hobby was gastronomy and in his masterpiece he laid down some excellent maxims concerning it. As will be seen he regarded it 'as something much more than the mere providing of good food, properly cooked'.

Let the number of guests not exceed twelve, so that the conversation may be constantly general.

Let them be so chosen that their occupations are various, their tastes analogous, and with such points of contact that one need not have recourse to that odious formality of introductions.

Let the dining-room be brilliantly lighted, the cloth as white as snow, and the temperature of the room from sixty to sixty-eight Fahrenheit.

Let the men be witty and not pedantic, and the women amiable without being too coquettish.

Let the dishes be served from the more substantial to the lighter; and from the simpler wines to those of finer bouquet.[9]

The last paragraph is perhaps the most important in laying down a rule which is now universally followed, but had not been in earlier days.

Brillat-Savarin was for a time mayor of his native town of Belley in southeast France and had to hand an abundance of game, delicious trout and *écrevisses de la rivière* (fresh-water crayfish), and, of course, the famous *poulet de Bresse*, the regional speciality, which, fed on cream and cooked with an abundance of fresh butter, is still one of the most succulent dishes in the world.

Some authors have doubted whether Brillat-Savarin's practice was as good as his theory. The Marquis de Cussy tells us that he 'ate copiously and ill, talked dully, and was preoccupied at the end of a repast'. But none can deny the persuasive charm of his book, and his name will always shine brightly in the annals of gastronomy.

However, he had been preceded by a man who certainly had more immediate influence: Grimod de la Reynière, the inspirer, and largely the author, of the *Almanach des Gourmands* which first appeared in 1804 and continued to be published annually until 1808. Alexandre Balthazar Laurent Grimod de la Reynière was born in Paris in 1758. He was trained in the law but did not pursue that profession with the persistence of Brillat-Savarin; instead he is said to have engaged in 'various artistic, literary and mercantile pursuits'. While editing a dramatic journal he fell in love with an actress, a certain Mademoiselle Mézeray, and when she rejected his advances he announced in verse, in his own paper, his '*Abnégation*' and declared that henceforth he was determined to devote himself to gastronomy. This was in the year 1796, by which time, we are told, he had belonged for many years to a club known as the Société des Mercredis, consisting of seventeen members who were in the habit of dining once a week at the Rocher de Concale, then the most celebrated restaurant in Paris.

There would be nothing astonishing in this if it were not for the date. 'For many years' implies that the dinners had continued throughout the whole period of the Revolution and the Terror. The history of the time is full of these surprises, and one can only conclude that in spite of all the upheavals it was still possible to live, discreetly, a fairly normal life.

The dinners were not mere convivial gatherings; those who took part constituted themselves a *jury dégustateur*, pronouncing verdicts on the dishes and wines submitted to them. The judges, never more than twelve or less than five, were presided over by the eminent physician Dr Gastaldy, with Grimod de la Reynière acting as secretary. Another member was the Marquis de Cussy, who was renowned as 'the first gastronomer of the age'. The meetings of the society took place at the residence of the secretary and usually lasted for five hours. What might be called the dinner proper was prepared by the secretary who was a *cordon bleu*.[10] One extra dish, often, it would seem, a pâté, was brought in from outside, the creator not being named until judgment had been passed. The judgments were printed in the *Almanach*, and it is plain that when they were favourable they provided valuable publicity for the *fournisseur* (caterer) in question and, when they were unfavourable, caused him to lose business. As may be imagined there were some angry reactions from unsuccessful competitors, but the reputation of the *Almanach* was so great, and the law of libel at that time so lax, that the only remedy was to try to do better next time.

It is a sobering experience for the modern reader to glance through the cookery books published in the early nineteenth century by such masters as Carême and Francatelli. All the recipes are extremely elaborate, hardly anything being sent to table without garnishes of mushrooms, truffles, quenelles and cocks' combs impaled on long silver skewers. Even sauces and soups were very complicated in their preparation. Turtle soup, for example, required not only the turtle, but '15 lbs. of leg of beef, 15 lbs. of knuckle of veal, 2 hens, 2 quarts of stock, ½ pottle of mushrooms, 4 onions, herbs and seasonings and a bottle of sherry'.

It is sad to think that while such delicacies were being consumed by kings and aldermen, most of the population of nearly every European country was on the verge of starvation in the difficult years following Waterloo.

13

FOOTNOTES

1 Samuel Pepys, *Diary*, 26 March 1660.
2 *Ibid.*, 26 January 1659.
3 George H. Ellwanger, *The Pleasures of the Table*, London 1903.

4 Strangely enough, this custom persisted even into the twentieth century. Lady Cynthia Asquith records that her lady's maid burst into tears when she heard that her mistress was going to marry a commoner. The unfortunate young woman saw herself at the bottom of the table in the servants' hall.

5 Rev. James Woodforde, *The Diary of a Country Parson* (1793–6), ed. John Beresford, London 1929.

6 R. Parkinson, *The Experienced Farmer's Tour in America*, London 1805.

7 M.D. George, *English Social Life*.

8 The drink 'geneva' has, of course, nothing to do with the city of Geneva. The word is derived from the old Dutch name for juniper.

9 Anthelme Brillat-Savarin, *Physiologie du Goût*, Paris 1826.

10 There has been some dispute concerning the origin of this term. Some think that it had originally nothing to do with gastronomy but was a reference to the blue ribbon awarded to the best pupils in Mme de Maintenon's academy for young ladies at Saint-Cyr.

14 Romanticism and Revolution

Romanticism has been described as the victory of sentiment over rationality, of emotion over thought, of mystery over classical clarity; as the free expression of individual sensibility, as the victory of the spirit of Chateaubriand over that of Voltaire. For our purposes it is perhaps sufficient to note that it was a literature of revolt.

The word 'literature' certainly imposes itself here, for the Romantic Movement was essentially literary, even in its painting, its interior decoration and its architecture. The literary element is plainly present in the work of men great in their own field, like Delacroix or Pugin. The names which come immediately to mind when thinking of Romanticism are the names of writers: Wordsworth, Byron, Shelley, Chateaubriand, Lamartine, Hugo. And they were all, in some sense, in revolt. At its highest, says Kitson Clark, Romanticism is 'the revolt of men profoundly dissatisfied with a shallow intellectualism which disdained emotion, or the intolerable complacency of a society which was at the same time artificial, self-satisfied and unjust'.[1]

Escape from such a society can be attained through exoticism – the 'far away and long ago' – or through physical rebellion and these alternatives do not exclude one another. If Chateaubriand looked back to the Middle Ages it was because he wanted '*Le Génie du Christianisme*' to be restored. If Byron found his spiritual home in the Middle East it was because he wanted to escape from the conventions and hypocrisies of London's West End. It was inevitable that the heroes both these great writers called into being should be cast in the mould of rebellion.

Such rebellion might take many forms. Chateaubriand was a liberal royalist, Byron a romantic nationalist (so long as the nation in question was Greece rather than England), Shelley an idealistic revolutionary – and Hugo? The evolution of Victor Hugo's thought and the application of his romantic principles to the real world of politics is a fascinating study.

Hugo's father was a general in the armies of Napoleon, out of employment after Waterloo. Victor himself, as a young man, professed himself a royalist.

He even brought out a book of royalist verses. He received a pension from both Louis XVIII and Charles X; and, with Lamartine, was chosen by Charles himself to attend his coronation and write an ode to celebrate the occasion. Hugo continued to write odes and in his third volume, composed between October 1825 and June 1828, his readers must have noticed something rather strange. For while the book opens with verses in honour of Charles X it concludes with a splendid poem in praise of Napoleon. Madame Duclaux tells us what had happened:

On the seventh of February in 1827 Victor Hugo, economically glancing at the *Gazette* on the bookseller's stall under the arcades of the Odeon Theatre, saw the report of a scandal which had occurred the night before at the Austrian Embassy, where there had been a gala. All Napoleon's marshals who bore Austrian titles[2] had been shorn of their foreign style. The Duke of Reggio had been announced as Duke Oudinot; the Duke of Treviso as Marshal Mortier; the Duke of Dalmatia as Marshal Soult; the Duke of Taranto by his name of Macdonald. The ambassador had calmly confiscated the souvenir of Napoleon's victories. Victor Hugo felt all the soldier's blood in his veins rise to his face as he read how Napoleon's generals, one after the other, had left the ball-room in solemn silence. He felt that his own father had been insulted, and he went home and wrote the first 'Ode à la Colonne', the first impassioned address to that great pillar on the Place Vendôme which supports the statue of Napoleon.[3]

Naturally, Victor Hugo's father was delighted that his son had come round to his point of view. The Ultras, those who wished for everything in the *ancien régime* to be restored, were outraged. He was accused of abjuring 'the sane tenets of the legitimate monarchy'. The Liberals on the whole were pleased, for, since Napoleon and the Duc de Reichstadt were both dead, there seemed no chance of a Bonaparte restoration. And then, in 1828, Hugo wrote another poem, in which, Napoleon for the time forgotten, he steps forward as the Poet Laureate of Democracy:

> Des révolutions j'ouvrais le gouffre immonde?
> C'est qu'il faut un chaos à qui veut faire un monde!
> C'est qu'une grande voix dans la nuit a parlé,
> C'est qu'enfin je voulais, menant au but la foule,
>   Avec le siècle qui s'écoule,
>   Confronter le siècle écoulé.[4]

We do not know what Charles X thought of his lapsed laureate, but he did not have very much longer to consider the matter. Apart from the Legitimist faction the French people had felt little enthusiasm for the return of the Bourbons. After all, they had come back, in the contemporary phrase, 'in the baggage waggons of the enemy'. The half-pay officers of the Imperial armies remembered only the victories of Napoleon and forgot that he had almost drained the country of manpower. It was this, however, which the bulk of the people *did* remember and they accepted the Bourbons out of lassitude.

Louis XVIII had had the wisdom to carry on the Imperial administrative system with as little change as possible, even of personnel. The *Code Napoléon* remained intact; and those who, under the Empire, had been given titles were allowed to keep them, however much the Faubourg St Germain might continue to believe itself the only authentic *noblesse*. All that had really been restored of the *ancien régime* was the hereditary King and his Court which, however, no longer revolved round Versailles. The monarch might call himself 'Louis XVIII, King of France and Navarre by the Grace of God'. He might substitute for the tricolour the white flag with its golden lilies, and date his acts 'in the eighteenth year of Our Reign', expunging, as it were, the very memory of the Revolution and the Empire – all these things were merely the trimmings of a regime which was in reality quite different. Louis steered a middle course and always refused to yield to the demands of the Ultras.

Charles X was himself an Ultra and when he succeeded his brother in 1820, he set himself to restore as much as possible of the *ancien régime*. He dissolved the elected Chamber before it had even had a chance to assemble; he changed the electoral system in favour of the conservative elements; and he re-established the censorship. Although he had been dissolute himself in his youth, he had now become pious and, it was said, was completely under the thumb of the Jesuits. He seemed determined to revive that alliance of 'Throne and Altar' which had existed before the Revolution.

In France, as elsewhere in Europe, the thirty years after 1815 were years of deprivation and poverty for the bulk of the people. In the country the wages of farm workers were below subsistence level. Even those peasants who owned their land owned too little for profitable exploitation and they lacked altogether the capital to enable them to purchase proper farm implements. Lack of transport made it difficult for them to market their produce. Most of them were unable to read or write.

Workers in the towns were even worse off, weavers who worked in their own homes being perhaps the most wretched of all as they had been undercut by the new methods. But even in factories which had begun to be established on the English model, and often with machinery imported from England, the hours were intolerably long and the wages extremely low. In great cities like Paris the housing problem was acute and the poor lived in conditions of horrifying squalor, without sanitation of any kind. In such conditions the seeds of discontent found a fertile soil.

Conditions in England were similar, with the Industrial Revolution more advanced than on the Continent, but with the condition of the workers little better. In rural areas the enclosures, if they had enormously increased agricultural yields, had depressed the living conditions of the men who had now become mere casual labourers almost beyond endurance. Indeed, quite beyond, for in 1830 there broke out what might be described as 'the last Peasants' Revolt' – if there had been, in England, any peasants left.[5]

It began in June 1830 with a rick fire at Orpington in Kent, followed by the destruction of a threshing machine near Canterbury. The movement spread rapidly through the southern and eastern counties; ricks were burned and agricultural implements destroyed. Landowners received threatening letters. The authorities grew alarmed. They saw a confederation of 'Papists, Frenchmen and Radicals' conspiring to take over the country, instead of what the movement really was, a spontaneous and unorganized uprising of men driven by poverty to desperation.

The revolt was firmly put down. Nearly 2,000 prisoners were taken: 19 were hanged, 481 transported and 664 imprisoned. No one was hurt on the other side, except financially, by the loss of some of their property. It is a savage – and almost forgotten – episode in English history.

In France bourgeois philanthropists began to be aware of the miserable conditions in which so many of their compatriots lived, and some of them began to wonder if improvement could ever come without a radical remodelling of society itself. Saint-Simon and his disciples, Fourier, Pierre Leroux and others, all produced 'systems' which involved what was just beginning to be called Socialism. The explosive phrase was coined: 'From each according to his powers; to each according to his needs.'

In contrast to what was happening in England where attempts at reform were concerned with practical issues, such as the formation of trades unions (in however primitive a form), co-operative societies, and demands for a shorter working day, the French movement was almost purely theoretical, concerned with the relationship between capital and labour and the radical reorganization of society. Already the words anarchism and communism began to be bruited about; the red flag was adopted as the revolutionary emblem. The 'Communist Manifesto' of Karl Marx was not issued until 1848, but the phrase 'Social Revolution' was already current in 1832. And two years before that the smouldering discontents had already burst into flame in the *Révolution de Juillet*.

While the storm was gathering Victor Hugo, who, as we have seen, had already announced in verse his readiness to create a chaos out of which a new world might be born, was in a somewhat equivocal position. He had written his play *Marion de Lorme*, had read it to a group of admiring friends,[6] and had already arranged for it to be staged at the Théâtre-Français. And then the censor intervened and forbade its production.

Hugo appealed to the King, who received him with great courtesy, but refused to override the censor. As a compensation he offered the poet a third pension in the Civil List – a pension of 4,000 francs. Hugo refused it but was careful in his letter to express his willingness to receive the two pensions he enjoyed already. And undeterred by his failure he began work on another play, *Hernani*.

The authorities did not interfere with *Hernani* in spite of the fact that the hero was a brigand. It was duly produced and resulted in an epic battle between those who disliked the Romantic Movement and those who supported it. Hugo refused to employ a hired claque, but he mobilized his supporters in the Latin Quarter and at one o'clock in the afternoon, with seven hours to wait, they swarmed into the theatre and occupied every place except the boxes. They were clad in every variety of fancy dress, Théophile Gautier being especially conspicuous in what is usually described as a *gilet rouge* (a red waistcoat), but was in reality a *pourpoint* (a doublet) of scarlet satin. They had brought provisions with them, garlic sausage, and beer, and they feasted and caroused and sang to pass the time. When the occupants of the boxes arrived in evening dress the *parterre* (the pit) was a shambles. The curtain went up and the play began, with the audience divided into hostile camps. But before the play was over there was no doubt of the final result. It was a tremendous success.

It has been called a 'rehearsal for revolution'; and so it proved. In March 1830 the King prorogued the Chamber and, relying on his chief minister Polignac, determined on extreme measures. Polignac told him that the Virgin had appeared to him in a vision and assured him that they would be successful. Paris rose. The city was still medieval in character with a maze of narrow and tortuous streets in which it was very easy to erect barricades – Baron Haussmann's wide boulevards were still in the future. The tricolour flag was hoisted again all over the city. Charles tried to resist. He had 12,000 soldiers, badly armed and led, and of doubtful loyalty. He said to Talleyrand (the inevitable Talleyrand): 'I see no middle way between the Throne and the Scaffold.' The old cynic murmured: 'Your Majesty forgets the post-chaise.' And the legitimate King of France took his advice.

What made the Revolution of 1830 possible was the alliance between the proletariat and the intellectuals. The latter, especially the students, had adopted with enthusiasm the doctrines of Romanticism. Charles Seignobos speaks of 'the revolt of a young generation against both academic tradition and bourgeois morality. It manifested itself by an eccentric costume, a provocative attitude and free love. In literature it involved a contempt for classical models, and *le style noble*, and an admiration for the work of foreign authors.'[7]

And, of course, they were all bearded. It is a curious fact of social history that there is always a tendency for those who wish to change the social structure to let their hair grow long and not to shave their faces. Presumably it has something to do with the idea of a return to Nature, a repudiation of artificiality of all kinds. It is safe to say that in the 1830s any bearded man was a revolutionary of some sort, and that every clean-shaven man was a reactionary. In the same way the clothes worn by the revolutionary were deliberately different from those of the fashionable man. They were in a sense 'working clothes': the inevitable wear of a proletariat, but deliberately adopted by their student allies. They also discarded stiff collars and neckcloths.

Those who fought in the Battle of the Barricades won. They had hoped for a Republic: what they got was Louis-Philippe. The new King accepted the tricolour flag and proclaimed himself 'King of the French, by the Grace of God and the Will of the People' – a slightly different formula from that of the *ancien régime*. Naturally, the Legitimists hated him, as the fox who had slipped into the farmyard while no one was looking and made off with his prey. The students and others who had made the Revolution of 1830 regarded him with contempt as the very symbol of the bourgeoisie against which they were in rebellion. Nevertheless he ruled for eighteen years and, except for one expedition in 1831 to help the Belgians in their revolt against Holland, he gave France peace.

Yet the regime was unpopular except among the bourgeoisie whose motto was: '*Enrichissez-vous* [enrich yourself]'. And it was the misfortune of the Bourgeois King, with his top hat and his umbrella – a kind of caricature of Joseph Prud'homme – to survive after the first ten years of his reign, into one of the most difficult periods of European history.

It is not for nothing that the decade is known as the 'Hungry Forties'. There was a bad harvest in 1841 and another in 1847. The poorer classes in Europe were starving; in France, in Germany and in England. But no country suffered more terribly than Ireland. It is a horrifying story. Conditions were bad enough before the Famine. Tyrannical landlords and rapacious agents kept the peasantry at bare subsistence level. A contemporary Government Report states that 'it would be impossible adequately to describe the privations which they habitually and silently endure . . . in many districts their only food is the potato, their only beverage water . . . their cabins are seldom a protection against the weather . . . a bed or a blanket is a rare luxury . . . their pig and a manure heap constitute their only property.' But they had not yet been driven to despair. Indeed, as Sir Walter Scott noted on his visit to Ireland in 1825: 'Their natural condition is turned towards gaiety and happiness,' and other observers remarked on 'the proverbial gaiety and lightheartedness of the peasant people'. And the report already quoted surely exaggerated in saying that their only drink was water. Poteen was being manufactured in illicit stills all over the country.

It is a curious fact that the population of Ireland had been for nearly a century increasing more rapidly than that of any other country in Europe. Various reasons have been adduced. An almost entirely rural population did not suffer from the ills of the urban slums in England. Life being so very simple was an encouragement to marry early. Girls married at sixteen, boys a couple of years later and Irishwomen, encouraged by the Catholic Church, were exceptionally fertile. Cecil Woodham-Smith remarks:

There was too one luxury enjoyed by the Irishman which favoured the survival and rearing of children – his cabin was usually well warmed by a turf fire. Ill-clothed though he was, sleeping as he did on a mud floor, with his pig in the corner, the Irish peasant did not have to endure cold, nor did his children die of cold. They were warm, they were abundantly fed – as long as the potato did not fail.[8]

It did fail and the tragedy that ensued is shown in the bare statistics of population. The census of 1841 showed that Ireland was inhabited by more than eight million people, and this was probably an under-estimate. By 1851, through starvation and emigration, the figure had dropped to six and a half million, and it continued to decline. Even today it has not reached half the figure of 1841.

The potato has been called 'the most dangerous of crops'. As it did not keep it could not be stored from one season to another; and in the summer gap when the last crop was finished and the new one not yet available, many labourers and their families suffered from famine even before 'the Famine'. In the preceding century the potato crop had failed several times. As long before as 1728 there was 'such a scarcity that on 26 February there was a great rising of the populace of Cork'. In the nineteenth century the crop failed, partly or entirely, in 1807, 1821, 1822, 1836 and 1837, and in 1839 there was famine throughout Ireland.

All these were failures due to frost, dry rot and curl, but in 1844 there was news from America of something much more sinister: the so-called American blight. It was tragic that 1845 promised an abundant crop. In August of that year the American blight crossed the Atlantic and affected the potato crops in the Isle of Wight and Kent; and in September it reached Ireland and spread rapidly. By the following year the famine was universal, with dysentry and other diseases in its wake. Also, as so many of the peasants were now unable to pay any rent, they were ruthlessly evicted and their cabins destroyed. Relief measures were promoted but only half-heartedly carried through. Sir Robert Peel, reversing the opinion of a lifetime, repealed the Corn Laws, and this enabled wheat to be imported. But this did not benefit the Irish for whom the cheapest bread was an unheard-of luxury. And the repeal caused so much political bitterness in England that it actually hampered the cause of Irish relief.

An attempt was made to employ the starving peasants on public works, but many of them were too weak to work. The winter of 1846–7 was exceptionally cold and wet, and the labour of breaking stones (which was all that most of them were capable of) very exacting. And not all the labourers were able-bodied men; many of them were women and children. The women worked for fourpence a day. It is not surprising that there were mutinies and acts of violence. Indeed it is astonishing that there were not more; but the bulk of the population was too weak and dispirited to revolt.

The authorities realized that the only possible solution was emigration. It was estimated that it cost much less to ship a labourer across the Atlantic than to keep him for a year in the poor-house. And so the great flight began: destitute families almost as tightly packed into the ships' holds as the Negro slaves had been in former days. The passage was long, food scanty and disease rife; and it is little wonder that the authorities in the United States and Canada were not at all anxious to receive the hordes of sick and indigent dumped upon their shores. The Americans had subscribed generously to famine relief, but to absorb large numbers of destitute persons who had never learned any trade (for the cultivation of a potato patch had required little skill) was another matter. The population of Boston at this time was little more than one hundred thousand and now, in a single year, it was increased by the arrival of nearly forty thousand immigrants. The effect on housing and public health was disastrous. It was estimated that more than fifty per cent of the children of the immigrants died before the age of five, and that the average age of persons buried in Boston during the late 'forties was thirteen and a half.

An added horror in Europe was the wave of epidemics which swept over it in the 'thirties and 'forties. Sanitary engineering had failed to keep pace with the rapid growth of towns, with the result that most of the water drunk by the poor was polluted. Cholera and typhus are both water-borne diseases. In 1832 cholera was raging all over the Continent and it kept returning every few years until slightly beyond the end of our period, when urban authorities at last began to take the matter in hand.

The United States had managed to absorb the immigration of Germans, Poles, French Huguenots, Swedes and Italians. The Irish were to present problems of integration not to be solved for the next two generations. In Ireland the Smith-O'Brien insurrection was a failure. In England the Chartist Movement, formed by a group of social and political reformers to demand a very modest programme of parliamentary reform, turned to ridicule. For the moment, all over Europe, reaction, or at least the maintenance of the *status quo*, had triumphed. But under the lava crust the subterranean fires were still burning and the rumblings could already be heard of an explosion to come.

Discontents mounted and it was plain that the men in France who, after the Revolution of 1830 had been fobbed off with the liberal monarchy of Louis-Philippe, were determined to try again to install a republic in his place. All over Europe revolutionary forces were gathering strength, and as the year 1847 drew to a close the entire Continent was on the verge of a catastrophic upheaval. The 'Year of Revolutions', 1848, was at hand.

14
FOOTNOTES

1 G.S.R. Kitson Clark, 'The Romantic Element, 1830 to 1850' in *Studies in Social History, A Tribute to G.M. Trevelyan*, ed. J.H. Plumb, London 1955.

2 And, of course, Italian and other titles.

3 Mme Duclaux, *Victor Hugo*, London 1921.

4 Which might be somewhat lamely translated:
  So, I unseal the abyss where all your thrones were hurled?
  Yes; we require a chaos who would frame a world!
  Yes; in the night a voice has spoken to my soul,
  Bidding me rise and lead the people to their goal,
    And confront the century gone
    With the century new begun.

5 As Michael Foot aptly remarks (in a review in the *Evening Standard* of *Captain Swing*, by E.J. Hobsbawn and George Rudé, London 1969) the title of the revolt 'in most history books has not earned the reward of capital letters.'

6 What a group! It consisted of Balzac, Musset, Nodier, Vigny, Dumas, Mérimée, Saint-Beuve and Delacroix!

7 Charles Seignobos, *Histoire Sincère de la Nation Française*, Paris 1933.

8 Cecil Woodham-Smith, *The Great Hunger*, London 1962.

Bibliography

General

Andrews, Alexander, *The Eighteenth Century*, London 1856
Ashton, J., *Social England*, London 1890
Beresford, J., *Gossip of the Seventeenth and Eighteenth Centuries*, London 1923
Burn, W.L., *The Age of Equipoise*, London 1964
Chamberlayne, John, *Magnae Britanniae Notitia, or The Present State of Great Britain*, London 1755
Cobban, A. (ed.), *The Eighteenth Century: The Age of Enlightenment*, London 1969
Dayot, A., *De la Régence à la Révolution*, Paris 1956
Duby, G., and Mandrou, R., *Histoire de la Civilisation Française*, Paris 1958
Franklin, Alfred, *La Vie privée d'Autrefois*, 27 vols, Paris 1887–1902
George, M.D., *London Life in the Eighteenth Century*, London 1930
Lacroix, Paul, *Le XVIIIᵉ Siècle*, Paris 1878
Lewis, W.S., *Three Tours through London in the Years 1748–1776–1799*, New Haven 1941
Morgan, R.B. (ed.), *Readings in English Social History*, Cambridge 1923
Paston, George, *Social Caricature in the Eighteenth Century*, London 1905
Robinson, J.H., *Medieval and Modern Times*, Boston 1919
Seignobos, Charles, *Histoire Sincère de la Nation Française*, Paris 1933
Traill, H.D., *Social England*, IV, London 1895
Trevelyan, G.M., *English Social History*, London 1947
Turberville, A.S., *English Men and Manners in the Eighteenth Century*, Oxford 1926
Turberville, A.S., *Johnson's England*, Oxford 1933
Walpole, Horace, *Letters*, ed. Mrs Paget Toynbee, Oxford 1914

1 Society and Religion in the Mid-Eighteenth Century

Clark, Adam, *Memoirs of the Wesley Family*, London 1823
George, M.D., *London Life in the Eighteenth Century*, London 1930
Goncourt, E. and J., *La Femme au XVIIIᵉ Siècle*, Paris 1890
Hervey, Lord, *Memoirs of the Reign of George II*, ed. J.W. Croker, London 1848

Kohn-Bramstedt, Ernst, *Aristocracy and the Middle Classes in Germany*, London 1937
Mavor, Elizabeth, *The Virgin Mistress, The Life of the Duchess of Kingston*, London 1964
Saussure, C. de, *A Foreign View of England in the Reigns of George I and George II*, London 1902
Southey, W., *Life of John Wesley*, London 1820
Walpole, Horace, *Memoirs of the Last Ten Years of the Reign of George II*, London 1822
Wesley, John, *Journal*, London 1909

2 *Crime and Punishment*

Anchel, Robert, *Crimes et Châtiments au XVIIIe Siècle*, Paris 1933
Andrews, Alexander, *The Eighteenth Century*, London 1856
Beccaria, Marquis, *An Essay on Crimes and Punishments with a Commentary by M. de Voltaire*, Glasgow 1770
Chamberlayne, John, *Magnae Britanniae Notitia, or The Present State of Great Britain*, London 1705
Fielding, Henry, *Works*, London 1762
Marks, Alfred, *Tyburn Tree. Its History and Annals*, London 1905
PERIODICALS: *Annual Register, Newgate Calendar, Tyburn Chronicle*

3 *Sports and Pastimes*

Altham, H.S., *The History of Cricket*, London 1926
Angelo, Henry, *Reminiscences*, London 1904
Anon., *The Art of English Shooting*, London 1777
Anon., *Fistiana, or The Oracle of the Ring*, London 1841
Beckford, Peter, *Thoughts on Hunting*, London 1781
Boulton, W.B., *The Amusements of Old London*, London 1901
Bowlker, Charles, *The Art of Angling*, London 1788
Browning, Robert, *A History of Golf*, London 1955
Carlyle, Alexander, *Autobiography*, Edinburgh 1860
Hackwood, F.W., *Old English Sports*, London 1907
Harris, S., *The Coaching Age*, London 1885
Hole, C., *English Sports and Pastimes*, London 1949
Hoyle's Games, Improved, London 1775
Markland, George, *Pteryplegia; or the Art of Shooting Flying*, London 1727
Marples, Morris, *A History of Football*, London 1954
Maxwell, Sir Herbert, *The Chase, The Road and The Turf*, London 1898
Misson, M., *Mémoires et Observations*, Paris 1689
Strutt, J., *The Sports and Pastimes of the People of England*, London 1801
Williams, J., *New Articles of Cricket*, London 1774
PERIODICALS: *Advertiser, Spectator, Gentleman's Magazine, Tatler, Protestant Mercury, British Champion*

4 Coffee Houses and Clubs

Bellamy, George Anne, *Apology for the Life of George Anne Bellamy*, London 1796
Escott, T.H.S., *Club Makers and Club Members*, London 1904
Fitzgerald, P., *The Garrick Club*, London 1903
Graves, Charles, *Leather Armchairs*, London 1963
McCormick, D., *The Hell-Fire Club*, London 1958
Ollier, Charles, *Original Views of London as it is, by Thomas Shotter Boys*, London 1842
Petrie, Sir Charles, *The Carlton Club*, London 1955
Smollett, T., *Works*, London 1797
Timbs, J., *Clubs and Club Life in London*, London 1872
PERIODICALS: *Connoisseur, Daily Journal, Old England, True Briton*

5 'Taking the Waters' and Other Diversions

Boulton, W.B., *The Amusements of Old London*, London 1901
Chancellor, E. Beresford, *Pleasure Haunts*, London 1925
Lawrence, W.J., *Johnson's England*, 2 vols, London 1933
Morley, H., *Memoirs of Bartholomew Fair*, London 1859
Scott, W.S., *Bygone Pleasures of London*, London 1948
PERIODICAL: *Spectator.*

6 Le Roi Bien-Aimé

Anon., *Anecdotes de la Cour de France pendant la faveur de Madame de Pompadour*, Paris 1802
Anon., *La Vie privée de Louis XV*, London 1788
Anon., *La Vie privée du Maréchal de Richelieu*, Paris 1791
Argenson, Marquis d', *Journal et Mémoires*, London 1909
Bachaumont, L.P. de (attributed to), *Mémoires secrets*, 36 vols, Paris 1777–89
Castries, Duc de, *Madame du Barry*, Paris 1967
Choiseul, Duc de, *Mémoires, 1719–85*, Paris 1790
Duchesne, Gaston, *Mademoiselle de Charollais, Procureuse du Roi*, Paris 1909
Kunstler, Charles, *La Vie Quotidienne sous Louis XV*, Paris n.d.
Levron, J., *Madame du Barry*, Paris 1961
Palacios, A.G., *The Age of Louis XV*, tr. H. Viden, London 1969
Peuchel, *Mémoires tirés des Archives de la Police de Paris*, Paris 1838
Saint-André, C., *Madame du Barry*, Paris 1909
Soulavie, J.L., *Anecdotes du règne de Louis XV*, Paris n.d.
Vèze, Raoul, *La Galanterie Parisienne au XVIIIᵉ Siècle*, Paris 1905

Walpole, Horace, *Letters*, ed. Mrs Paget Toynbee, Oxford 1914

7 The Pursuit of Love

Anon., *Le Porte-Feuille de Madame Gourdan*, Paris 1783

Anon., *Les Sérails de Paris*, Paris 1802

Anon., *Nocturnal Revels: or the History of King's Place by a Monk of the Order of St Francis*, 2 vols, London 1779

Bachaumont, L.P. de, *Mémoires secrets*, 36 vols, Paris 1777-89

Béranger, L.P., *De la Prostitution*, Paris 1789

Bloch, Iwan, *Sexual Life in England*, London 1938

Casanova, Giacomo, *History of My Life*, tr. Willard R. Trask, London 1969

Chancellor, E. Beresford, *Lives of the Rakes*, London 1925

Ellis, Havelock, *Sex in Relation to Society*, London 1910

Fuller, R., *Hell-Fire Francis*, London 1937

Glenbervie, Lord, *Diaries*, London 1928

Gorer, Geoffrey, *The Life and Ideas of the Marquis de Sade*, London 1953

Hunt, Morton N., *The Natural History of Love*, New York 1959

Jones, L.C., *The Clubs of the Georgian Rakes*, Columbia 1942

'Junius', *Letters of Junius*, London 1770

Lauzun, Duc de, *Mémoires, 1747-83*, Paris 1858

Molmenti, P.G., *Storia di Venezia nella vita privata*, Turin 1880

Partridge, B., *A History of Orgies*, London 1958

Peuchel, *Mémoires tirés des Archives de la Police de Paris*, Paris 1838

Restif de la Bretonne, *Monsieur Nicolas, or The Human Heart Unveiled*, tr. R. Crowdy, London 1930

Richelieu, Maréchal de, *Mémoires*, Paris 1790

Ryan, M., *Prostitution in London*, London 1839

Taylor, G. Rattray, *Sex in History*, London 1953

Vèze, Raoul, *La Galanterie Parisienne au XVIIIe Siècle*, Paris 1905

Ward, N., *The Secret History of Clubs*, London 1709

PERIODICAL: *Morning Post*

8 *Before the Deluge*

Behrens, C.B.A., *The Ancien Régime*, London 1967

Cagliostro, Alexandre, *Vie de Joseph Balsamo*, Paris 1791

Campan, J.L.H., *Memoirs of the Private Life of Marie-Antoinette*, 2 vols, London 1823

Egret, Jean, *La Pré-Révolution française, 1787-88* Paris 1962

Ethenville, Botte d', *Complete Collection of all the Memoirs which have appeared in the Famous Affair of the Necklace*, 6 vols, Paris 1786

Fay, Bernard, *Louis XVI ou la Fin d'un Monde*, Paris 1961

Fleischman, H., *Madame de Polignac et la Cour Galante de Marie-Antoinette*, Paris 1910

Fox, Henry, fourth Lord Holland, *Diary*, ed. the Earl of Ilchester, London 1923

Funck-Brentano, F., *The Diamond Necklace*, tr. H. Sutherland Edwards, London 1901

Goncourt, E. and J., *Histoire de Marie-Antoinette*, new ed., Paris 1884

Guérin, René, *Jean-Jacques Rousseau*, Paris 1930

Jabez, Alphonse, *La France sous Louis XVI*, 3 vols, Paris 1877-93

Kunstler, Charles, *La Vie Quotidienne sous Louis XVI*, Paris n.d.

Lévis, Duc de, *Souvenirs et Portraits, 1780–89*, London 1813

Maugras, G., *Le Duc de Lauzun et la Cour de Marie-Antoinette*, Paris 1895

Nolhac, P. de, *La Reine Marie-Antoinette*, Paris 1922

Mayer, Dorothy Moulton, *The Tragic Queen, Marie-Antoinette*, London 1968

Mercy-Argenteau, Comte de, *Correspondence secrète, entre Marie-Thérèse et le Comte de Mercy-Argenteau*, Paris 1874

Oberkirch, Baroness d', *Mémoires*, written by herself and edited by her grandson the Comte de Montbrisson, London 1852

Rétaux de Villette, *Mémoires historiques des intriguess de la Cour*, Venice 1790

Rochefort, Henri, *Les Aventures de ma Vie*, 5 vols, Paris 1896

Sagnac, Philippe, *La Fin de l'Ancien Régime et la Révolution Américaine, 1763–1789*, Paris 1947

Viel Castel, H. de, *Commérages*, Paris 1930

Viel Castel, H. de, *Marie-Antoinette et la Révolution Française*, Paris 1859

Walpole, Horace, *Letters*, ed. Mrs Paget Toynbee, Oxford 1914

Ward, Marion, *The Du Barry Inheritance*, London 1969

Young, Arthur, *Travels in France*, London 1892

9 *The Broken Link*

Fitzpatrick, J.C., *The Spirit of the Revolution*, Boston 1924

Gottschalk, L., *Lafayette joins the American Army*, Chicago 1937

Holstein, D., *Memoir of La Fayette*, New York 1824

Jones, C.Sheridan, *A Short Life of Washington*, London 1920

Kayser, J., *La Vie de La Fayette*, Paris 1928

La Fayette, Marquis de, *Mémoires*, Paris 1837–8

Nevins, A., and Commager, H.S., *A Pocket History of the United States*, new enlarged ed., New York 1960

Parkes, H.B., *The American People*, London 1949

Sears, L.M., *George Washington*, New York 1932

Tower, C., *La Fayette in the American Revolution*, Philadelphia 1895

Trevelyan, G.O., *The American Revolution*, London 1899

10 *The Great Upheaval*

Bareste, E., *Nostradamus*, Paris 1840

Boswell, J., *Life of Johnson*, London 1791

Bouillé, Marquis de, *Mémoires sur la Révolution Française*, Paris 1802

Bizard, Léon, 'La Prison de Saint-Lazare sous la Révolution' in *Les Œuvres Libres*, clxxiii, Paris 1935

Caron, P., *Les Massacres de Septembre*, Paris 1935

Dayot, A., *La Révolution Française*, Paris 1905

Dussane, Mme, *La Célimène de Thermidor, Louise Contat*, Paris 1929

Greville, C., *Diary*, ed. P.W. Wilson, London 1937

Guérin, R., *Jean-Jacques Rousseau*, Paris 1930

Jette, M.H., *France religieuse sous la Révolution et l'Empire*, Paris 1958

Lenôtre, G., *En France Jadis*, Paris 1938
Lockray, E., *Journal d'une Bourgeoise pendant la Révolution*, Paris 1881
Mayer, Dorothy Moulton, *The Tragic Queen, Marie-Antoinette*, London 1968
Michelet, Jules, *History of the French Revolution*, London 1847–8
Mornet, D., *Les Origines Intellectuelles de la Révolution Française*, Paris 1932
Rigby, Dr, *Letters from France . . . in 1789*, London 1880
Robiquet, Jean, *La Vie Quotidienne en Temps de la Révolution*, Paris n.d.
Smith, Thomas, *A Book for a Rainy Day*, London 1905
Soboul, A., *Paysans, Sans-culottes et Jacobins*, Paris 1960
Staël, Mme de, *Considérations sur la Révolution Française*, Paris 1818
Viel Castel, H. de, *Marie-Antoinette et la Révolution Française*, Paris 1859
Ward, Marion, *The Du Barry Inheritance*, London 1969
Wraxall, Sir Nathaniel, *Historical and Posthumous Memoirs*, ed. H.B. Wheatley, London 1884

11 *After the Deluge*

Abrantès, Duchesse d', *Mémoires*, Paris 1893
Alméras, H. d', *Barras et son Temps*, Paris 1929
Alméras, H. d', *Une Amoureuse: Pauline Bonaparte*, Paris n.d.
Amateur, an., *Real Life in London*, London, 1821, 1822
Barras, Vicomte de, *Mémoires*, ed. Georges Duray, Paris 1896
Boigne, Comtesse de, *Mémoires*, Paris 1907
Boigne, Comtesse de, *Récits d'une Tante*, Paris 1921–7
Bonaparte-Wyse, *The Spurious Brood*, London 1969
Bouillé, Baron de, *Mémoires et Chronique scandaleuse sous l'Empire*, Paris n.d.
Bourienne, L.A.F. de, *Mémoires*, Paris 1910
Breton, Guy, *Napoleon and his Ladies*, tr. Frederick Holt, London 1865
Chéramy, Paul (ed.), *A Favourite of Napoleon, Memoirs of Mademoiselle George*, London 1909
Chimay, Princesse de, *Mme Tallien, royaliste et révolutionnaire*, Paris 1934
Croker, J.W., *Papers*, ed. L.J. Jennings, London 1882
Doris, C., *Amours et Aventures du Vicomte de Barras*, Paris 1816–17
Dumas, Alexandre *père*, *Mes Mémoires*, Paris 1890
Fabre de l'Aude, Comte, *Histoire secrète du Directoire*, Paris 1832
Fleischman, H., *Une Maîtresse de Napoléon*, Paris 1908
Forneron, H., *Les Emigrés et la Société Française sous Napoléon*, Paris 1890
Fox, Henry, fourth Lord Holland, *Journal*, London 1923
Gastin, L., *La Belle Tallien – Reine du Directoire*, Paris 1909
Goncourt, E. and J., *Histoire de la Société Française sous le Directoire*, Paris 1929
Gosselin, T., *Histoire anecdotique des Salons de Peinture depuis 1673*, Paris 1881
Houssaye, Arsène, *Notre-Dame de Thermidor*, Paris 1866
Pasquier, Etienne-Denis, *Mémoires*, Paris 1893
Récamier, Mme de, *Mémoires et Correspondence*, ed. J.M. Luyster, London 1867
Rémusat, Mme de, *Memoirs*, tr. Mrs Cashel Hoey and John Lillie, 4th ed., London 1880
Rochefort, H., *Les Aventures de ma Vie*, Paris 1896

Sainte-Elme, Ida, *Mémoires d'une Contemporaine*, Paris 1897
Vivent, J., *Barras*, Paris 1939

12 *The Regency*

Angelo, Henry, *Reminiscences*, London 1830
Archenholz, J.W.von, *A Picture of England*, London 1789
Barrington, Sir Jonah, *Personal Sketches of His Own Times*, 3rd ed., London 1869
Beloe, Rev. William, *The Sexagenarian, or the Recollections of a Literary Life*, London 1817
Crapelet, G.A., *Souvenirs de Londres en 1814 et 1816*, Paris 1817
Creevey, Thomas, *Memoirs, Diaries and Correspondence*, ed. Sir Herbert Maxwell, London, 1903
Croker, J.W., *Papers*, ed. L.J. Jennings, London 1882
Defauconpret, A.J.B., *Quinze Jours à Londres à la fin de 1815*, Paris 1816
Egon, Pierce, *Life in London*, London 1821
Falk, Bernard, *'Old Q's' Daughter*, London 1937
Glenbervie, Lord, *Diaries*, London 1928
Grego, Joseph, *Rowlandson the Caricaturist*, London 1880
Gronow, Captain R.H., *Reminiscences*, London 1847
Huish, Robert, *Memoirs of George IV*, London 1821
Lauzun, Duc de, *Mémoires*, Paris 1858
MacFarlane, Charles, *Reminiscences of a Literary Life*, London 1917
Peillart, Léonce, *La Vie Quotidienne à Londres au Temps de Nelson et de Wellington, 1774–1852* Paris n.d.
Smith, J.T., *A Book for a Rainy Day, or Recollections of the Events of the Years 1766–1833*, London 1905
Trench, Charles Chenevix, *The Royal Malady*, London 1964
Wilson, Harriet, *Memoirs*, London 1825
Wraxall, Sir Nathaniel, *Historical and Posthumous Memoirs*, London 1884

13 *The Inner Man*

Almanach des Gourmands, Paris 1803–12
Almanach Perpétuel des Pauvres Diables pour servir de Correctif à l'Almanach des Gourmands, Paris 1803
Anon., *La Cuisinière Bourgeoise*, Paris 1746
Anon., *Les Soupers de la Cour, ou l'Art de Travailler toutes sortes d'Aliments pour servir les meilleurs Tables*, Paris 1755
Beauvilliers, A., *L'Art du Cuisinier*, Paris 1824
Brillat-Savarin, A., *Physiologie du Goût*, 2 vols, Paris 1826
Carême, A., *L'Art de la Cuisine Française*, 3 vols, Paris 1833–5
Carter, Charles, *The Compleat City and Country Cook*, London 1732
Demoiresterres, G., *Grimod de la Reynière et son Groupe*, Paris 1877
Ellwanger, G.H., *The Pleasures of the Table*, London 1903
Franklin, A., *La Vie privée d'Autrefois*, Paris 1887–1902

Grimod de la Reynière, *Manuel des Amphitryons*, Paris 1808
Harrison, Mrs Sarah, *The Housekeeper's Pocket Book and Complete Family Cook*, London 1751
Lenôtre, G., *En France Jadis*, Paris 1938
Mackay, A., *A Journey through England*, London 1724
Martin, A., *Le Cuisinier des Gourmands*, Paris 1829
Peckham, Ann, *The Complete English Cook; or Prudent Housewife*, London 1770
Thompson, Sir Henry, *Food and Feeding*, London 1899
Woodforde, Rev. James, *The Diary of a Country Parson*, ed. John Beresford, London 1924

14 *Romanticism and Revolution*

Adams, W.F., *Ireland and Irish Emigration*, London 1932
Burnand, R., *La Vie Quotidienne en France en 1830*, Paris n.d.
Chastenet, J., *La Vie Quotidienne en Angleterre au Début du Règne de Victorie*, Paris 1961
Clark, G.S.R. Kitson, 'The Romantic Element, 1830 to 1850' in *Studies in Social History*, ed. J.H. Plumb, London 1955
Duclaux, Mme. *Victor Hugo*, London 1921
Engels, F., *The Condition of the Working Classes in 1842*, London 1892
Fish, C.R., *The Rise of the Common Man, 1830-50*, London 1927
Furst, L.R., *Romanticism in Perspective*, London 1969
Guichen, Vicomte de, *La Révolution de Juillet 1830 et l'Europe*, Paris 1917
Hobsbaum, Eric and Rudé, George, *Captain Swing*, London 1969
Hovell, Mark, *The Chartist Movement*, Manchester 1925
Praz, Mario, *The Romantic Agony*, London 1933
Talmon, J.L., *Romanticism and Revolt*, London 1967
Woodham-Smith, Cecil, *The Great Hunger*, London 1962

Acknowledgements

The author and publisher would like to thank the following for permission to quote from their works: H. Bamford Parkes, *The American People*, Associated Book Publishers Ltd.; Burgo Partridge, *A History of Orgies*, Anthony Blond Ltd.; Charles Seignobos, *A History of the French People*, Jonathan Cape Ltd. and Alfred A. Knopf Inc.; Rev. James Woodforde, *The Diary of a Country Parson*, Clarendon Press; Lord Glenbervie, *Diaries*, ed. F. Bickley, Constable Publishers; Robert Parkes, *History of Golf*, J. M. Dent & Sons and E. P. Dutton & Co. Inc.; Cecil Woodham-Smith, *The Great Hunger*, Hamish Hamilton Ltd. and Harper & Row Inc.; Charles Greville, Diaries, ed. P. W. Wilson, William Heinemann Ltd. and Doubleday & Co. Inc.; *Studies in Social History, A Tribute to G. M. Trevelyan*, ed. J. H. Plumb, Longman Ltd.; M. D. George, *English Social Life*, The Society for Promoting Christian Knowledge.

Index